SINGLE SCENE

short stories

SINGLE SCENE

short stories
edited by Margaret Bishop

GIBBS SMITH
TO ENRICH AND INSPIRE HUMANKIND

© Gibbs Smith
Text © as noted on pages 251–53

Published by
Gibbs Smith, Publisher
P.O. Box 667
Layton, Utah 84041

Orders: 1.800.835.4993
www.gibbs-smith.com

Cover designed by Ron Stucki
Interior designed by m:GraphicDesign/ Maralee Oleson
Printed and bound in U.S.A.

Library of Congress Cataloging-in-Publication Data
2007920936

ISBN 13: 978-1-4236-0062-6

For Bill Miller,
who believed in me long before I did.
That has meant everything.

Contents

Acknowledgments

Thank you to all the people who made this possible. Alan Cheuse, for the original idea, for his guidance in collecting the stories—"Start reading and ask everyone," for his wisdom in finalizing the collection—"Three Dorothy Parker's? Really?" for his ongoing support—helping me to find a publisher, to understand the bewildering and daunting process of tracking down copyright holders, and especially for his great belief and patience—"When will you have a manuscript?" "When will you have a manuscript?" "OK, well, let me know when you have a manuscript." There might never have been a finished manuscript without him.

Dr. Noel Schweig makes all things possible. My friends, Chris, Christiana, Julia, Kelli, Teresa, Tracey. My family with their unflappable faith.

Thank you to the writers for their lovely and inspired single scenes.

Introduction

What is a scene? When a scene occurs on stage or in a story, it provides a fixed setting in an unbroken stream of time. Poe's essay "The Philosophy of Composition" emphasized that any short narrative must present a "unity of impression." Aristotle, in *Poetics,* contended that a story, to be complete, needs three parts: (1) an action or purpose, (2) passion, and (3) perception or recognition. Essentially the protagonist has a motive or desire, thrashes about pursuing it, and arrives at an enhanced recognition of his or her plight. This recognition, in the best stories, is often accompanied by a reversal, and both the recognition and the reversal spring organically from the tension between the character's action and passion.

In the traditional short story, these three parts are rendered across several scenes, with one arc, and when well executed the effect is timeless and brilliant. This requires a narrative rigor, a ruthless dispensing with any and all stray bits of back story, unnecessary modifiers, cluttering subplots. A loyalty to the heart of the story is mandatory, and any other diverting dalliance signals fear, uncertainty, faithlessness. This form stood for years as admirable, even untouchable.

In the 1980s, writers, growing restless with traditional forms and casting about for new ways to turn narrative upside down, embraced sudden fiction, the short-short story. And then, the inexorable urge to take every good idea much too far, lead to flash fiction. Flash fiction is an "emergency flare" sort of story, based on a blind faith that less is better, when sometimes, less is just less. The form was then ground down beyond all sense to micro-fiction, stories told in one sentence, a few lines, the prose equivalent of half a haiku—and about that satisfying. The story was lost and only the short remained.

The single scene story, in contrast, holds a fully developed purpose, passion, and perception. It is a full story, yet it is all heart. A writer chooses the one scene that makes the story and presents us with that scene, little or no ramp up, the barest allowable back story, a thin line here and there to locate the reader to character and situation. Freitag's diagram, a means of graphing the plot of a story, shows the rising action as an up-sloping line—the crisis forms the peak and the resolution or falling action is the down slope. In a single scene story, the first leg of Freitag's diagram is very short. As Vonnegut recommended, the story truly begins as close to the end as possible.

In a single scene short story, the desire, the thrashing, the reversal—all of this takes place in one scene, one geographical coordinate, one window of time. It is useful to think of it dramatically, presented on a stage with no change of setting or costume, no voiceover summarizing or carrying the viewer from here to there.

The stories in this collection were chosen with that definition in mind. Not all are short-short, there is no micro among them. The length of the stories was not at issue, only the strictures on setting and time. Having begun with a strict and unforgiving definition of what could be considered truly a single scene story, I modified that definition to include stories that adhered to the spirit of the form if not the letter. The heart of the story is of a piece, and a brief break in time is allowable, a framed story is acceptable, a meandering about within a small physical space, such as from one room to another in the same house, came to seem suitable.

Maupassant's story, "The Ruse," is a framed narrative beginning and ending with the doctor relating an account of an unusual experience with a patient. This story is included because the story itself, the narrative arc, is embedded in the larger story, while that frame, the beginning and ending setting and brief dialogue, provide an opportunity for the telling of the story.

I have also included a few stories where the time is not one unbroken jet stream. In "The Jilting of Granny Weatherall," time lapses correspond to Granny's waking and dozing, but the movement and the arc are seamless.

In Chabon's story, "House Hunting," the characters move all over the house—together, separately, in and out, essentially on and off stage—but the time is continuous, and the story is told as one scene, albeit a particularly busy and involved scene. The set is larger and allows for more concrete physical action. The passion, as Aristotle defined it, spreads further, covers more ground, both literally and figuratively.

Some stories rely heavily on a character's thoughts ranging around, across time and place. I included stories with long passages of such rumination, emoting, and remembering if the effect of all that mental activity was in the moment. Joyce's "Eveline" is such a story, as the protagonist spends almost the entire scene remembering parts of her past and imagining her future. These thoughts lead to her sole action, which is a refusal to act. Wolff's "Bullet in the Brain" uses a similar technique to great effect. Wolff delineates a comprehensive inventory of occurrences and individuals not remembered as the bullet enters and exits Anders' brain, and finally allows for the one phrase that reverberated as a golden joy in that drawn-out dying moment. It is a single scene fraught with far reaching dramatic impact.

For all of these stories, the unity of effect is both compressed and deepened by the seamless action. The before and after is left to the reader's imagination, but that imagination is helped considerably by the scene we are given. At the end of "Hills Like White Elephants," the reader has a chilling picture of how the future looks for the girl and the American. It is a line drawing expertly rendered, which suggests motion, flight, terror, but is literally no more than a few dark squiggles on a blank page.

Working within a single scene the writer must accomplish more with less. The satisfaction for the reader comes from the emotional impact of the story and also from a slightly more removed appreciation of the form, of the writer's artistry in all that is accomplished with one scene.

The content is at least partially in the form. As in poetry, form echoes and reverberates the effect for the reader. Hempel's story "San Francisco" accomplishes this to a wonderful end. The repressed anger and despair, the loss, the *absence*—of the watch, of the mother, is reinforced by the brevity of the narrative. The structure acts as a meta-metaphor for the story's theme of subverted grief. The reader's experience is informed by the lapidary rendering of the single scene.

When writing poetry in form, the accepted rule is that a poet can deviate from the strictures of the form a time or two, and such departures enhance the poem's power. An extra foot, an off-rhyme, maybe a double envoi at the end of a sonnet, all have the potential to lift the poem off the page, to transport the reader beyond himself. Similarly, a few allowances in what constitutes a single scene has enabled this collection to be more exemplar than example.

A tighter form allows the writer to express emotions—conflict, dissonance, fear, or love—that could be overwhelming or trite given too much free-form space. Perhaps that is why so many of these stories are about disturbed relationships or moments right before the end of life. Love and death and making a scene. The single scene story allows these experiences to go directly into our hearts where they enrich and inform our own awareness of being in this world.

The Soul Molecule

STEVE ALMOND

I was on my way to see Wilkes. We were going to have brunch. Wilkes was a minor friend from college. He played number one on the squash team. I'd challenged him once, during a round-robin, but he annihilated me with lobs. Afterward, in the showers, he told me his secret.

"Vision," he said. "You have to see what's going to happen."

Now it is five years on, and I still felt sort of indebted to him. This was idiotic, but I couldn't unpersuade myself. I kept remembering those lobs, one after another, as elegant as parasols.

Wilkes was in the back of the restaurant, in a booth. We said our hellos and he picked up his menu and set it down again.

"We've known each other a long time, haven't we, Jim?"

"Sure," I said.

"Eight years now, coming up on eight."

"That sounds about right."

"You wouldn't think less of me if I told you something, would you?"

"Heck no," I said. Mostly, I was wondering how much breakfast would cost, and whether I'd have to pay.

"I've got a cartridge in my head," Wilkes said.

He had that drowsy pinch around the eyes you see in certain leading men. He was wearing a blue blazer with discreet buttons. He looked like the sort of guy from whom other guys would buy bonds. That was his business. He was in bonds.

"A cartridge has been placed in my head for surveillance purposes. This was done a number of years ago by a race of superior beings. I don't know if you know anything about abduction, Jim. Do you know anything about abduction?"

"Wait a second," I said.

"An abduction can take one of two forms. The first—you don't need to know the technical terms—the first is purely for research purposes. Cell harvesting, that kind of thing. The second involves implants, Jim, such as the one in my brain."

Wilkes was from Maryland, the Chesapeake Bay area. He spoke in these crisp, prepared sentences. I'd always thought he'd be a corporate lawyer, with an office in a glass tower and a secretary better looking than anyone I knew.

"You're telling me you've been abducted," I said.

Wilkes nodded. He picked up his fork and balanced it on his thumb. "The cartridges can be thought of as visual recorders, something like cameras. They allow the caretakers to monitor human activity without causing alarm."

"The caretakers," I said.

"They see whatever I see." Wilkes gazed at me for a long moment. It was eerie, like I was staring into the big black space where an audience might be. Finally, he looked up and half-rose out of his seat. "Mom," he said. "Dad. Hey, there they are. You remember Jim."

"Why, of course," said his mother. She was a Southern lady with one of those soft handshakes.

"Pleasure" Mr. Wilkes said. "Unexpected pleasure. No no. Don't make a fuss. We'll just settle in. What are you up to, Jim? How're you bringing in the pesos?"

"Research," I said.

His face brightened. "Research, eh? The research game. What's that, biotech?"

"Yeah, sort of."

I'd never done any research. But I liked the way the word sounded. It sounded broad and scientific and beyond reproach.

"Your folks?" Mr. Wilkes said.

"You'll remember us to them, I hope," Mrs. Wilkes said.

I had no recollection of my parents having met the Wilkeses.

"What are you two bird dogs up to?" Mr. Wilkes said. He was from Connecticut, but he sometimes enjoyed speaking like a Texan.

Wilkes was squeezed next to his dad and his voice was full of that miserable complicated family shit. "We were talking," he said. "I was telling Jim about the cartridge in my head."

Mr. Wilkes fixed him with a look, and I thought for a second of that Goya painting, Saturn wolfing down his kids like they were chicken fingers. Mrs. Wilkes began fiddling with the salt and pepper, as if she might want to knit with them eventually.

"How about that?" Mr. Wilkes said. "What do you think of that, Jim?"

"Interesting," I said.

"*Interesting?* That the best you can do? Come on now. This is the old cartridge in the head. The old implant-a-roony."

I started to think, right then, about this one class I'd taken sophomore year, the Biology of Religion. The professor was a young guy who was doing research at the medical school. He told us that the belief in a higher power was a function of biological desire, a glandular thing. The whole topic got him very worked up.

Mr. Wilkes said: "Do you know why they do it, Jim?"

"Sir?"

He turned to his son again. "Did you explain the integration phases to him? The hybrids? The grays? Anything?"

"He just got here," Wilkes said.

Mr. Wilkes was sitting across from me. He was one of these big Republicans you sometimes see. The gin blossoms, the blue blazer. His whole aura screamed *yacht.*

"They teach you any folklore in that fancy college of yours? Fairy, dybbuk, goblin, sprite. Ring a bell, Jim? These are the names the ancients used to describe our extraterrestrial caretakers. 'Their appearance was like burning coals of fire and like the appearance of lamps: It went up and down among the living creatures, and the fire was bright and out of the fire went forth lightning.' That's straight from the Book of Ezekiel. What's that sound like to you, Son? Does that sound like God on his throne of glory?"

"No," I said. "I guess not."

"There's a reason Uncle Sam launched Project Blue Book," Mr. Wilkes said. "He was forced to, Jim. Without some kind of coherent response, there'd be no way to stem the panic. Let me ask you something. Do you know how many sightings have been reported to the Department of Defense in the past ten years? Guess. Two point five million. Abductions? Seven hundred thousand plus. They are among us, Jim."

Our waitress had appeared.

"Do you serve Egg Beaters?" Mr. Wilkes said. The waitress shook her head.

"Toast," Mrs. Wilkes said. "You can have some toast, dear."

"I don't want toast," Mr. Wilkes said.

Wilkes looked pretty much entirely miserable.

"What about egg whites," Mr. Wilkes said. "Can you whip me up an omelet with egg whites?"

The waitress shifted her weight from one haunch to the other. She was quite beautiful, though a bit dragged down by circumstance. "An omelet with what?" she said.

"The white part of the egg. The part that isn't the yolk." Mr. Wilkes picked up his fork and began to simulate the act of scrambling eggs.

"I'm asking what you want in the omelet, Sir."

"Oh. I see. Ok. How about mushroom, swiss, and bacon."

"*Bacon?*" said Mrs. Wilkes.

I didn't know what the hell to order.

The waitress left, and Mr. Wilkes turned right back to me. He'd done some fund-raising for the GOP and I could see now just how effective he might be in this capacity. "Mrs. Wilkes and I, we both have implants. It's no secret. Not uncommon for them to tag an entire family. Did Jonathon already explain this?"

"I didn't explain anything," Wilkes said. "You didn't give me a chance."

"Yes," Mrs. Wilkes said. "You mustn't dominate the conversation, Warren."

"Remember Briggs?" Wilkes said.

"Who?"

"Briggs. Ron Briggs. Played number four on the team. He's got an implant. He lives out in Sedona now."

"Do we know him?" Mrs. Wilkes said.

Mr. Wilkes waved his hand impatiently. "Now I'm not going to bore you with some long story about our abductions, Jim. How would that be? You show up for breakfast and you have to listen to *that*. What you need to understand is the role these beings play. If they wanted to destroy us, if that was their intent, hell, I wouldn't be talking to you right now. They're caretakers, Jim. An entire race of caretakers. I'm not trying to suggest that these implants are any bed of roses, mind you. You've got all the beta waves to contend with, the ringing. Val's got a hell of a scar."

Mrs. Wilkes blushed. She had an expensive hairstyle and skin that looked a bit irradiated. "He's going to think we're kooks," she said.

"Not at all," I said quietly.

"Hell, we are kooks," Mr. Wilkes said. "The whole damn species is kooks. Only a fool would deny it."

I waited for the silence to sort of subside and excused myself I needed some cold water on my ears. I filled the sink and did a quick dunk and stared at the bathroom mirror—really *stared*—until my face got all big-eyed and desperate.

When I got back to the table, the food had arrived and the Wilkeses were eating in this extremely polite manner. I'd visited them once, on the way back from a squash match at Penn. All I could remember about their home was the carpets. They must have had about a thousand of them, beautiful and severe, the kind you didn't even want to step on. I couldn't imagine a kid growing up in that place.

My French toast was sitting there, with some strawberries, but I wasn't hungry.

Mrs. Wilkes frowned. "Is something wrong with your food, dear? We can order you something else."

"That was pretty funny," I said finally. "You guys really had me going. You must be quite the charades family."

The Wilkeses, all of them, looked at me. It was that look you get from any kind of true believer, this mountain of pity sort of wobbling on a pea of doubt.

I thought about my biology professor again. Toward the end of class, just before I dropped out in fact, he gave us a lecture about this one chemical that gets released by the pineal gland. He called it the soul molecule, because it triggered all kinds of mystical thoughts. Just a pinch was enough to have people talking to angels. It was the stuff that squirted out at death, when the spirit is said to rise from the body.

Mr. Wilkes was talking about the binary star system Zeta Reticuli and the Taos hum and the Oz effect. But you could tell he wasn't saying what he really wanted to. His face was red with the disappointed blood.

The waitress came and cleared the dishes.

Wilkes started to mention a few mutual friends, guys who made me think of loud cologne and urinals.

Mrs. Wilkes excused herself and returned a few minutes later with fresh makeup.

Mr. Wilkes laid down a fifty. It was one of his rituals and, like all our rituals, it gave him this little window of expansiveness.

"I don't know the exact game plan, Jim. Anyone tells you they do, head the other direction. But I do know that these beings, these grays, they are essentially good. Why else would they travel thirty-seven light-years just to bail our sorry asses out? It's the mission that affects me," he said. "Mrs. Wilkes and Jonathon and I, all of us, we feel a part of something larger." He gazed at his wife and son and smiled with a tremendous vulnerability. "I know how it looks from the outside. But we don't know everything. We all make mistakes." He tried to say something else, but his big schmoozy baritone faltered.

Mrs. Wilkes put her hand on his.

"What the hell do I know?" Mr. Wilkes said.

"We all make mistakes," his wife said.

"I'm not perfect."

"Nobody's perfect, love."

There was a lot passing between them. Wilkes started to blush. His father seemed to want to touch his cheek. "They're just trying to save us from ourselves, so we don't ruin everything."

The waitress had come and gone and left change on the table. All around us people were charging through their mornings, toward God knows what.

The Wilkeses were sitting there, in their nice clothing, but I was seeing something else now, these whitish blobs at the centers of their bodies. It was their spirits I was seeing. I wasn't scared or anything. Everyone's a saint when it comes to the naked spirit. The other stuff just sort of grows over us, like weeds.

I thought about that crazy professor again. He'd called me to his office after Thanksgiving to tell me I was flunking. He was all torn up, as if he'd somehow betrayed me. He asked if I'd learned anything at all in his class. I said of course I had, I'd learned plenty of things, but when he pressed me to name one or two, I drew a blank. Just before I left, he came over to my side of the desk and put his hand on my shoulder and said, *We all need someone to watch over us, James.*

"Do you believe that?" Mr. Wilkes said.

I was pretty sure I'd never see the three of them again and it made me a little sad, a little reluctant to leave.

Wilkes was smoothing down his lapels. Mrs. Wilkes smiled with her gentle teeth and Mr. Wilkes began softly, invisibly, to weep. His spirit was like a little kerchief tucked into that big blue suit.

"I think we're going to be all right," I said. "That's the feeling I get." This was true. I was, in fact, having some kind of clairvoyant moment. Everything that was about to happen I could see just before it did.

Outside, up in the sky, above even the murmuring satellites, an entire race of benevolent yayas was maybe peering down at me with glassy black eyes. I started waving. The waitress breezed by and blew me a kiss. Mr. Wilkes slid another fifty across the table and winked. The sun lanced through a bank of clouds and lit the passing traffic like tinsel. I waved like hell.

Ad Infinitum: A Short Story

JOHN BARTH

A t the far end of their lawn, down by the large pond or small marshy lake, he is at work in "his" daylily garden—weeding, feeding, clearing out dead growth to make room for new—when the ring of the telephone bell begins this story. They spend so much of their day outdoors, in the season, that years ago they installed an outside phone bell under the porch roof overhang. As a rule, they bring a cordless phone out with them, too, onto the sundeck or the patio, where they can usually reach it before the answering machine takes over. It is too early in the season, however, for them to have resumed that convenient habit. Anyhow, this is a weekday midmorning; she's indoors still, in her studio. She'll take the call.

The telephone rings a second time, but not a third. On his knees in the daylily garden, he has paused, trowel in hand, and straightened his back. He returns to his homely work, which he always finds mildly agreeable but now suddenly relishes: simple physical work with clean soil in fine air and sunlight. The call could be routine: some bit of business, some service person. In the season, he's the one who normally takes weekday morning calls, not to interrupt her concentration in the studio; but it's not quite the season yet. The caller could be a friend—although their friends generally don't call them before noon. It could be a telephone solicitor: There seem to be more of those every year, enough to lead them to consider unlisting their number, but not quite yet to unlist it. It could be a misdial.

If presently she steps out onto the sundeck, looking for him, whether to bring him the cordless phone if the call is for him or to report some news, this story's beginning will have ended, its middle begun.

Presently she steps out onto the sundeck, overlooking their lawn and the large pond or small lake beyond it. She had been at her big old drafting-table, working—trying to work, anyhow; pretending to work; maybe actually almost really working—when that phone call began this story. From her upholstered swivel chair, through one of the water-facing windows of her studio, she could see him on hands and knees down in his daylily gar-den along the water's edge. Indeed, she had been more or less watching him, preoccupied in his old jeans and sweatshirt and gardening gloves, while she worked or tried or pretended to work at her worktable. At the first ring, she saw him straighten his back and square his shoulders, his trowel-hand rest-ing on his thigh-top, and at the second (which she had waited for before picking up the receiver) look houseward and remove one glove. At the non-third ring, as she said hello to the caller, he pushed back his eyeglasses with his ungloved hand. She had continued then to watch him—returning to his task, his left hand still ungloved for picking out the weeds troweled up with his right—as she received the caller's news.

The news is bad indeed. Not quite so bad, perhaps, as her very-worst-case scenario, but considerably worse than her average-feared scenarios, and enor-mously worse than her best-case, hoped-against-hope scenarios. The news is of the sort that in one stroke eliminates all agreeable plans and expectations—indeed, all prospect of real pleasure from the moment of its communication. In effect, the news puts a period to this pair's prevailingly happy though cer-tainly not carefree life; there cannot imaginably be further delight in it, of the sort that they have been amply blessed with through their years together. All that is over now: for her already; for him and for them as soon as she relays the news to him—which, of course, she must and promptly will.

Gone. Finished. Done with.

Meanwhile, *she* knows the news, but he does not, yet. From her work-table she sees him poke at the lily-bed mulch with the point of his trowel and pinch out by the roots, with his ungloved other hand, a bit of chickweed, wire grass, or ground ivy. She accepts the caller's terse expression of sympa-thy and duly expresses in return her appreciation for that unenviable bit of message-bearing. She has asked only a few questions—there aren't many to be asked—and has attended the courteous, pained, terrible but unsurprising replies. Presently she replaces the cordless telephone on its base and leans back for a moment in her comfortable desk chair to watch her mate at his ordinary, satisfying work and to assimilate what she has just been told.

There is, however, no assimilating what she has just been told—or, if there is, that assimilation is to be measured in years, even decades, not in moments, days, weeks, months, seasons. She must now get up from her chair, walk through their modest, pleasant house to the sundeck, cross the lawn to the daylily garden down by the lake or pond, and tell him the news. She regards him for some moments longer, aware that as he proceeds with his gardening, his mind is almost certainly on the phone call. He will be wondering whether she's still speaking with the caller or has already hung up the telephone and is en route to tell him the news. Perhaps the call was merely a routine bit of business, not worth reporting until their paths recross at coffee break or lunchtime. A wrong number, even, it might have been, or another pesky telephone solicitor. He may perhaps be half-deciding by now that it was, after all, one of those innocuous possibilities.

She compresses her lips, closes and reopens her eyes, exhales, rises, and goes to tell him the news.

He sees her, presently, step out onto the sundeck, and signals his where-abouts with a wave of his trowel in case she hasn't yet spotted him down on his knees in the daylily garden. At that distance, he can read nothing in her expression or carriage, but he notes that she isn't bringing with her the cord-less telephone. Not impossibly, of course, she could be simply taking a break from her studio work to stretch her muscles, refill her coffee mug, use the toilet, enjoy a breath of fresh springtime air, and report to him that the phone call was nothing—a misdial, or one more canvasser. She has stepped from the deck and begun to cross the lawn, himward, unurgently. He resumes weeding out the wire grass that perennially invades their flower beds, its rhizomes spreading under the mulch, secretly reticulating the clean soil and choking the lily bulbs. A weed, he would agree, is not an organism wicked in itself; it's simply one of nature's creatures going vigorously about its natural business in a place where one wishes that it would not. He finds something impressive, even awesome, in the intricacy and tenacity of those rhizomes and their countless interconnections; uproot one carefully and it seems to network the whole bed—the whole lawn, probably. Break it off at any point and it redoubles like the monster Whatsitsname in Greek mythol-ogy. The Hydra. So it's terrible, too, in its way, as well as splendid, that blind tenacity, that evolved persistence and virtual ineradicability, heedless of the daylilies that it competes with and vitiates, indifferent to everything except its mindless self-proliferation. It occurs to him that, on the other hand, that same persistence is exactly what he cultivates in their flowers, pinching back the rhododendrons and dead-heading yesterday's lilies to encourage multiple blooms. An asset here, a liability there, from the gardener's point of view, while Nature shrugs its non-judgmental shoulders. Unquestionably, however, it would be easier to raise a healthy crop of wire grass by weeding out the daylilies than vice versa.

With such reflections he distracts himself, or tries or pretends to distract himself, as she steps unhurriedly from the sundeck and begins to cross the lawn, himward.

She is, decidedly, in no hurry to cross the lawn and say what she must say. There is her partner, lover, best friend and companion, at his innocent, agreeable work: half chore, half hobby, a respite from his own busy professional life. Apprehensive as he will have been since the telephone call, he is still *as if* all right; she, too, and their life and foreseeable future—*as if* still all right. In order to report to him the dreadful news, she must cross the entire lawn, with its central Kwanzan cherry tree: a magnificently spreading, fully mature specimen, just now at the absolute pink peak of its glorious bloom. About halfway between the sundeck and that Kwanzan cherry stands a younger and smaller, but equally vigorous, Zumi crab apple that they themselves put in a few seasons past to replace a storm-damaged predecessor. It, too, is a near-perfect specimen of its kind, and likewise at or just past the peak of its flowering, the new green leaves thrusting already through the white clustered petals. To reach her husband with the news, she must pass under that Kwanzan cherry—the centerpiece of their property, really, whose great widespread limbs they fear for in summer thunder squalls. For her to reach that cherry tree will take a certain small time: perhaps twenty seconds, as she's in no hurry. To stroll leisurely even to the Zumi crab apple takes ten or a dozen seconds—about as long as it takes to read this sentence aloud. Walking past that perfect crab apple, passing under that resplendent cherry, crossing the remaining half of the lawn down to the lily garden and telling him the news—these sequential actions will comprise the middle of this story, already in progress.

In the third of a minute required for her to amble from sundeck to cherry tree—even in the dozen seconds from deck to crab apple (she's passing that crab apple now)—her companion will have weeded his way perhaps one trowels-length farther through his lily bed, which borders that particular stretch of pond- or lakeside for several yards, to the far corner of their lot, where the woods begin. Musing upon this circumstance—a reflex of insulation, perhaps, from the devastating news—puts her in mind of Zeno's famous paradox of Achilles and the tortoise. Swift Achilles, Zeno teases, can never catch the tortoise, for in whatever short time required for him to close half the hundred yards between them, the sluggish animal will have moved perhaps a few inches; and in the very short time required to halve that remaining distance, an inch or two more, et cetera—ad infinitum, inasmuch as finite distances, however small, can be halved forever. It occurs to her, indeed—although she is neither philosopher nor mathematician—that her husband needn't even necessarily be moving away from her, so to speak, as she passes now under the incredibly full-blossomed canopy of the Kwanzan cherry and pauses to be quietly reastonished, if scarcely soothed, by its splendor. He (likewise Zeno's tortoise) could remain fixed in the same spot; he could even rise and stroll to meet her, *run* to meet her under that flowered canopy; in every case and at whatever clip, the intervening distances must be halved, re-halved, and re-re-halved forever, ad infinitum. Like the figured lovers in Keats's "Ode on a Grecian Urn" (another image from her college days), she and he will never touch, although unlike those, these are living people en route to the how-many-thousandth tête-a-tête of their years together—when, alas, she must convey to him her happiness-ending news. In John Keats's words and by the terms of Zeno's paradox, *forever* will he love, and she be fair. Forever they'll go on closing the distance between them—as they have in effect been doing, like any well-bonded pair, since Day One of their connection—yet never close it altogether: asymptotic curves that eternally approach, but never meet.

But of course they will meet, very shortly, and before even then they'll come within hailing distance, speaking distance, murmuring distance. Here in the middle of the middle of the story, as she re-emerges from under the bridal-like canopy of cherry blossoms into the tender midmorning sunlight, an osprey suddenly plummets from the sky to snatch a small fish from the shallows. They both turn to look. He, the nearer, can see the fish flip vainly in the raptor's talons; the osprey aligns its prey adroitly fore-and-aft, head to wind, to minimize drag, and flaps off with it toward its rickety treetop nest across the pond or lake.

The fish is dying. The fish is dying. The fish is dead.

When he was a small boy being driven in his parents' car to something he feared—a piano recital for which he felt unready, a medical procedure that might hurt, some new town or neighborhood that the family was moving to—he used to tell himself that as long as the car-ride lasted, all would be well, and wish it would last forever. The condemned en route to execution must feel the same, he supposes, while at the same time wanting the dread thing done with: The tumbril has not yet arrived at the guillotine; until it does, we are immortal, and here meanwhile is this once pleasing avenue, this handsome small park with its central fountain, this plane-tree-shaded corner where, in happier times.

A gruesome image occurs to him, from his reading of Dante's *Inferno* back in college days: The Simoniacs, traffickers in sacraments and holy offices, are punished in hell by being thrust head-downward for all eternity into holes in the infernal rock. Kneeling to speak with them in that miserable position, Dante is reminded of the similar fate of convicted assassins in his native Florence, executed by being bound hand and foot and buried alive head-down in a hole. Before that hole is filled, the officiating priest bends down as the poet is doing, to hear the condemned man's last confession—which, in desperation, the poor wretch no doubt prolongs, perhaps adding fictitious sins to his factual ones in order to postpone the end—and in so doing (it occurs to him now, turning another trowelsworth of soil as his wife approaches from the cherry tree) appending one more real though venial sin, the sin of lying, to the list yet to be confessed.

Distracted, he breaks off a wire-grass root.

"Time," declares the Russian critic Mikhail Bakhtin, "is the true hero of every feast." It is also the final dramaturge of every story. History is a Mandelbrot set, as infinitely subdivisible as is space in Zeno's paradox. No interval past or future but can be partitioned and sub-partitioned, articulated down through ever finer, self-similar scales like the infinitely indented coastlines of fractal geometry. This intelligent, as if-still-happy couple in late mid-story—what are they doing with such reflections as these but attempting unsuccessfully to kill time, as Time is unhurriedly but surely killing them? In narrated life, even here (halfway between cherry tree and daylily garden) we could suspend and protract the remaining action indefinitely, without "freeze-framing" it as on Keats's urn; we need only slow it, delay it, atomize it, flash back in time as the woman strolls forward in space with her terrible news. Where exactly on our planet are these people, for example? What pond or lake is that beyond their pleasant lawn, its olive surface just now marbled with springtime yellow pollen? Other than one osprey nest in a dead but still-standing oak, what is the prospect of its farther shore? We have mentioned the man's jeans, sweatshirt, gloves, and eyeglasses, but nothing further of his appearance, age, ethnicity, character, temperament, and history (other than that he once attended college), and (but for that same detail) nothing whatever of hers; nor anything, really, of their life together, its gratifications and tribulations, adventures large or small, careers, corner-turnings. Have they children? Grandchildren, even? What sort of telephone solicitors disturb their evidently rural peace? What of their house's architecture and furnishings, its past owners, if any, and the history of the land on which it sits—back to the last glaciation, say, which configured "their" pond or lake and its topographical surround? Without our woman's pausing for an instant in her hasteless but steady course across those few remaining yards of lawn, the narrative of her final steps might suspend indefinitely their completion. What variety of grasses does that lawn comprise, interspersed with what weeds, habitating what insecta and visited by what birds? How, exactly, does the spring air feel on her sober-visaged face? Are his muscles sore from gardening, and, if so, is that degree of soreness, from that source, agreeable to him or otherwise? What is the relevance, if any, of their uncertainty whether that water beyond their lawn is properly to be denominated a large pond or a small lake, and has that uncertainty been a running levity through their years there? Is yonder osprey's nest truly rickety, or only apparently so? The middle of this story nears its end, but has not reached it yet, not yet. There's time still, still world enough and time. There are narrative possibilities still unforeclosed. If our lives are stories, and if this story is three-fourths told, it is not yet four-fifths told; if four-fifths, not yet five-sixths, et cetera, et cetera—and meanwhile, meanwhile it is *as if* all were still well.

In non-narrated life, alas, it is a different story, as in the world of actual tortoises, times, and coastlines. It might appear that in Time's infinite sub-segmentation, 11:00 A.M. can never reach 11:30, far less noon; it might appear that Achilles can never reach the tortoise, nor any story its end, nor any news its destined hearer—yet reach it they do, in the world we know. Stories attain their denouement by selective omission, as do real-world coastline measurements; Achilles swiftly overtakes the tortoise by ignoring the terms of Zeno's paradox. Time, however, more wonderful than these, omits nothing, ignores nothing, yet moves inexorably from hour to hour in just five dozen minutes.

The story of our life is not our life; it is our story. Soon she must tell him the news.

Our lives are not stories. Now she must tell him the news.

This story will never end. This story ends.

The Voices from the Other Room

RICHARD BAUSCH

appy?
Mmm.
That was lovely.
. . .
Wasn't that lovely?
Sweet.
So sweet.
. . .
I've been so miserable.
. . .
Are you warm?
I'm toasty.
Love me?
What do you think?
It was good for you?
You were nice.
Nice?
. . .
Just nice?
Nice is wonderful, Larry. It's more than good, for instance. You're always
so insecure about it. Why is that?
I'm not insecure. I just like to know I gave you pleasure.
You did.
That's all I wanted to know.
. . .
I mean it's a simple thing.

Okay.

Ellen?

What.

Nothing.

No, tell me.

Well—if it was wonderful, why didn't you say wonderful?

Is this a test?

Okay, you're right. I'm sorry. I wish we could get together more often. I've been so miserable. You have no idea.

I think I have an idea.

I don't mean you haven't suffered too.

Good thing.

Yeah, but I can't help it—I feel so guilty about Janice and the boys. I'm afraid they'll see the unhappiness in my face over the dinner table. I wish I could find a way to tell her and get the whole thing settled.

. . .

I just wish I could see you more than once a week.

Larry, don't.

I know you're busy.

Oh, God.

I guess I made it sound like this is a lunch date or something, I'm sorry. I'm such a wreck.

Oh, Larry, why do you have to pick at everything like that?

I said I was sorry.

Well, let's just be quiet awhile, okay? Please?

I'm sorry.

. . .

You comfy?

I think I just said I was.

Okay.

Look, really, why don't we just drift a little now. I'm sleepy. I don't feel like talking.

It seems you never feel like talking anymore.

What would be the point?

That's kind of harsh, don't you think?

We just keep going over the same ground, don't we? We always come back to the same things. You talk about how miserable you are, and then you worry about Janice and the boys, and I talk about how my life, which I can hardly bear, is so busy.

Are you trying to tell me something?

God, I don't think so.

Well, really, Ellen.

I'm not blaming anybody. I want to sleep a little, okay?

Okay.

. . .

But I know I won't sleep.

You sound determined.

I just know myself.

. . .

Ellen?

What?

Nothing.

What?

It's silly.

I expect nothing less. Tell me.

You wanted to sleep.

Just say it, Larry.

. . .

Will you just say it?

It's—well—it's just that okay is okay, and wonderful is wonderful, and nice is nice. They all mean different things.

. . .

I told you it was silly.

What sort of reassurance are you looking for here? I thought it was nice. I thought it was wonderful. I'm here, exactly as I have been every Friday for the last two months. Nothing has changed. All right?

. . .

You're such a worrier.

I'm sorry.

. . .

But was it nice or wonderful?

Lord. Pick one. You were that.

You're pretty glib about it, don't you think?

Really?

Okay, never mind.

Look, what is this?

I was just asking. Nice is not wonderful.

Is this a grammar lesson?

I'm just saying a true thing, that's all.

God! You were wonderful. Great. Terrific. Magnificent. And glorious. The fucking earth moved.

. . .

Okay?

. . .

Don't tell me I hurt your feelings now.

. . .

Come on. Is his iddy-biddy feelings hurt?

Don't do that. It tickles.

This?

Cut it out, Ellen.

I'm tickling you. It's supposed to tickle.

Well don't. I'm not in the mood.

All right.

And don't be mad.

I'm *not* mad.

Sorry.

. . .

Whole thing's silly.

Whatever you say, Mr. Man.

There's no need to take an attitude.

. . .

Ellen?

Darling, I think it's a little late to be worrying about whether or not we've been okay in bed, isn't it?

Oh, so now I was just okay.

My God!

It's never too late to worry about a thing like that.

Oh, for Christ's sake. I didn't mean it that way. Light me a cigarette.

What way did you mean it?

Light me a cigarette, would you?

. . .

Boy, this is some afterglow we've got here.
I can't help it.
. . .
Ellen?
What?
Do you ever think of him when we're—together like this?
Stop it, Larry.
I told you I can't help it.
You're being ridiculous.
. . .
I can't believe you'd bring him up that way.
You do think about him, then.
This isn't a movie, Larry.
No, I know.
. . .
Why'd you say this isn't a movie—what's that supposed to mean?
I don't know. Forget it.
You think I'm being overly dramatic.
. . .
That's natural enough, isn't it? Under the circumstances?
You know, I really don't want to talk about it.
Well, I'll tell you something. I can't get him out of my head.
You? You think about him?
Of course I do.
While we're—when we're—
All the time. Sure.
God.
. . .
Light me a cigarette, would you?
You mean you don't think of him? He never enters your mind?
He never enters my mind. I have trouble remembering him *while he's*
speaking to me.
And you don't—compare?
Compare what?
Nothing.
Oh, for Christ's sake, Larry.
Don't be mad.

Look, I don't think about him. Okay?

He used to tell me things. In those first years you were married.

What things?

Forget it.

Jesus Christ, what are you talking about? What things? What things did he tell you?

Never mind about it, okay? It's nothing.

If it's nothing, why can't you tell me about it?

Don't get up.

I want a cigarette.

I'll get you one.

. . .

There.

Now tell me what fucking things he talked to you about, Larry.

Well—well he's my brother. Men talk about their sexual—about sex. You know.

You mean he would tell you what we *did?* Oh, boy! Give me an example.

Look, I'm sorry I brought it up.

No—come on now. I want to know. You tell me.

Don't cry.

I'm not crying, goddamn you. Tell me.

He—well, he—he said you did oral things, and that you were excitable.

Excitable.

That you—you'd cry out.

Oh, Jesus God. Oh, boy. This is funny. This is classic.

. . .

Larry?

I know.

You're really an asshole, you know that?

Okay, okay. I'm sorry. It was a long time ago. It was boys talking.

Well, but—now—let me see if I can get this straight. Now, I'm not living up to your fantasies, based on what Joe told you about me. Is that it?

No. Christ—you make it sound—

But you are. You're thinking of what Joe told you, right?

I don't know.

If that isn't men for you.

Now don't start on all that crap. There's nothing to extrapolate from the fact that my brother told me a few things a long time ago.

Yeah, well maybe Joe was lying. Did that ever occur to you? Maybe I wouldn't be here with you now if Joe was half as good as he must've said he was.

You mean that's the only reason we—you and I—

Boy, is this ever a fun conversation.

. . .

Tell me what I'm apparently lacking according to the legends you've heard.

Stop it, Ellen. I just wanted to be sure I was giving you as much pleasure as—hell, never mind.

No, this is interesting. You want to know if I think you're as good. Right?

I wanted to be sure I was giving you pleasure. Is that such a terrible thing?

And there was no thought of gratifying your male ego?

Please don't hand me that feminist shit. Not now.

Well, isn't that it?

No, that is *not* it.

You couldn't tell from what we just did that I was getting pleasure out of it?

Okay.

This whole thing bothers you more than it does me, right?

Well, he's my brother, after all.

He never deigned to remind himself of that fact, why should you?

Because he *is* my brother.

When was the last time he played that role with you?

This isn't about roles or role-playing, okay? This is blood.

. . .

No, don't, Ellen. Stay, please.

When was the last time he had anything to do with you, besides ordering you around and berating you for the fact that you don't make a hundred seventy thousand dollars a year setting up contracts for corporate giants?

. . .

Remember when I got interested in astronomy, and he bought me the telescope and we started looking at the stars, making calculations and charting the heavenly bodies in flight? Remember that?

I guess.

I was looking through the thing one night, and it came to me that the distances between those stars, that was like the distances I felt between him and me. And it didn't have anything to do with sex. The sex was fine, then. Back then. At least I thought it was fine.

Fine. Not nice or wonderful?

Jesus, you're beginning to sound pathetic.

It was a joke, Ellen. Can't you take a joke?

I wasn't joking. I was trying to tell you something.

. . .

If this was a movie, I think I'd be trying to get you to kill him or something. Make it look like an accident.

Good Lord.

Why not? It happens all the time. We could play Hamlet.

. . .

The classic love triangle.

Stop this.

Hey, Larry. It's just talk, right? I'm babbling on because I'm so happy.

Why'd you marry him, anyway?

I loved him.

You *thought* you loved him.

No, goddamn you—I *did* love him.

Okay, I'm sorry.

. . .

Can you forgive me?

I don't know what kind of person you think I am.

It's just that all this is so strange for me. And I can't keep from thinking about him.

You mean you can't stop thinking about what he told you about me in bed.

I wish I hadn't mentioned that. I'm not talking about that now. That isn't all we talked about.

You told him about all your adventures with Janice.

Stop it, Ellen.

Well, tell me. Give me an example of whatever else you talked about.

I don't know. When I was in Texas that time, and he came through on one of his trips. You and he had been married the year before, I think. He was so—glad. He told me stuff you guys were doing together. Places you went. He even had pictures. You looked so happy in the pictures.

I *was* happy.

. . .

We've been married ten years. What do you think? It's all been torture?

. . .

Jesus, Larry.

Well, I feel bad for him.

He's happy. He's got his work. His travels, his pals. His life is organized about the way he likes it. You know what he said to me on our last anniversary? He said he wasn't sure he was as heterosexual as other men. Imagine that.

What the hell was he talking about?

He doesn't feel drawn to me that way. He hasn't touched me in months, okay? Do you want me to be as graphic about all this as he was back when we were twenty-five years old and I believed that what happened between us was private?

No, don't—come on. I'm sorry. Don't cry.

I'm not crying.

. . .

Anyway, this doesn't really have anything to do with him.

I wish we could stop talking about him.

You're the one who brought him up, Larry.

Don't be mad. Come on, please.

Well, for Christ's sake, can't you just enjoy something for what it is, without tearing it all to pieces? You know what you are? You're morbid.

I'm scared.

. . .

I am. I'm scared.

Scared of what? Joe? He's in another time zone, remember? He won't be home for another week.

I think I'm scared of you.

. . .

It's like I'm on the outside of you some way. Like there's walls I can't see through. I don't know what effect I have on you. Or if I really mean anything to you.

Do you want me to simper and tell you how I can't live without you?

. . .

Well?

I don't know what I want. It's like you're a drug, and I can't get enough of you. But I get the feeling sometimes—I can't express it exactly—like—well, like you could do without me very easily.

. . .

I do. I get that feeling.

Poor Larry.

I can't help it.

And now you expect me to reassure you about that, too.

There's nothing wrong with saying you love someone.

And that's what you want?

Never mind.

No, really. We started with you worrying about whether or not you were as sexy as Joe—or whether or not I found you as sexy as Joe.

Let's just forget it, okay?

Are you afraid of what my answer might be?

I thought you *had* answered it.

. . .

Look, why did you want to get involved in the first place?

I think it just happened, didn't it, Larry?

. . .

Didn't it?

That's the way it felt.

Then why question it now?

You said you looked through the telescope and saw the distances between the stars—

Are we going to talk about this all night?

Well, why haven't you divorced him?

I might. Someday I might.

But why not now?

Do you want me to?

Do you want to?

Where would I go?

You could come to me.

I'm here now.

But we could get married, Ellen.

Oh, please. Can we change the subject? Can we talk about all this later? Surely you can see that this is not the time.

You don't believe me?

. . .

It would be terrible to leave Janice and the boys. But I think I would. If I could have you. I really think I would.

You do. You *think* you would.

. . .

Well, would you or wouldn't you?

I said I think I would.

You're hilarious. Truly a stitch, you know it?

I believe that I would.

Ah, an article of faith.

There's no reason to be sarcastic, Ellen.

I know, Larry, let's talk about the stars, crossing through the blackness of space. Let's talk about the moons of Jupiter and Mars.

You're being sarcastic.

I'm simply trying to change the subject.

Okay, we'll change the subject.

. . .

If that's what you want. We'll just change it.

It's what I want.

. . .

Well?

I'm thinking. Jesus, you don't give a man a chance.

Terrific.

Just wait a minute, can't you?

. . .

Ellen?

I'm listening.

Did you ever think you'd end up here?

I don't think I'm going to *end up* here, particularly. You make it sound awful.

You know how I mean it.

All right, darling, let's just say that from where I started, I would never have predicted it. You're right about that.

I feel the same way.

Now if you don't mind, sir, can we sleep a little?
I'm sorry.
And stop apologizing. I swear you're the most apologetic man I know.
Do you know how many times a day you say you're sorry about something?
You're right, sweetie, I'm sor—Jesus. Listen to me.
. . .
I've been so miserable, Ellen.
Oh, Christ.
Okay, I won't talk about it anymore.
Is that a promise?
I promise, sweetie, really.
Thanks.
. . .
I think I should go soon.
I guess so.
. . .
Sweetie?
What, Larry.
Do you love me?
. . .
I just need to hear it once.
. . .
Honey?
. . .
Aren't you going to?
. . .
Ellen?
. . .
Sweetie, please.
. . .
Ellen?

August 25, 1983

JORGE LUIS BORGES

saw by the clock at the little station that it was past eleven. I began walking through the night toward the hotel. I experienced, as I had at other times in the past, the resignation and relief we are made to feel by those places most familiar to us. The wide gate was open; the large country house itself, in darkness. I went into the vestibule, whose pale mirrors echoed back the plants of the salon. Strangely, the owner did not recognize me; he turned the guest register around for me to sign. I picked up the pen chained to the register stand, dipped it in the brass inkwell, and then, as I leaned over the open book, there occurred the first of the many surprises the night would have in store for me—my name, Jorge Luis Borges, had already been written there, and the ink was not yet dry.

"I thought you'd already gone upstairs," the owner said to me. Then he looked at me more closely and corrected himself: "Oh, I beg your pardon, sir. You look so much like the other gentleman, but you are younger."

"What room is he in?" I asked.

"He asked for Room 19," came the reply.

It was as I had feared.

I dropped the pen and hurried up the stairs. Room 19 was on the third floor; it opened onto a sad, run-down sort of terrace with a park bench and, as I recall, a railing running around it. It was the hotel's most secluded room. I tried the door; it opened at my touch. The overhead light still burned. In the pitiless light, I came face to face with myself. There, in the narrow iron bed—older, withered, and very pale—lay I, on my back, my eyes turned up vacantly toward the high plaster moldings of the ceiling. Then I heard the voice. It was not exactly my own; it was the one I often hear in my recordings, unpleasant and without modulation.

"How odd," it was saying, "we are two yet we are one. But then nothing is odd in dreams."

"Then. . ." I asked fearfully, "all this is a dream?"

"It is, I am sure, my last dream." He gestured toward the empty bottle on the marble nightstand. "You, however, shall have much to dream, before you come to this night. What date is it for you?"

"I'm not sure," I said, rattled. "But yesterday was my sixty-first birthday."

"When in your waking state you reach this night again, yesterday will have been your eighty-fourth. Today is August 25, 1983."

"So long to wait," I murmured.

"Not for me," he said shortly. "For me, there's almost no time left. At any moment I may die, at any moment I may fade into that which is unknown to me, and still I dream these dreams of my double . . . that tiresome subject I got from Stevenson and mirrors."

I sensed that the evocation of Stevenson's name was a farewell, not some empty stroke of pedantry. I was he, and I understood. It takes more than life's most dramatic moments to make a Shakespeare, hitting upon memorable phrases. To distract him, I said:

"I knew this was going to happen to you. Right here in this hotel, years ago, in one of the rooms below, we began the draft of the story of this suicide."

"Yes," he replied slowly, as though piecing together the memories, "but I don't see the connection. In that draft I bought a one-way ticket for Adrogué, and when I got to the Hotel Las Delicias I went up to Room 19, the room farthest from all the rest. It was there that I committed suicide."

"That's why I'm here," I said.

"*Here*? We've always been *here*. It's here in this house on Calle Maipú that I am dreaming you. It is here, in this room that belonged to Mother, that I am taking my departure?"

". . . that belonged to Mother," I repeated, not wanting to understand. "I am dreaming you in Room 19, on the top floor, next to the rooftop terrace?"

"Who is dreaming whom? I know I am dreaming you—I do not know whether you are dreaming me. That hotel in Adrogué was torn down years and years ago—twenty, maybe thirty. Who knows?"

"I am the dreamer," I replied, with a touch of defiance.

"Don't you realize that the first thing to find out is whether there is only one man dreaming, or two men dreaming each other?"

"I am Borges. I saw your name in the register and I came upstairs."

"But I am Borges, and I am dying in a house on Calle Maipú."

There was a silence, and then he said to me:

"Let's try a test. What was the most terrible moment of our life?"

I leaned over him and the two of us spoke at once. I know that neither of us spoke the truth.

A faint smile lit up the aged face. I felt that that smile somehow reflected my own.

"We've lied to each other," he said, "because we feel that we are two, not one. The truth is that we are two yet we are one."

I was beginning to be irritated by this conversation, and I told him so. Then I added: "And you, there in 1983—are you not going to tell me anything about the years I have left?"

"What can I tell you, poor Borges? The misfortunes you are already accustomed to will repeat themselves. You will be left alone in this house. You will touch the books that have no letters and the Swedenborg medallion and the wooden tray with the Federal Cross. Blindness is not darkness; it is a form of solitude. You will return to Iceland."

"Iceland! Sea-girt Iceland!"

"In Rome, you will once more recite the poetry of Keats, whose name, like all men's names, was writ in water."

"I've never been in Rome."

"There are other things. You will write our best poem—an elegy."

"On the death of . . . " I began. I could not bring myself to say the name.

"No. She will outlive *you*."

We grew silent. Then he went on:

"You will write the book we've dreamed of for so long. In 1979 you will see that your supposed career has been nothing but a series of drafts, miscellaneous drafts, and you will give in to the vain and superstitious temptation to write your great book—the superstition that inflicted upon us Goethe's *Faust*, and *Salammbô*, and *Ulysses*. I filled, incredible to tell, many, many pages."

"And in the end you realized that you had failed."

"Worse. I realized that it was a masterpiece in the most overwhelming sense of the word. My good intentions hadn't lasted beyond the first pages; those that followed held the labyrinths, the knives, the man who thinks he's an image, the reflection that thinks it's real, the tiger that stalks in the night, the battles that are in one's blood, the blind and fatal Juan Muraña, the voice of Macedonio Fernández, the ship made with the fingernails of the dead, Old English repeated in the evening."

"That museum rings a bell," I remarked sarcastically.

"Not to mention false recollections, the doubleness of symbols, the long catalogs, the skilled handling of prosaic reality, the imperfect symmetries that critics so jubilantly discover, the not always apocryphal quotations?"

"Did you publish it?"

"I toyed, without conviction, with the melodramatic possibility of destroying the book, perhaps by fire. But I wound up publishing it in Madrid, under a pseudonym. I was taken for a clumsy imitator of Borges— a person who had the defect of not actually being Borges yet of mirroring all the outward appearances of the original."

"I'm not surprised," I said. "Every writer sooner or later becomes his own least intelligent disciple."

"That book was one of the roads that led me to this night. The others . . . The humiliation of old age, the conviction of having already lived each day . . ."

"I will not write that book," I said.

"You will, though. My words, which are now your present, will one day be but the vaguest memory of a dream."

I found myself annoyed by his dogmatic tone, the tone that I myself no doubt use in my classes. I was annoyed by the fact that we resembled each other so much and that he was taking advantage of the impunity lent him by the nearness of death.

"Are you so sure," I said, to get back at him a bit, "that you're going to die?"

"Yes," he replied. "I feel a sort of sweetness and relief I've never felt before. I can't describe it; all words require a shared experience. Why do you seem so annoyed at what I'm saying?"

"Because we're too much like each other. I loathe your face, which is a caricature of mine, I loathe your voice, which is a mockery of mine, I loathe your pathetic syntax, which is my own."

"So do I," he smiled. "Which is why I decided to kill myself."

A bird sang from the garden.

"It's the last one," the other man said.

He motioned me toward him. His hand sought mine. I stepped back; I was afraid the two hands would merge.

"The Stoics teach," he said to me, "that we should not complain of life—the door of the prison is open. I have always understood that; I myself saw life that way, but laziness and cowardice held me back. About twelve days ago, I was giving a lecture in La Plata on Book VI of the *Æneid*. Suddenly, as I was scanning a hexameter, I discovered what my path was to be. I made this decision—and since that moment, I have felt myself invulnerable. You shall one day meet that fate—you shall receive that sudden revelation, in the midst of Latin and Virgil, yet you will have utterly forgotten this curious prophetic dialogue that is taking place in two times and two places. When you next dream it, you shall be who I am, and you shall be my dream."

"I won't forget it—I'm going to write it down tomorrow."

"It will lie in the depths of your memory, beneath the tides of your dreams. When you write it, you will think that you're weaving a tale of fantasy. And it won't be tomorrow, either—it will be many years from now."

He stopped talking; I realized that he had died. In a way, I died with him—in grief I leaned over his pillow, but there was no one there anymore.

I fled the room. Outside, there was no patio, no marble staircase, no great silent house, no eucalyptus trees, no statues, no gazebo in a garden, no fountains, no gate in the fence surrounding the hotel in the town of Adrogué.

Outside awaited other dreams.

The Ninth, in E Minor

FREDERICK BUSCH

The morning after I drove to his newest town, I met my father for break-fast. He was wearing hunter's camouflage clothing and looked as if he hadn't slept for a couple of nights. He reminded me of one of those militia clowns you see on television news shows, very watchful and radiating a kind of high seriousness about imminent execution by minions of the state.

I knew he had deeper worries than execution. And I was pleased for him that he wore trousers and T-shirt, a soft, wide-brimmed cap, and hip-length jacket that would help him disappear into the stony landscape of upstate New York. He *needs* the camouflage, I thought, although where we stood—in the lobby of the James Fenimore Cooper Inn—he seemed a little out of place among the college kids and commercial travelers. The inn advertised itself as The Last of the Great Upstate Taverns. My father looked like The Last of the Great Upstate Guerrilla Fighters. Still, I thought, he's got the gear, and one of these days he will blend right in.

"Hi, Baby," he said. He tried to give me one of the old daddy-to-daughter penetrating stares, but his eyes bounced away from mine, and his glance slid down my nose to my chin, then down the front of my shirt to the oval silver belt buckle I had bought in Santa Fe.

"How are you, Daddy?"

He fired off another stare, but it ricocheted. "I have to tell you," he said, "half of the time I'm flat scared."

His shave was smooth, but he'd missed a couple of whiskers, which looked more gray than black. His face had gone all wrinkled and squinty. He looked like my father's older brother, who was shaky and possibly ill and commuting from the farthest suburbs of central mental health. He took his cap off—doffed it, you would have to say. His hair looked soft. You could see how someone would want to reach over and touch it.

"But I don't like to complain," he said.

I got hold of his arm and pulled my way along his brown-and-sand-and-olive-green sleeve until I had his hand, which I held in both of mine. He used enough muscle to keep his arm in that position, but the hand was loose and cool, a kid's.

I asked him, "Do you know what you're scared of?"

He shrugged, and, when he did, I saw a familiar expression inside his tired, frightened face. He made one of those French frowns that suggested not giving a good goddamn, and it pleased me so much, even as it disappeared into his newer face, that I brought his hand up and kissed the backs of his fingers.

"Aw," he said. I thought he was going to cry. I think he thought so too.

"Look," I said, letting go of his hand, "I saw Mommy in New York. That's where I drove up from. We had dinner two days ago. She asked me to remember her to you. She's fine."

He studied my words as if they had formed a complex thought. And then, as if I hadn't said what he was already considering, he asked, "How is she?"

"She's fine. I told you."

"And she asked to be remembered to me."

"Right."

"You're lying, Baby."

"Correct."

"She didn't mention me."

"Oh, she mentioned you."

"Not in a friendly way."

"No."

"She was hostile, then?"

"Hurt, I'd say."

He nodded. "I hate that—I didn't want to hurt anybody," he said. "I just wanted to feel better."

"I know. Do you feel better?"

"Do I look it?"

"Well, with the outfit and all . . ."

"This stuff's practical. You can wear it for weeks before you need to wash it. The rain runs off the coat. You don't need to carry a lot of clothing with you."

"Traveling light, then, is how you would describe yourself?"

"Yes," my father said. "I would say I'm traveling light. But you didn't answer me. How do I look?"

I walked past matching club chairs upholstered in maroon-and-aqua challis, and I looked out a window. A crew had taken down an old, broad maple tree. The sidewalk was buried under branches and bark, and a cat-walk of plywood led from the street, around the downed tree, and into the inn. The tree was cut into round sections three or four feet across, and a man in a sweated undershirt was using a long-handled splitting maul to break up one of the sections. Behind him stood another man, who wore a yellow hard hat and an orange shirt and a yellow fluorescent safety vest. He held a long chain saw that shook as it idled. A woman wearing a man's old-fashioned undervest, work gloves, and battered boots watched them both. Occasionally, she directed the man with the splitting maul. Her hair beneath her yellow hard hat looked reddish-gold. The one with the chain saw stared at the front of her shirt. She looked up and saw me. She looked at me through her safety goggles for a while and then she smiled. I couldn't help smiling back.

"You look fine," I said. "It's a beautiful spring morning. Let's eat."

In the Natty Bumppo Room, we were served our juice and coffee by a chunky woman with a happy red face. My father ordered waffles, and I remembered how, when I was in elementary school, he heated frozen waffles in the toaster for me and spread on margarine and syrup. I remembered how broad his hands had seemed. Now, they shook as he spread the margarine. One of his camouflage cuffs had picked up some syrup, and he dripped a little as he worked at his meal. I kept sipping the black coffee, which tasted like my conception of a broth made from long-simmered laundry.

"The hardest part," he said, "it drives me nuts. The thing with the checks."

"Sure," I said, watching the margarine and maple syrup coat his lips. "Mommy has to endorse your checks, then she has to deposit them, then she has to draw a bank check, and then she has to figure out where you are so she can send it along. It's complicated."

"I'm not making it that way on purpose," he said.

"No. But it's complicated." He looked young enough to have been his son, sometimes, and then, suddenly, he looked more like his father. I understood that the man I had thought of as my father, looking like himself, was no longer available. He was several new selves, and I would have to think of him that way.

"I'm just trying to get better," he said.

"Daddy, do you hear from her?"

He went still. He held himself so that—in his camouflage outfit—he suggested a hunter waiting on something skittish, a wild turkey, say, said to be stupid and shy. "I don't see the point of this," he said. "Why not talk about you? That's what fathers want to hear. About their kids. Why not talk about you?"

"All right," I said. "Me. I went to Santa Fe. I had a show in a gallery in Taos, and then I drove down to Santa Fe and I hung out. I walked on the Santa Fe Trail. It goes along the streets there. I ate too much with too much chili in it, and I bought too many pots. Most of the people in the restaurants are important unknown Hollywood celebrities from outside Hollywood."

"Did you sell any pictures?"

"Yes, I did."

"Did you make a lot of money?"

"Some. You want any?"

"Because of how long it takes for your mother to cash my check and send a new one."

"Are you *allowed* to not live at home and still get money from the state?"

"I think you're supposed to stay at home," he said.

"So she's being illegal along with you? To help you out?" He chewed on the last of his waffle. He nodded.

"Pretty good," I said.

"She's excellent to me."

"Considering," I said. "So how much money could you use?"

"Given the complications of the transmission process," he said.

"Given that," I said. "They sit outside the state office building, the Indians off the pueblos. They hate the people who come, but they all sit there all day long, showing you the silver and the pots all arranged on these beautiful blankets. I bought too much. But I felt embarrassed. One woman with a fly swatter, she kept spanking at the jewelry she was selling. She'd made it. She kept hitting it, and the earrings jumped on the blanket. The rings scattered, and she kept hitting away, pretending she was swatting flies, but she wasn't. She was furious."

"Displacement," my father said.

"It's just a story, Daddy."

"But you told it."

"Yes, but it didn't have a message or anything."

"What did it have?"

"*In situ* Native American displacement, and handmade jewelry. A tourist's usual guilt. Me, on the road, looking around. Me, on my way northeast."

"Did you drive?"

"I did."

"All by yourself?"

"Like you, Daddy."

"No," he said, fitting his mouth to the trembling cup. "We're both together here, so we aren't alone now."

"No." I heard the splitting maul, and I imagined the concussion up his fingers and along his forearm, up through the shoulder and into the top of the spine. It would make your brain shake, I thought.

"A hundred or two?" he said.

"What? Dollars?"

"Is that too much?"

"No," I said, "I have that."

"Thanks, Baby."

"But do you hear from her, Daddy?"

He slumped. He stared at the syrup on his plate. It looked like a pool of sewage where something had drowned.

He said, "Did I tell you I went to Maine?"

I shook my head and signaled for more coffee. When she brought it, I asked if I could smoke in the Natty Bumppo Room, and she said no. I lit a cigarette and when I was done, and had clicked the lighter shut, she took a deep breath of the smoke I exhaled and she grinned.

"What's in Maine?" I asked him.

"Cabins. Very cheap cabins in a place on the coast that nobody knows about. I met a man in New Hampshire—Portsmouth, New Hampshire? He was on the road, like me. He was a former dentist of some special kind. We were very similar. Taking medication, putting the pieces back together, at cetera. And he told me about these cabins. A little smelly with mildew, a little unglamorous, but cheap, and heated if you need, and near the sea. I really wanted to get to the sea."

"So you drove there, and what?"

"I slept for most of the week."

"You still need to sleep a lot."

"Always," he said. "Consciousness," he said, "is very hard work."

"So you slept. You ate lobster."

"A lot."

"And what did you do when you weren't sleeping or eating lobsters or driving?"

"I counted girls in Jeeps."

"There are that many?"

"All over New England," he said, raising a cup that shook. "They're blond, most of them, and they seem very attractive, but I think that's because of the contrast—you know, the elegant, longlegged girl and the stubby, utilitarian vehicle. I found it quite exciting."

"Exciting. Jesus, Daddy, you sound so adolescent. Exciting. Blondes in Jeeps. Well, you're a single man, for the most part. What the hell. Why not. Did you date any?"

"Come on," he said.

"You're not ancient. You could have a date."

"I've had them," he said.

"That's who I was asking you about. Do you hear from her?"

"I'm telling you about the girls in their Jeeps on the coast of Maine, and you keep asking—"

"About the woman you had an affair with who caused you to divorce my mother. Yes."

"That's wrong," he said. "We separated. That's all that I did—I moved away. It was your *mother* sued for divorce."

"I recollect. But you do understand how she felt. There you were, shacking up with a praying mantis from Fort Lee, New Jersey, and not living at home for the better part of two years."

"Do I have to talk about this?"

"Not for my two hundred bucks. We're just having an on-the-road visit, and I'm leaving soon enough, and probably you are too."

"I drift around. But that's a little unkind about the money. *And* about the praying mantis thing. Really, to just bring it up."

"Because all you want to do is feel better," I said, lighting another cigarette. By this time, there were several other diners in the Natty Bumppo

Room, and one of them was looking over the tops of her gray-tinted lenses to indicate to me her impending death from secondary smoke. *Oh, I'm sorry!* I mouthed to her. I held the cigarette as if I were going to crush it onto my saucer, then I raised it to my mouth and sucked in smoke.

I blew it out as I said to him, "She's the one who led you into your nose-dive. She's the reason you crashed in flames when she left you."

"This is not productive for me," he said.

"You're supposed to be productive for *me*," I said. I heard the echo of my voice and, speaking more calmly, I said, "Sorry. I didn't mean to shout. This still fucks me up, though."

"Don't use that kind of language," he said, wiping his eyes.

"No."

"I thought we were going to have a *visit*. A father-and-daughter reunion."

"Well, we are," I said.

"All right. Then tell me about yourself. Tell me what's become of you."

I was working hard to keep his face in focus. He kept looking like somebody else who was related to him, but he was not the him I had known. I was twenty-eight years old, of no fixed abode, and my father, also without his own address, was wearing camouflage clothing in an upstate town a long enough drive from the New York State Thruway to be nothing more than the home of old, rotting trees, a campus in the state's junior college system, and the site of the James Fenimore Cooper Inn.

"What's become of me," I said. "All right. I have two galleries that represent me. One's in Philadelphia and one's in Columbia County, outside New York. I think the owner, who also runs what you would call a big-time gallery on Greene Street, in Manhattan, may be just around the corner from offering me a show in New York City. Which would be very good. I got some attention in Taos, and a lot of New York people were there, along with the usual Hollywood producer-*manqué* people, both has-beens and would-bes, and the editorial stars who hire agents to get their names in the gossip columns. It was very heady for me to be hit on by such upper-echelon minor leaguers."

"When you say *hit on*," he said, "what are you telling me?"

"Exactly what you think. A number of men fancied fucking me."

He let his head droop toward his plate. "That's a terrible way to live," he said. "I'm supposed to be protecting you from that."

"But why start now?"

"That's what you came for," he said. "I've been waiting, since you phoned me, to figure out why you would look me up *now*, when you might suspect I'm down on my luck and in unheroic circumstances."

"Unheroic," I said. "But you're wrong. I mean, as far as I *know*, you're wrong. I asked Mommy for your address because I hadn't seen you since I was in graduate school. And you're my father. And I guess I was missing you."

"And because you wanted to tell me the thing about men trying to—you know. Because it would hurt me. And you're angry with me."

"Well, you could say the way you left your wife was a little disappointing to me."

He'd been rubbing at his forehead with the stiffened fingers of his right hand. He stopped, and he looked around his hand, like a kid peeking through a fence, his expression merry and, suddenly, quite demented. Then the merriment left him, and then the craziness, and he looked like a man growing old very quickly. He said, "I have to tell you, the whole thing was disappointing for me as well."

"You mean, leaving your wife for the great adventure and then being dumped."

"And then being dumped," he said.

"Mommy said you were doing drugs when that happened."

"There was nothing we didn't do except heroin," he said. "If we could have bought it safely, I'd have stuffed it up my nose, shot it into my eyeballs, anything."

"Because of the sex?"

He looked right at me. "The best, the most astonishing. I haven't been able to acknowledge a physical sensation since then. Everything I've felt since then is, I don't know—as if it was *reported*. From a long way away."

"Jesus. *And* you loved her?"

"I've dealt with a therapist who says maybe I didn't. Maybe it was the danger. I seem to act self-destructively, from time to time. I seem to possibly not approve of myself. I seem to need to call it love whether that's what I feel or not. I seem to have conflated sex with love."

"A conflatable sex doll," I said. I snickered. He managed to look hurt. "I'm sorry."

"It doesn't matter much. I'm working on my health. It doesn't have to hurt to hear that kind of laughter. I suppose it's good for me. A kind of practice at coping with difficulties."

"No," I said, "I apologize. It just seemed like a very good damned pun, the conflatable sex doll. I am nobody's spokeswoman for reality. I apologize."

"Tell me how your mother is."

"She's fine. She's living a life. I'd feel uncomfortable if I gave you any details. I think she wants to keep that stuff to herself."

"So she's fine, and you've managed to endure the attentions of men with press agents."

"Mostly to evade them, as a matter of fact."

"Mostly?"

"Daddy, if anyone around here's fine, it's me. Nobody has to worry about men, nutrition, the upkeep of my car, or the management of my career. I do my own taxes, I wrote my own will, and I navigate my own cross-country trips."

"Why do you have a will? A legal last will and testament, you're saying? Why?"

"I'm not getting any younger," I said.

"Nonsense. You don't have a family to provide for."

"You know that, do you?"

"You *do*?"

I nodded. I found it difficult to say much.

"What, Baby?"

"A son. His name is Vaughan."

"Vaughan? As in the singer Vaughan Monroe?"

"As in Ralph Vaughan Williams. One of his symphonies was playing when, you know."

"I know nothing," he said. He was pale, and his lips trembled as his hands did, though in a few seconds his mouth calmed down. His fingers didn't.

"He's with Mommy."

"But he lives with you?"

"I'm thinking of living with someone downstate. We would stay together there."

"His father?"

"No. But a man I like. A photographer."

"Criminies," he whispered. "There are all those gaps, all those *facts* I don't know. This is like looking at the family picture album, but most of the pictures aren't in the book. Are you *happy* about this child?"

"Are you happy about me?"

"Sure," he said. "Of course I am."

"Then I'm happy about my boy. Did you really say criminies?"

He clasped his hands at the edge of the table, but they upset his breakfast plate. Syrup went into the air, and soggy crumbs, and his stained napkin. The waitress came over to sponge at the mess and remove our dishes. She came back with more coffee and the check.

"Criminies," my father said. "I haven't heard that word for years."

I was counting out money which I slid across the table to him. "I hope this helps," I said, "really."

"I regret needing to accept it," he said. "I regret not seeing you more. I regret your having to leave."

"That's the thing with those family albums, Daddy. People are always leaving them."

"Yes. But I'm a grandfather, right?"

"Yes, you are."

"Could I see him?"

"Ever get downstate?"

"Oh, sure," he said. "I get to plenty of places. I told you, I was all the way up in Maine just a few weeks ago."

"All those girls in Jeeps. I remember. So, sure. Yes. Of course. He's your grandson."

"Big and sloppy like me?"

"His father was a kind of fine-boned man. But he'll have my arms and legs."

"He'll look like a spider monkey."

"You haven't called me a spider monkey for an awfully long time."

"But that's what he look like? I want to think of him with you."

"Very light brown hair, and a long, delicate neck. And great big paws, like a puppy."

"He'll be tall."

We sat, and maybe we were waiting to find some words. But then my father pulled on his camouflage cap, and tugged at the brim. He was ready, I suppose. I left the dining room and then the inn a couple of steps ahead of him. We stopped outside the front doors and watched the man, now shirtless, as he swung, working his way through a chunk of a hundred and fifty years. Splinters flew, and I heard him grunt as the wedge-shaped maul head landed. The woman in the cotton vest was watching it batter the wood.

I put my arms around his neck and hugged him. I kissed his cheek.

"Baby, when does everybody get together again?"

I hugged him again, and then I backed a couple of steps away. I could only shrug.

He said, "I was thinking roughly the same."

I heard the maul. I watched my father zip, then unzip his camouflage hunting coat.

He turned to the woman in the cotton vest and tipped his camouflage cap. She stared at him through her safety goggles.

He was giving a demonstration, I realized. With his helpless, implausible smile, he was showing me his lapsed world of women. He was broken, and he shook with medication, but he dreamed, it was clear, of one more splintered vial of amyl nitrate on the sweaty bedclothes of a praying mantis from Fort Lee, New Jersey. He had confected a ride with a leggy blonde in a black, convertible Jeep on US 1 in Maine. And if the foreman of the forestry crew would talk to him in front of her tired and resentful men, he would chat up that lady and touch, as if by accident, the flesh of her sturdy, tanned arms.

That was why I backed another pace. That was why I turned and went along the duckwalk behind my father, leaving the wreckage of the maple tree and walking toward my car. I wanted to be driving away from him—locked inside with the windows shut and the radio up—before he could tip his cap, and show me his ruined, innocent face, and steal what was left of my life.

Crickets

ROBERT OLEN BUTLER

They call me Ted where I work and they've called me that for over a decade now and it still bothers me, though I'm not very happy about my real name being the same as the former President of the former Republic of Vietnam. Thiệu is not an uncommon name in my homeland and my mother had nothing more in mind than a long-dead uncle when she gave it to me. But in Lake Charles, Louisiana, I am Ted. I guess the other Mr. Thiệu has enough of my former country's former gold bullion tucked away so that in London, where he probably wears a bowler and carries a rolled umbrella, nobody's calling him anything but Mr. Thiệu.

I hear myself sometimes and I sound pretty bitter, I guess. But I don't let that out at the refinery, where I'm the best chemical engineer they've got and they even admit it once in a while. They're good-hearted people, really. I've done enough fighting in my life. I was eighteen when Saigon fell and I was only recently mustered into the Army, and when my unit dissolved and everybody ran, I stripped off my uniform and put on my civilian clothes again and I threw rocks at the North's tanks when they rolled through the streets. Very few of my people did likewise. I stayed in the mouths of alleys so I could run and then return and throw more rocks, but because what I did seemed so isolated and so pathetic a gesture, the gunners in the tanks didn't even take notice. But I didn't care about their scorn. At least my right arm had said no to them.

And then there were Thai Pirates in the South China Sea and idiots running the refugee centers and more idiots running the agencies in the U.S. to find a place for me and my new bride, who braved with me the midnight escape by boat and the terrible sea and all the rest. We ended up here in the flat bayou land of Louisiana, where there are rice paddies and where the water and the land are in the most delicate balance with each other, very much like the Mekong Delta, where I grew up. These people who work around me are good people and maybe they call me Ted because they want to think of me as one of them, though sometimes it bothers me that these men are so much bigger than me. I am the size of a woman in this country and these American men are all massive and they speak so slowly, even to one another, even though English is their native language. I've heard New Yorkers on television and I speak as fast as they do.

My son is beginning to speak like the others here in Louisiana. He is ten, the product of the first night my wife and I spent in Lake Charles, in a cheap motel with the sky outside red from the refineries. He is proud to have been born in America, and when he leaves us in the morning to walk to the Catholic school, he says, "Have a good day, y'all." Sometimes I say good-bye to him in Vietnamese and he wrinkles his nose at me and says, "Aw, Pop," like I'd just cracked a corny joke. He doesn't speak Vietnamese at all and my wife says not to worry about that. He's an American.

But I do worry about that, though I understand why I should be content. I even understood ten years ago, so much so that I agreed with my wife and gave my son an American name. Bill. Bill and his father Ted. But this past summer I found my son hanging around the house bored in the middle of vacation and I was suddenly his father Thiệu with a wonderful idea for him. It was an idea that had come to me in the first week of every February we'd been in Lake Charles, because that's when the crickets always begin to crow here. This place is rich in crickets, which always make me think of my own childhood in Vietnam. But I never said anything to my son until last summer.

I came to him after watching him slouch around the yard one Sunday pulling the Spanish moss off the lowest branches of our big oak tree and then throwing rocks against the stop sign on our corner. "Do you want to do something fun?" I said to him.

"Sure, Pop," he said, though there was a certain suspicion in his voice, like he didn't trust me on the subject of fun. He threw all the rocks at once that were left in his hand and the stop sign shivered at their impact.

I said, "If you keep that up, they will arrest me for the destruction of city property and then they will deport us all."

My son laughed at this. I, of course, knew that he would know I was bluffing. I didn't want to be too hard on him for the boyish impulses that I myself had found to be so satisfying when I was young, especially since I was about to share something of my own childhood with him.

"So what've you got, Pop?" my son asked me.

"Fighting crickets," I said.

"What?"

Now, my son was like any of his fellow ten-year-olds, devoted to super-heroes and the mighty clash of good and evil in all of its high-tech forms in the Saturday-morning cartoons. Just to make sure he was in the right frame of mind, I explained it to him with one word, "Cricketmen," and I thought this was a pretty good ploy. He cocked his head in interest at this and I took him to the side porch and sat him down and I explained.

I told him how, when I was a boy, my friends and I would prowl the undergrowth and capture crickets and keep them in matchboxes. We would feed them leaves and bits of watermelon and bean sprouts, and we'd train them to fight by keeping them in a constant state of agitation by blowing on them and gently flicking the ends of their antennas with a sliver of wood. So each of us would have a stable of fighting crickets, and there were two kinds.

At this point my son was squirming a little bit and his eyes were shift-ing away into the yard and I knew that my Cricketman trick had run its course. I fought back the urge to challenge his set of interests. Why should the stiff and foolish fights of his cartoon characters absorb him and the real clash—real life and death—that went on in the natural world bore him? But I realized that I hadn't cut to the chase yet, as they say on the TV. "They fight to the death," I said with as much gravity as I could put into my voice, like I was James Earl Jones.

The announcement won me a glance and a brief lift of his eyebrows. This gave me a little scrabble of panic, because I still hadn't told him about the two types of crickets and I suddenly knew that was a real important part for me. I tried not to despair at his understanding and I put my hands on his shoulders and turned him around to face me. "Listen," I said. "You need to understand this if you are to have fighting crickets. There are two types, and all of us had some of each. One type we called the charcoal crickets. These were very large and strong, but they were slow and they could become con-fused. The other type was small and brown and we called them fire crickets. They weren't as strong, but they were very smart and quick."

"So who would win?" my son said.

"Sometimes one and sometimes the other. The fights were very long and full of hard struggle. We'd have a little tunnel made of paper and we'd slip a sliver of wood under the cowling of our cricket's head to make him mad and we'd twirl him by his antenna, and then we'd each put our cricket into the tunnel at opposite ends. Inside, they'd approach each other and begin to fight and then we'd lift the paper tunnel and watch."

"Sounds neat," my son said, though his enthusiasm was at best moderate, and I knew I had to act quickly.

So we got a shoe box and we started looking for crickets. It's better at night, but I knew for sure his interest wouldn't last that long. Our house is up on blocks because of the high water table in town and we crawled along the edge, pulling back the bigger tufts of grass and turning over rocks. It was one of the rocks that gave us our first crickets, and my son saw them and cried in my ear, "There, there," but he waited for me to grab them. I cupped first one and then the other and dropped them into the shoe box and I felt a vague disappointment, not so much because it was clear that my boy did not want to touch the insects, but that they were both the big black ones, the charcoal crickets. We crawled on and we found another one in the grass and another sitting in the muddy shadow of the house behind the hose faucet and then we caught two more under an azalea bush.

"Isn't that enough?" my son demanded. "How many do we need?"

I sat with my back against the house and put the shoe box in my lap and my boy sat beside me, his head stretching this way so he could look into the box. There was no more vagueness to my feeling. I was actually weak with disappointment because all six of these were charcoal crickets, big and inert and just looking around like they didn't even know anything was wrong.

"Oh, no," my son said with real force, and for a second I thought he had read my mind and shared my feeling, but I looked at him and he was pointing at the toes of his white sneakers. "My Reeboks are ruined!" he cried, and on the toe of each sneaker was a smudge of grass.

I glanced back into the box and the crickets had not moved and I looked at my son and he was still staring at his sneakers. "Listen," I said, "this was a big mistake. You can go on and do something else."

He jumped up at once. "Do you think Mom can clean these?" he said.

"Sure," I said. "Sure."

He was gone at once and the side door slammed and I put the box on the grass. But I didn't go in. I got back on my hands and knees and I circled the entire house and then I turned over every stone in the yard and dug around all the trees. I found probably two dozen more crickets, but they were all the same. In Louisiana there are rice paddies and some of the bayous look like the Delta, but many of the birds are different, and why shouldn't the insects be different, too? This is another country, after all. It was just funny about the fire crickets. All of us kids rooted for them, even if we were fighting with one of our own charcoal crickets. A fire cricket was a very precious and admirable thing.

The next morning my son stood before me as I finished my breakfast and once he had my attention, he looked down at his feet, drawing my eyes down as well. "See?" he said. "Mom got them clean."

Then he was out the door and I called after him, "See you later, Bill."

Olympus Hills

RON CARLSON

left the party early finding my coat on the bed surprising Karen and Darrel, who stood when I entered. "It's funny," I said, trying to ease their embarrassment, "but I know every coat in this pile." I lifted Cindy's rabbit fur jacket. "For five points. Careful: she does not wear this thing to work."

"Cindy," Karen said, her voice husky.

I had just left Cindy in the kitchen. She and Tom were sitting on the counter drinking tequila and having a heart to heart. Whenever people drink tequila, they always talk about it, the worm, a war story or two, and then maybe mushroom experience and it's a heart to heart. Cindy was wearing a white silk dress, sprayed with little red dots which turned out to be strawberries. I have been in these kitchens before and when Cindy hoists her bottom onto the kitchen counter and, nursing a tequila and lemon between her knees, starts telling drug experiences, it's just enough. Even Tom sitting up there by her looked a little spent. He's too big a guy to sit on a kitchen counter and look natural anyway.

Karen and Darrel had forgotten to let go of each other's hands and their faces were smashed red from all the kissing. They looked like the two healthiest people at the party. I was surprised, because I'd seen Karen with another guy from the firm, a programmer named Chuck who does our board overlays, at a dozen lunches in the last month. And I admired Darrel's ability to struggle in there with Karen, while we could all hear his wife, Ellen, singing along with Tommy James and the Shondells in the other room. It was a small house for Olympus Hills.

"Victor, Ted, Sharon, Tom, Ellen," I said, laying the coats aside, until I found the tan raincoat. "Lisa," I said, looking at it. The bed was a little archaeology of the party: all those layers of beautiful coats. Victor and his new leather flight jacket. Tom and his bright swollen parka. And Lisa's classy raincoat second from the bottom. She must have arrived early.

"My coat," I looked up and said to Darrel, and when I saw how embarrassed he still was, leaning there against the wall as if I was going to scold them, I added, "I'm leaving early. No problem." I patted my coat. "I'd say you've got an hour before another coat is touched. I'll close the door. Happy Valentines."

I didn't put my coat on in the hall, because I didn't want Ted or Sharon to make a fuss, to cry out, "Hal, you're leaving! Before charades! You can't leave before charades!"

I wanted to leave before charades. I'd played charades with this group before and it was worse than college. Victor, Ted, and about five others played solely to humiliate everyone. They would select unproduced plays from Gilbert and Sullivan, and then explode when people would claim to have not heard of them. "You ignorami!" I'd heard Victor scream. "You aborigines! Swinesnouts! This is incredible."

My wife, Lisa, could be wicked too. She would always write the sexiest titles she could, knowing that some woman on the other team, in the drunken spirit of camaraderie that sometimes waved over the group, would embarrass herself fully doing How to Make Love to a Man and be the talk of the office for a week. I remember in detail the vision of Cindy writhing before the group one night, clutching both her breasts with her hands, thrusting her pelvis at her team as if to drive them back on the couch. I don't remember the name of the literary work she was describing.

I wanted to slip through the living room as if I were getting some fresh air and then be gone. Lisa had come from work tonight and she had her own car; I'd see her at home later. There was a time when we had one car, and we used to go places together. It was a used silver Tempest, the car I had in graduate school. The original owner had applied zodiac stickers in circles on all the doors.

Lisa always claims to hate these parties. We'll be dressing at home and she'll wave the hairdrier at me, making predictions. "Karen will wear that blue mini and go after Lou. They'll have a clam dip diluted with sour cream. Generic sour cream. Did I say generic sour cream? Wayne will move in on me when I sit on the couch and tell me about his kids for two hours. He thinks that's the way you flirt. Ted will bring his oldies tape. Ellen will be the first one to sing. Tom will be the first one drunk. You'll get drunk too and come on to Cindy, and we'll have our little quarrel on the way home. Are you ready? Let's go."

And she used to be right. I would get drunk. I'd end up singing with Ellen and, later, making my three point five crass comments to some of the women. Wayne would do his sincerity routine for Lisa on the couch. He was no dummy; she was always the loveliest woman in the whole house. I'd end up in the kitchen, leaning against the counter with Cindy, sometimes leaning against Cindy and then the counter. It was a party, wasn't it?

That was then. Lisa wouldn't be right tonight, about me. February. It had been a long winter already: five, six parties since New Year's. No wonder Karen had been able to spot Cindy's coat. Too much snow, too much fog; by Friday night, no one wanted to go home. Everybody was kind of surprised suddenly to have money, but no one knew what to do about it. Most of us had Ted's oldies tape memorized the way you come to know an album; when a song ends, you know what's coming next. We knew what brand everyone smoked and who would lend you a cigarette gladly. We knew that Ted smoked Kools because he'd learned in college that no one would borrow them. We knew what everyone drank and how much. We knew where people would be sitting by eleven o'clock. I knew it all and I just wanted to go home. I was trying.

I eased by a group standing by the kitchen door, and edged around the two couples dancing to the Supremes. Ellen waved at me from across the buffet table with the breadstick she was using as a microphone. Baby Love. I could see Lisa sitting on the couch. She was smiling at Wayne who sat on the carpet by her knees. I know all her smiles and this was a real one. I had to thread between Victor and his new girlfriend to reach the door and then I was out in the snow.

Pulling on my coat, I walked down the trail in the falling snow, right into the deer. I didn't actually hit him, but by the time we both looked up we were at most three feet apart. It was a young male. He had a fine pair of forked antlers and a broad black nose, wet and shiny in the light from the yard lamp. I immediately backed up four or five steps to give him room, but he stood there, casually, looking at me. There were deer all over the city because of the snowfall, but I had never, ever, seen one this close.

I backed to the door, slowly, thinking to show someone. I forgot myself. I wanted Lisa to come out and see this guy. I wanted Lisa to come out and see this deer and come home with me. She could say, "We'll pick up my car tomorrow or the day after that," and steam up the dark with her laugh. I hadn't realized how lonely I was until I saw his face, his moist eyes, the bone grain of his antlers.

I pushed the door inward and said, "Hey, come see this deer." Cindy's face appeared in the opening. Behind her the party seemed to rage; Ellen was singing "Satisfaction," and the din of conversation was loud and raw and alien.

"What?"

"Look at this deer."

"What are you talking about?"

"What are you talking about?"

"This deer." I turned and he was gone. I stepped to the corner of the house and was able to glimpse his gray back pass under a yard lamp two houses up.

"Right," Cindy said, taking my arm. "The deer." She lobbed her drink, glass and all, into the snowbank, and turned fully to me. Her mouth was warm with tequila, and I could feel the flesh of her back perfectly through the cold silk of her dress. She rose against me, ignoring the cold, or frantic against it, I couldn't tell which. It was funny there outside the party. When she went for me, I did nothing to stop her. I had made it outside, leaving early, but that was all I could do.

Intimacy

RAYMOND CARVER

have some business out west anyway, so I stop off in this little town where my former wife lives. We haven't seen each other in four years. But from time to time, when something of mine appeared, or was written about me in the magazines or papers—a profile or an interview—I sent her these things. I don't know what I had in mind except I thought she might be interested. In any case, she never responded.

It is nine in the morning. I haven't called, and it's true I don't know what I am going to find.

But she lets me in. She doesn't seem surprised. We don't shake hands, much less kiss each other. She takes me into the living room. As soon as I sit down she brings me some coffee. Then she comes out with what's on her mind. She says I've caused her anguish, made her feel exposed and humiliated.

Make no mistake, I feel I'm home.

She says, But then you were into betrayal early. You always felt comfortable with betrayal. No, she says, that's not true. Not in the beginning, at any rate. You were different then. But I guess I was different too. Everything was different, she says. No, it was after you turned thirty-five, or thirty-six, whenever it was, around in there anyway, your mid-thirties somewhere, then you started in. You really started in. You turned on me. You did it up pretty then. You must be proud of yourself.

She says, Sometimes I could scream.

She says she wishes I'd forget about the hard times, the bad times, when I talk about back then. Spend some time on the good times, she says. Weren't there some good times? She wishes I'd get off that other subject. She's bored with it. Sick of hearing about it. Your private hobby horse, she says. What's done is done and water under the bridge, she says. A tragedy, yes. God knows it was a tragedy and then some. But why keep it going? Don't you ever get tired of dredging up that old business?

She says, Let go of the past, for Christ's sake. Those old hurts. You must have some other arrows in your quiver, she says.

She says, You know something? I think you're sick. I think you're crazy as a bedbug. Hey, you don't believe the things they're saying about you, do you? Don't believe them for a minute, she says. Listen, I could tell them a thing or two. Let them talk to me about it, if they want to hear a story.

She says, Are you listening to me?

I'm listening, I say. I'm all ears, I say.

She says, I've really had a bellyful of it, buster! Who asked you here today anyway? I sure as hell didn't. You just show up and walk in. What the hell do you want from me? Blood? You want more blood? I thought you had your fill by now.

She says, Think of me as dead. I want to be left in peace now. That's all I want anymore is to be left in peace and forgotten about. Hey, I'm forty-five years old, she says. Forty-five going on fifty-five, or sixty-five. Lay off, will you.

She says, Why don't you wipe the blackboard clean and see what you have left after that? Why don't you start with a clean slate? See how far that gets you, she says.

She has to laugh at this. I laugh too, but it's nerves.

She says, You know something? I had my chance once, but I let it go. I just let it go. I don't guess I ever told you. But now look at me. Look! Take a good look while you're at it. You threw me away, you son of a bitch.

She says, I was younger then and a better person. Maybe you were too, she says. A better person, I mean. You had to be. You were better then or I wouldn't have had anything to do with you.

She says, I loved you so much once. I loved you to the point of distraction. I did. More than anything in the whole wide world. Imagine that. What a laugh that is now. Can you imagine it? We were so *intimate* once upon a time I can't believe it now. I think that's the strangest thing of all now. The memory of being that intimate with somebody. We were so intimate I could puke. I can't imagine ever being that intimate with somebody else. I haven't been.

She says, Frankly, and I mean this, I want to be kept out of it from here

on out. Who do you think you are anyway? You think you're God or somebody? You're not fit to lick God's boots, or anybody else's for that matter.
Mister, you've been hanging out with the wrong people. But what do I know?
I don't even know what I know any longer. I know I don't like what you've
been dishing out. I know that much. You know what I'm talking about, don't
you? Am I right?

Right, I say. Right as rain.

She says, You'll agree to anything, won't you? You give in too easy. You
always did. You don't have any principles, not one. Anything to avoid a fuss.
But that's neither here nor there.

She says, You remember that time I pulled the knife on you?

She says this as if in passing, as if it's not important.

Vaguely, I say. I must have deserved it, but I don't remember much
about it. Go ahead, why don't you, and tell me about it.

She says, I'm beginning to understand something now. I think I know
why you're here. Yes. I know why you're here, even if you don't. But you're
a slyboots. You know why you're here. You're on a fishing expedition. You're
hunting for *material*. Am I getting warm? Am I right?

Tell me about the knife, I say.

She says, If you want to know, I'm real sorry I didn't use that knife. I
am. I really and truly am. I've thought and thought about it, and I'm sorry I
didn't use it. I had the chance. But I hesitated. I hesitated and was lost, as
somebody or other said. But I should have used it, the hell with everything
and everybody. I should have nicked your arm with it at least. At least that.

Well, you didn't, I say. I thought you were going to cut me with it, but
you didn't. I took it away from you.

She says, You were always lucky. You took it away and then you slapped
me. Still, I regret I didn't use that knife just a little bit. Even a little would
have been something to remember me by.

I remember a lot, I say. I say that, then wish I hadn't.

She says, Amen, brother. That's the bone of contention here, if you hadn't
noticed. That's the whole problem. But like I said, in my opinion you remember the wrong things. You remember the low, shameful things. That's why you
got interested when I brought up the knife.

She says, I wonder if you ever have any regret. For whatever that's worth
on the market these days. Not much, I guess. But you ought to be a special-
ist in it by now.

Regret, I say. It doesn't interest me much, to tell the truth. Regret is not a word I use very often. I guess I mainly don't have it. I admit I hold to the dark view of things. Sometimes, anyway. But regret? I don't think so.

She says, You're a real son of a bitch, did you know that? A ruthless, coldhearted son of a bitch. Did anybody ever tell you that?

You did, I say. Plenty of times.

She says, I always speak the truth. Even when it hurts. You'll never catch me in a lie.

She says, My eyes were opened a long time ago, but by then it was too late. I had my chance but I let it slide through my fingers. I even thought for a while you'd come back. Why'd I think that anyway? I must have been out of my mind. I could cry my eyes out now, but I wouldn't give you that satisfaction.

She says, You know what? I think if you were on fire right now, if you suddenly burst into flame this minute, I wouldn't throw a bucket of water on you.

She laughs at this. Then her face closes down again.

She says, Why in hell *are* you here? You want to hear some more? I could go on for days. I think I know why you turned up, but I want to hear it from you.

When I don't answer, when I just keep sitting there, she goes on.

She says, After that time, when you went away, nothing much mattered after that. Not the kids, not God, not anything. It was like I didn't know what hit me. It was like I had *stopped living*. My life had been going along, going along, and then it just stopped. It didn't just come to a stop, it screeched to a stop. I thought, If I'm not worth anything to him, well, I'm not worth anything to myself or anybody else either. That was the worst thing I felt. I thought my heart would break. What am I saying? It did break. Of course it broke. It broke, just like that. It's still broke, if you want to know. And so there you have it in a nutshell. My eggs in one basket, she says. A tisket, a tasket. All my rotten eggs in one basket.

She says, You found somebody else for yourself, didn't you? It didn't take long. And you're happy now. That's what they say about you anyway: "He's happy now." Hey, I read everything you send! You think I don't? Listen, I know your heart, mister. I always did. I knew it back then, and I know it now. I know your heart inside and out, and don't you ever forget it. Your heart is a jungle, a dark forest, it's a garbage pail, if you want to know. Let them talk to me if they want to ask somebody something. I know how you operate. Just let them come around here, and I'll give them an earful. I was there. I served, buddy boy. Then you held me up for display and ridicule in your so-called work. For any Tom or Harry to pity or pass judgment on. Ask me if I cared. Ask me if it embarrassed me. Go ahead, ask.

No, I say, I won't ask that. I don't want to get into that, I say.

Damn straight you don't! she says. And you know *why*, too!

She says, Honey, no offense, but sometimes I think I could shoot you and watch you kick.

She says, You can't look me in the eyes, can you?

She says, and this is exactly what she says, You can't even look me in the eyes when I'm talking to you.

So, okay, I look her in the eyes.

She says, Right. Okay, she says. Now we're getting someplace, maybe. That's better. You can tell a lot about the person you're talking to from his eyes. Everybody knows that. But you know something else? There's nobody in this whole world who would tell you this, but I can tell you. I have the right. I *earned* that right, sonny. You have yourself confused with somebody else. And that's the pure truth of it. But what do I know? they'll say in a hundred years. They'll say, Who was she anyway?

She says, In any case, you sure as hell have *me* confused with somebody else. Hey, I don't even have the same name anymore! Not the name I was born with, not the name I lived with you with, not even the name I had two years ago. What is this? What is this in hell all about anyway? Let me say something. I want to be left alone now. Please. That's not a crime.

She says, Don't you have someplace else you should be? Some plane to catch? Shouldn't you be somewhere far from here at this very minute?

No, I say. I say it again: No. No place, I say. I don't have anyplace I have to be.

And then I do something. I reach over and take the sleeve of her blouse between my thumb and forefinger. That's all. I just touch it that way, and then I just bring my hand back. She doesn't draw away. She doesn't move.

Then here's the thing I do next. I get down on my knees, a big guy like me, and I take the hem of her dress. What am I doing on the floor? I wish I could say. But I know it's where I ought to be, and I'm there on my knees holding on to the hem of her dress.

She is still for a minute. But in a minute she says, Hey, it's all right, stupid.

You're so dumb, sometimes. Get up now. I'm telling you to get up. Listen, it's okay. I'm over it now. It took me a while to get over it. What do you think? Did you think it wouldn't? Then you walk in here and suddenly the whole cruddy business is back. I felt a need to ventilate. But you know, and I know, it's over and done with now.

She says, For the longest while, honey, I was inconsolable. *Inconsolable*, she says. Put that word in your little notebook. I can tell you from experience that's the saddest word in the English language. Anyway, I got over it finally. Time is a gentleman, a wise man said. Or else maybe a worn-out old woman, one or the other anyway.

She says, I have a life now. It's a different kind of life than yours, but I guess we don't need to compare. It's my life, and that's the important thing I have to realize as I get older. Don't feel *too* bad, anyway, she says. I mean, it's all right to feel a *little* bad, maybe. That won't hurt you, that's only to be expected after all. Even if you can't move yourself to regret.

She says, Now you have to get up and get out of here. My husband will be along pretty soon for his lunch. How would I explain this kind of thing?

It's crazy, but I'm still on my knees holding the hem of her dress. I won't let it go. I'm like a terrier, and it's like I'm stuck to the floor. It's like I can't move.

She says, Get up now. What is it? You still want something from me. What do you want? Want me to forgive you? Is that why you're doing this? That's it, isn't it? That's the reason you came all this way. The knife thing kind of perked you up, too. I think you'd forgotten about that. But you needed me to remind you. Okay, I'll say something if you'll just go.

She says, I forgive you.

She says, Are you satisfied now? Is that better? Are you happy? He's happy now, she says.

But I'm still there, knees to the floor.

She says, Did you hear what I said? You have to go now. Hey, stupid. Honey, I said I forgive you. And I even reminded you about the knife thing. I can't think what else I can do now. You got it made in the shade, baby. Come *on* now, you have to get out of here. Get up. That's right. You're still a big guy, aren't you. Here's your hat, don't forget your hat. You never used to wear a hat. I never in my life saw you in a hat before.

She says, Listen to me now. Look at me. Listen carefully to what I'm going to tell you.

She moves closer. She's about three inches from my face. We haven't been this close in a long time. I take these little breaths that she can't hear, and I wait. I think my heart slows way down, I think.

She says, You just tell it like you have to, I guess, and forget the rest. Like always. You been doing that for so long now anyway it shouldn't be hard for you.

She says, There, I've done it. You're free, aren't you? At least you think you are anyway. Free at last. That's a joke, but don't laugh. Anyway, you feel better, don't you?

She walks with me down the hall.

She says, I can't imagine how I'd explain this if my husband was to walk in this very minute. But who really cares anymore, right? In the final analysis, nobody gives a damn anymore. Besides which, I think everything that can happen that way has already happened. His name is Fred, by the way. He's a decent guy and works hard for his living. He cares for me.

So she walks me to the front door, which has been standing open all this while. The door that was letting in light and fresh air this morning, and sounds off the street, all of which we had ignored. I look outside and, Jesus, there's this white moon hanging in the morning sky. I can't think when I've ever seen anything so remarkable. But I'm afraid to comment on it. I am. I don't know what might happen. I might break into tears even. I might not understand a word I'd say.

She says, Maybe you'll be back sometime, and maybe you won't. This'll wear off, you know. Pretty soon you'll start feeling bad again. Maybe it'll make a good story she says. But I don't want to know about it if it does.

I say good-bye. She doesn't say anything more. She looks at her hands, and then she puts them into the pockets of her dress. She shakes her head. She goes back inside, and this time she closes the door.

I move off down the sidewalk. Some kids are tossing a football at the end of the street. But they aren't my kids, and they aren't her kids either. There are these leaves everywhere, even in the gutters. Piles of leaves wherever I look. They're falling off the limbs as I walk. I can't take a step without putting my shoe into leaves. Somebody ought to make an effort here. Somebody ought to get a rake and take care of this.

House Hunting

MICHAEL CHABON

The house was all wrong for them. An ivy-covered Norman country manor with an eccentric roofline, a fat, pointed tower, and latticed mullions in the downstairs windows, it sat perched on the northwest shoulder of Lake Washington, a few blocks to the east of the house in which Christy had grown up. The neighborhood was subject to regular invasion by armies of gardeners, landscape contractors, and installers of genuine Umbrian granite paving stone, but nevertheless it was obvious the house had been got up to be sold. The blue paint on the shutters looked slick and wet, fresh black mulch churned around the pansies by the driveway, and the immense front lawn had been polished to a hard shine. The listing agent's sign was a discreet red-and-white escutcheon, on a black iron stake, that read simply, "Herman Silk," with a telephone number, in an elegant sans serif type.

"This?" Daniel Diamond said, his heart sinking in a kind of giddy fizz within him. Although they had all the windows open, Mr. Hogue's car was choked with the smell of his cologne, a harsh extract of wintergreen and brine which the realtor had been emitting more fiercely, like flop sweat, the nearer they got to the house. It was aggravating Daniel's allergies, and he wished he'd thought to pop a Claritin before leaving the apartment that morning. "This is the one?"

"That's the one," Hogue said, sounding weary, as though he had spent the entire day dragging them around town in his ancient Mercedes sedan, showing them one perfectly good house after another, each of which they had rejected with the most arbitrary and picayune of rationales. In fact, it was only ten o'clock in the morning, and this was the very first place he'd brought them to see. Bob Hogue was a leathery man of indefinite middle age, wearing a green polo shirt, tan chinos, and a madras blazer in the palette favored by manufacturers of the cellophane grass that goes into Easter baskets. His rectilinear wrinkles, his crew cut, his chin like a couple of knuckles, his nose lettered with minute red script, gave him the look of a jet pilot gone to seed. "What's the matter with it? Not good enough for you?"

Daniel and his wife, Christy Kite, looked at each other across the back of Christy's seat—Christy could never ride in the rear of any vehicle without experiencing acute motion sickness.

"Well, it's awfully big, Mr. Hogue," she said, tentatively, leaning to look past the realtor at the house. Christy had gone to college in Palo Alto, where she studied French and led cheers for a football team that lost all the big games. She had the Stanford graduate's aggressive nice manners, and the eyes of a cheerleader atop a struggling pyramid of girls. She had been the Apple Queen of Roosevelt High. From her mother, she had learned to try very hard to arrange everything in life with the flawlessness of a photograph in a house-and-garden magazine, and then to take it just as hard when the black plums went uneaten in the red McCoy bowl and filled the kitchen with a stink of garbage, or when the dazzling white masses of Shasta daisies in the backyard were eaten by aphids.

"Yeah, I don't know, Mr. Hogue," Daniel said. "I think—"

"Oh, but it is beautiful," Christy said. She furrowed her brow and narrowed her eyes. She poked her tongue gamely from a corner of her mouth. She was trying her hardest, Daniel could see, to imagine living in that house with him. House hunting, like all their efforts to improve things between them—the counseling, the long walks, the watching of a movie called *Spanking Brittany Blue*—had been her idea. But after a moment her face went slack, and her eyes sought Daniel's, and in them he saw, for the first time since their wedding the summer before last, the luster of real despair, as if she feared they would find no home for their marriage, not in Seattle or anywhere in the world. Then she shrugged and reached up to retie her scarf, a sheer white piece of Italian silk patterned with lemons and limes. She opened her door, and started to get out of the car.

"Just a minute, you," Hogue said, taking her arm. She fell back into the car at once, and favored Hogue with her calmest and most obliging Apple Queen smile, but Daniel could see her nostrils flaring like a rabbit's. "Don't be in such a rush," Hogue went on irritably. "You're always running off half-cocked." He leaned over to open the glove compartment and rummaged

around inside it until he found a package of Pall Malls. He pushed in the cigarette lighter and tapped one end of a wrinkled cigarette against the
dashboard. "You can't rush into a thing like this. It could turn out to be a
terrible mistake."

At once, like people trapped in an empty bus station with a fanatical
pamphleteer, Daniel and Christy agreed with Hogue.

"We're careful people," Christy said. Carefully, she averted her face from
Hogue's gaze, and gave her husband a brief grimace of not quite mock alarm.

"Careful people with limited resources," Daniel said. He hadn't decided
whether to tell Christy that, two days earlier, her father had taken him to
lunch at the University Club and offered to make a present of any reasonably priced house they might choose. After the war, Mr. Kite had founded
an industrial advertising agency, landed the accounts of several major sup-
pliers to Boeing, and then, at the age of sixty-two, sold his company for
enough money to buy a condominium on the ninth hole at Salishan and a
little cabana down on the beach at Cabo San Lucas. Daniel, a graduate stu-
dent in astronomy at U.W., where Christy taught psychology, didn't have any
money of his own. Neither, for that matter, did his father, who, in the years
of Mr. Kite's prosperity, had run two liquor stores, a printshop, and a five-
and-dime into the ground, and now lived with Daniel's mother amid the
coconut palms and peeling white stucco of an internment camp for impov-
erished old people not far from Delray Beach. "Maybe we ought to just—"

Christy cut him off with a sharp look. The lighter popped out, and
Hogue reached for it, and they watched in uncomfortable silence as, hands
shaking, he tried to light his cigarette. After several seconds and a great deal
of fearsome wheezing, the few frayed strands of tobacco he had succeeded
in getting lit fell out of the end of the cigarette, landed in his lap, and began
to burn his chinos. He slapped at his thigh, scowling all the while at the
house, as if it, or its occupants, were somehow responsible for his ignition.

"Maybe we ought to take a look at it, Mr. Hogue," Christy said.

Mr. Hogue looked back over at the house. He took a deep breath.

"I guess we'd better," he said. He opened his door and got out of the car,
eyeing the house warily.

Daniel and Christy lingered a moment by the Mercedes, whispering.

"He looks like he's seen a ghost," Christy observed, buttoning the top
button of her white cardigan. "He looks awful."

"Did he look better at our wedding?"

Daniel understood that Bob Hogue had been among the guests at their wedding, the summer before last, but his recollection of that remote afternoon had grown vague. In fact, the great event itself had, at the time, unfolded around him at a certain vague remove. He had felt not like the star attraction, along with Christy, of a moderately lavish civil ceremony held on the slope of a Laurelhurst lawn so much as like a tourist, lost in a foreign country, who had turned in to an unfamiliar street and found himself swallowed up in the clamor of a parade marking the feast day of some silken and barbarous religion. He remembered this Bob Hogue and his handsome wife, Monica, no better than he remembered Bill and Sylvia Bond, Roger and Evelyn Holsapple, Ralph and Betsy Lindstrom, or any of the three hundred other handsome old friends of his in-laws who had made up the bulk of the wedding guests. He knew that Hogue was a college chum and occasional golfing partner of his father-in-law's, and he was aware that an acrid ribbon of bad news was sent curling toward the ceiling of any room in which Bob Hogue's name was brought up, though he could never keep straight whether Hogue had married the lush, or fathered the Scientologist, or lost a piece of his left lung to cancer.

"To tell you the truth," Christy said, "I don't remember him at our wedding. I don't really know the Hogues very well. I just kind of remember how he looked when I was little."

"Well, no wonder he looks awful, then." He stepped back to admire her in her smart green Vittadini dress. Her bare legs were new-shaven, so smooth that they glinted in the sun, and through the gaps in her open-toed flats you could see a couple of slender toes, nails painted pink. "You, however, look very nice."

She smiled, and her pupils dilated, flooding her eyes with a darkness. "I liked what we did last night."

"So did I," Daniel said at once. Last night they had lain on top of their down comforter, with their heads at opposite ends of their bed, and massaged each other's feet with fragrant oil, by candlelight, while Al Green cooed to them in the background. This was an activity recommended to them by their couples therapist as a means of generating a nonthreatening sense of physical closeness between them. Daniel blushed now at this recollection, which he found painful and sad. To his great regret there was nothing even remotely erotic to him about feet, his wife's or anyone's. You might have permitted him to anoint the graceful foot of Semiramis or Hedy Lamarr, and he would not have popped a boner. He slid a hand up under the hem of Christy's dress and tried to skate his index and middle fingers up the smooth, hard surface of her right thigh, but she moved, and somehow Daniel's entire hand ended up thrust between her legs, as though he were attempting to hold open the doors of an elevator.

"Ouch," said Christy. "You don't have to be so rough."

"Sorry," said Daniel.

They started up the driveway after Mr. Hogue.

"Who's Herman Silk?" Daniel said, as they passed the discreet little sign.

"Who's Herman Silk?" Hogue wove a puzzling thread of bitterness into the question. "That's a good one." Daniel wondered if he should recognize the name from some local real estate scandal or recent round of litigation in the neighborhood. He tried to keep track of such mainstays of Kite-family conversation, but it was hard, in particular since they were generally served up, in the Kite house, with liberal amounts of Canadian Club and soda. "That's very funny," said Hogue.

When they got to the front door, Mr. Hogue could not seem to work the combination of the lockbox there. He tried several different permutations of what he thought was the code and then, in a display of bafflement at once childish and elderly, reached into his pocket and attempted to stick one of his own keys in the lock.

"Funny," he muttered, as this hopeless stratagem in due course failed. "Herman Silk. Ha."

Christy looked at Daniel, her eyes filled with apology for having led them into this intensifying disaster. Daniel smiled and gave his shoulders an attenuated shrug, characteristic of him, that did not quite absolve her of blame.

"Uh, why don't you tell me the combination, Mr. Hogue?" Christy suggested, yanking the lockbox out of his hands. She, who was willing to lie for hours listening to Reverend Al while Daniel worked over her oiled foot like a desperate man trying to summon a djinn, was finally losing patience. Daniel's heart was stirred by a wan hope that very soon now they would have to give up on old Mr. Hogue, on buying a house, on Christy's entire project of addressing and finding solutions for their problem. Now that things were starting to go so wrong, he hoped they could just return to their apartment on Queen Anne Hill and resume ignoring their problem, the strategy he preferred.

Hogue fed Christy the combination one digit at a time, and she worked the tumblers. She gave a sharp tug on the lockbox. It held firm.

"Are you sure that's the right number?" she said.

"Of course it's the right number," Hogue snapped. All at once his face had turned as red as the wrapper of his Pall Malls. One would have said that he was furious with Christy and Daniel, that he had had his fill of the unreasonable demands and the cruel hectoring to which they had subjected him over the last forty years. "Why are you always pestering me like that? Don't you know I'm doing my best?"

Daniel and Christy looked at each other. Christy bit her lip, and Daniel saw that she had been afraid something like this might happen. A sudden clear memory of Mr. Hogue at the wedding returned to him. There had been a series of toasts after dinner, and Mr. Hogue had risen to say a few words. His face had gone full of blood and he looked unsteady on his feet. The woman sitting beside him, Monica Hogue—slender, youthful, with red spectacles and a cute gray bob—had given his elbow a discreet tug. For a moment the air under the great white tent had grown still and sour, and the guests had looked down at their plates.

"Well, sure we do, Mr. Hogue," Christy said. "We know you've been doing a great job for us, and we really appreciate it. Don't we, Daniel?"

"Well, yeah. We really do."

The blood went out of Hogue's face.

"Excuse me," he said. "I—I'm sorry, you kids. I'm not feeling very well today." He ran a hand across the close-cropped top of his head. "Here. Let me see something. There used to be—" He backed down the steps and, half crouched, hands on his knees, scanned the ground under the long rhododendron hedges that flanked the door. He moved crabwise along the row of shrubbery until he disappeared around the corner of the house.

"I remember him now," said Daniel.

Christy laughed, through her nose, and then sadly shook her head.

"I hope he's all right."

"I think he just needs a drink."

"Hush, Daniel, please."

"Do you remember the toast he gave at the wedding?"

"Did he make a toast?"

"It was 'To our wives and lovers, may they never meet.'"

"I don't remember that."

"Pretty fucking appropriate wedding-toast material, I thought."

"Daniel."

"This is a waste."

"Daniel, please don't say that. We're going to work this all out."

"Christy," Daniel said. "Please don't say that."

"What else can I say?"

"Nothing," Daniel said. "I don't think you know how to say anything else."

"Found it!" Hogue came back around the house toward them, favoring the young couple with his realtor's smile—the smile of someone who knows that he has been discussed unfavorably in his absence. He was brandishing a medium-sized, mottled gray stone, and for a wild instant Daniel thought he intended somehow to smash his way in. But Hogue only turned the stone over, slid aside a small plastic panel that was attached to it, and pulled from its interior a shiny gold key. Then he slipped the false stone into the hip pocket of his jacket.

"Neat little things," he said. He slid the key into the lock without difficulty, and let them into the house. "Don't worry, it's quite all right," he added, when he saw how they were looking at him. "I'll just have to call about the lockbox. Happens all the time. Come on in."

They found themselves in a small foyer with plaster walls that were streaked like thick cake frosting, fir floors, and a built-in hatstand festooned with all manner of hats. Hogue hitched up the back of his trousers and stood looking around, blinking, mouth pinched, expression gone blank. The profusion of hats on the hatstand—three berets in the colors of sherbets, a tweedy homburg, a new-looking Stetson with a snakeskin band, several billed golf caps bearing the crest of Mr. Kite's club—seemed to bewilder him. He cleared his throat, and the young people waited for him to begin his spiel. But Hogue said nothing. Without gesturing for them to follow, he shuffled off into the living room.

It was like a page out of one of Mrs. Kite's magazines, furnished with a crewel love seat, two old-fashioned easy chairs that had been re-covered with pieces of a Persian kilim, a low Moroccan table with a hammered-brass top, an old blue Chinese Deco rug, and a small collection of art books and local Indian basketry, arranged with mock haphazardness on the built-in shelves. The desired effect was doubtless an eclectic yet contemporary spareness, but the room was very large, and to Daniel it just looked emptied.

"Are you all right, Mr. Hogue?" Christy said, elbowing Daniel.

Mr. Hogue stood on the Chinese rug, surveying the living room with his eyes wide and his mouth open, a hand pressed to his midsection as though he had been sandbagged.

"Eh? Oh, why, yes, it's just—they just—they changed things around a little bit," he said. "Since the last time I was here."

From his astonished expression it was hard to believe that Hogue had ever seen the place before. Daniel wondered if Hogue hadn't simply plucked it at random out of a listing book and driven them over here to satisfy some sense of obligation to Christy's parents. Clearly the owners had not been expecting anyone to come through this morning; there was an old knit afghan lying twisted on the love seat, a splayed magazine on one of the chairs, and a half-empty glass of tomato juice on the brass table.

"Mr. Hogue?" said Christy. "Are you sure this is okay?"

"Fine," said Hogue. He pointed to a pair of French doors at the far end of the living room. "I believe you'll find the dining room through there." Daniel followed Christy into the dining room, which was cool and shady and furnished with whitewashed birch chairs and a birchwood table with an immense glass top. In the center of the table sat a small black lacquer bowl in which a gardenia floated, its petals scorched at the edges by decay.

"Nice," Daniel said, although he always misgave at the odor of gardenias, which tempted with a promise of apples and vanilla beans but finished in a bitter blast of vitamins and burnt wire.

"Come on, Daniel. We can't afford this."

"Did I say we could?"

"Please don't be a bastard."

"Was I being a bastard?"

Christy sighed and looked back toward the living room. Hogue hadn't joined them yet; he seemed to have disappeared. He was probably back in the foyer, Daniel thought, looking around for the fact sheet on the house, so that he could pretend to be knowledgeable about it. Christy lowered her voice and spoke into Daniel's ear. Her breath played across the inner hairs of his ear and raised gooseflesh all down his forearms.

"Do you think he's not supposed to be doing this anymore?"

"What do you mean?" Daniel said, taking an involuntary step away from her. Her scarf had come loose at the back, allowing a thick lank strand of her unwashed dark hair to dangle alongside her face. It was not healthy to over-wash the hair—that was why she was wearing the jazzy scarf—and Daniel imagined he could still smell smoke on it from the Astronomy Department barbecue they had attended the night before.

"I mean, with the lockbox, and all—do you think he's been disbarred? Or whatever they do to realtors?"

"They make them unreal," Daniel suggested. He reached up and took hold of her scarf, and teased it loose. All of her smoky hair spilled down around her head.

"Why did you do that?" she said.

"I don't know," he admitted. He handed her the scarf, and she bound up her hair once more. "I'll go check on Mr. Hogue."

He went through the French doors back into the living room. Hogue was standing at the far end, where it opened onto the foyer, with his back to Daniel. There were built in shelves on this side of the room, also, peopled with a sparse collection of small *objets* and half a dozen framed photographs of infants and graduates and an Irish setter in an orange life preserver. As Daniel came in, Hogue was fingering something small and glittering, a piece of crystal or a glass animal. He picked it up, examined it, and then slipped it into the right hip pocket of his jacket.

"Coming," he said, after Daniel, rendered speechless, managed to clear his throat in alarm. Hogue turned, and for an instant, before his face resumed its habitual clench-jawed jet-pilot tautness, he looked grimly, mysteriously pleased with himself, like a man who had just exacted a small and glittering measure of revenge. Then he accompanied Daniel into the dining room, and Daniel tried to think of something plausible to ask him. What did normal husbands say to normal real estate agents at this stage of the game? It occurred to him that Hogue had not yet mentioned the asking price of the house.

"So what do they want, anyway, Mr. Hogue?" he tried.

"God only knows," Hogue said. He reached down toward the black lacquer bowl and picked up the gardenia, holding it by the clipped, dripping stem underneath. He brought it to his nose, took a deep draft of it, and then let out a long artificial sigh of delight. With Daniel looking right at him, he slipped the flower into the pocket of his jacket, too. "Let's have a look at that kitchen, shall we?"

So Daniel followed him into the kitchen, where Christy was exclaiming with a purely formal enthusiasm over the alderwood cabinets, the ceramic stove burners, the wavering light off the lake.

"What a waste, eh?" Hogue said. A dark patch of dampness was spreading across the fabric of his pocket. "They put I don't know how many thousands of dollars into it." He reached over to a sliding rheostat on the wall and made the track lighting bloom and dwindle and bloom. He shook his head. "Now then, this way to the family room. TV room. It amounts to the same thing, doesn't it?"

He slid a louvered door aside and went into the next room. Christy gestured to Daniel to come and stand beside her. Daniel looked back at the dining room. A lone leaf spun on the surface of the water in the lacquer bowl.

"Daniel, are you coming?" said Christy.

"There's something weird about this house," said Daniel.

"I wonder what," Christy said, giving her eyes a theatrical roll toward the family room and Mr. Hogue. As he passed through the kitchen, Daniel looked around, trying to see if anything portable was missing—a paradoxical exercise, given that he had never laid eyes on the room before. Sugar bowl, saltshaker, pepper mill, tea tongs trailing a winding rusty ribbon of dried tea. On the kitchen counter, under the telephone, lay a neat pile of letters and envelopes, and Daniel thought Hogue might have grabbed some of these, but they had been rubber-banded together and they looked undisturbed. A business card was affixed with a paper clip to the uppermost letter, printed with the name and telephone number of a Sergeant Matt Reedy of the Domestic Violence Unit of the Seattle Police Department. Daniel peeled back the pleat of the letter it was clipped to—it was out of its envelope—and peeked at its salutation, typed on an old typewriter that dropped its O's.

"DEAR BITCH," he read. "ARE YOU AND HERMAN HAPPY NOW, YOU—"

"Daniel! What are you doing?"

"Nothing," Daniel said, letting the letter fall shut again. "They, uh, they seem to be having some problems, the people who live in this house."

"Nothing that's our business, Daniel," Christy said, with what seemed to him excessive primness, taking hold of his hand.

Daniel yanked his hand free. He could hear Mr. Hogue muttering to himself in the other room.

"Ouch!" said Christy, bringing her fingers to her lips to kiss the joints he'd wrenched. She eyed the pile of letters on the counter. "What did it say?"

"It said maybe they ought to try rubbing each other's feet a little more often."

Now Christy really looked hurt.

"If you didn't want to do it, Daniel, I wish—"

"What's going on in here?" said Mr. Hogue, returning from the family room.

"We're just coming now," Daniel said. "Sorry. It's just—man, this kitchen is incredible."

Hogue gave a sour nod, lips pressed together. There was an obvious bulge in his right hip pocket now, and what appeared to be a table-tennis paddle protruding from the left one.

"Incredible," he agreed.

In the family room, when they joined him there, Hogue stole a well-thumbed paperback copy of Donald Trump's autobiography which was lying out on the coffee table, and in the small, tobacco-stained den off the foyer he took a little brass paperweight in the shape of a reclining pasha with curled slippers. When they went out to the garage, where, along with a long, slender automobile hidden under a canvas cover, there was a well-stocked workbench, he filched a box of nails, a Lufkin tape measure, and something else that Daniel couldn't quite determine the nature of. The thefts were blatant and apparently unself-conscious, and by the time they got upstairs to the second guest bedroom, Christy, too, was watching in a kind of jolly dread as Mr. Hogue worked the place over. He took a souvenir Space Needle, and a rubber coin purse, and a package of deodorizing shoe inserts. When he led the young couple at last into the master bedroom, his pockets were jangling.

He stopped short as he entered the room, so that Daniel and Christy nearly collided with him. He looked around at the big four-poster bed, the heavy Eastlake dresser and wardrobe, the walls covered in an unusual dark paper the red of old leather books. Once again Hogue marveled, in the same openmouthed, oddly crestfallen manner, as if the bedroom's decor, like the living room's, came to him, somehow, as a blow. As in the living room, there was no indication that the sellers had been expecting anyone to come through. The bed was unmade, and there were some ruffled white blouses and several bras and pairs of women's underpants heaped on the floor by the door. Hogue crossed the dark red room to a door opposite, which appeared to give onto a screened-in sleeping porch. Windows on either side of the door let in some of the bright September light pouring through the outer windows of the porch.

"I'd sure like to lie down in that hammock out there," Hogue said, with surprising wistfulness. He gave the knob an experimental twist. It was locked. He pressed his face to the glass. "God, I'm tired."

He reached into his breast pocket for a cigarette and found nothing there. He looked back and smiled thinly at Daniel and Christy, as if they had played a cruel trick on him, hiding the only solace of a weary and over-worked man. Then he patted down all his clattering pockets until he came up with a tattered Pall Mall. He went over to a marble-topped nightstand beside the bed and pulled open its drawer. He scrabbled around inside until he found a book of matches. His hands were shaking so badly now that he dropped the cigarette. Then he dropped the burning match. At last he succeeded in getting the thing lit. He blew a plume of smoke toward the pillows of the big, disorderly bed.

"You'll get the sun almost all day long in this room," he said, dreamily. "It's a shame to paper it over so dark." Then he flicked ashes onto the polished fir floor.

"All right, Mr. Hogue," said Christy, with all the sharpness of tone she was capable of mustering. "I guess we've seen enough."

"All right," said Hogue, though he didn't move. He just stood there, looking out at the canvas hammock that was hung between two pillars of the sleeping porch.

"We'll meet you downstairs, how about?" Daniel said. "How about you just give us a minute to talk things over between ourselves. You know. Look around one more time. You can't rush into something like this, right?"

Hogue swallowed, and some of the old flush of anger seemed to return now to the tips of his ears and to the skin at the back of his neck. Daniel could see that it was Hogue who wanted to be left alone here, in this bedroom, contemplating all his untold mistakes and whatever it was that was eating at him. He wanted them out of there. Christy sidled up to Daniel and pressed herself against him, hip to his thigh, cheek against his shoulder. He put his arm around her, and pressed his fingers against the slight bulge of skin under the strap of her bra.

"You know how important the bedroom is," Christy said, in a strangled voice.

Hogue took a thoughtful drag on his cigarette, eyeing them. Then, as before, the fire seemed to go out of him, and he nodded.

"I'll meet you downstairs," he said. "You kids take all the time you want."

He went out of the room, but before he did so, he stopped by the pile of laundry, picked up a rather large pair of lobelia blue panties with a lace waistband, and stuffed them into his pocket with the rest of his loot. They heard his tread on the stairs, and then, a moment later, the sound of a cabinet door squealing open on its hinges.

"He's going for the silver," Daniel said.

"Daniel, what are we going to do?"

Daniel shrugged. He sat down on the unmade bed, beside the nightstand that Hogue had rifled for matches.

"Maybe I should call my parents," Christy said. "They know Bob. Maybe they know what to do when he gets this way."

"I think it's a little too late for us to snub him," said Daniel.

Christy looked at him, angry and puzzled by the persistence of his nastiness toward her.

"That's not fair," she said. "God! Just because my parents—"

"Check this out." Daniel had been rummaging around in the nightstand drawer, where he had found, in addition to a bag of Ricola cough drops, a silver police whistle, and a small plastic vial of a popular genital lubricant, a greeting card, in a pink envelope that was laconically addressed "Monkey." He pulled out the card, on the cover of which Greta Garbo and John Gilbert were locked in a passionate black-and-white embrace. The greeting was handwritten: "I have tripped and fallen in love with you. Herman." After a moment Daniel looked up, feeling a little confused, and handed it to Christy. She took it with a disapproving frown.

"Herman," she read. "Herman Silk?"

"I guess it's a little extra service he provides."

"He must be selling his own house." She sat down on the bed beside him. "Do they do that?"

"Why not?" Daniel said. "Plenty of people sell their own houses."

"True."

He showed her the vial of lubricant.

"Maybe he should have said, 'I have *slipped* and fallen.'"

"Daniel, put that back. I mean it." She gestured downstairs. "Just because he's doing it doesn't mean you should." She snatched the little plastic bottle out of his hand, tossed it and the greeting card into the drawer, and then slammed the drawer shut. "Come on. Let's just get out of here."

They glared at each other, and then Daniel stood up. He felt a strong desire for his wife. He wanted to push her down onto the bed and pound her until his bones hurt and the smell of smoke from her hair filled the bedroom. But he would never do anything like that. And neither would she. Not in someone else's house, in someone else's bed. They were, both of them, hypochondriacs and low rollers, habitual occupants of the right lane on freeways, inveterate savers of receipts, subscribers to *Consumer Reports*, filterers of tap water, wearers of helmets and goggles and kneepads. And yet their prudence—prudence itself, it now seemed to Daniel, watching Christy's freckled breast fall and rise and fall—was an illusion, a thin padded blanket they drew around themselves to cushion the impact from the string of bad decisions each of them had made. For all their apparent caution, they had nonetheless married each other, willingly and without material compulsion, in the presence of the three hundred people. Christy had agreed to join herself in perpetuity to a man whose touch left her vagina as dry as a fist, and Daniel had consigned himself to a life spent as a hundred and sixty-two pounds of hair in her mouth and elbows in her rib cage and hot breath in her nostrils.

"I hate you," he said.

For a moment she looked very surprised by this admission. Then she stuck out her jaw and narrowed her eyes.

"Well, I hate you, too," she said.

Daniel fell on top of her. He was a little self-conscious at first about the animal sounds he heard them making and the way they were biting and tearing at each other's clothes. It was uncomfortably reminiscent of a key scene in *Spanking Brittany Blue*. Then some spasm sent Christy's hand flying, and she smacked Daniel in the eye. Inside his skull a bright red star flared and then winked out. After that, he forgot to pay attention to what they were doing. The bed underneath them smelled of its right occupants, of the night sweat and the aftershave and the skin lotion of Herman Silk and his Monkey. A loose board in the old fir floor rhythmically creaked. When the proper time came, Daniel reached into the drawer for Herman's little bottle of lubricant. He turned Christy over on her belly, and spread her legs with his knee, and greased her freely with the cold, clear stuff. His entry into her was, for the first time, effortless and quick.

"That was fun," Christy said, when it was over. She stretched her limbs across the wrecked bed as if to embrace it, and rolled, like a cat, back and forth, until it was smeared with the manifold compound of their lovemaking.

"Still hate me?" said Daniel.

She nodded, and that was when Daniel saw the mistake that they had made. Although sex was something they both regarded as perilous, marriage had, by contrast, seemed safe—a safe house in a world of danger; the ultimate haven of two solitary, fearful souls. When you were single, this was what everyone who was already married was always telling you. Daniel himself had said it to his unmarried friends. It was, however, a lie. Sex had everything to do with violence, that was true, and marriage was at once a container for the madness between men and women and a fragile hedge against it, as religion was to death, and the laws of physics to the immense quantity of utter emptiness of which the universe was made. But there was nothing at all safe about marriage. It was a doubtful enterprise, a voyage in an untested craft, across a hostile ocean, with a map that was a forgery and with no particular destination but the grave.

"I had lunch with your father the other day," he began.

"Shh!" Christy said.

He lay beside her, listening. From downstairs they could hear the sound of raised voices. A man and a woman were shouting at each other. The man was Mr. Hogue.

"I'm going to call the police, Bob," the woman said.

Daniel and Christy looked at each other. They stood up and scrambled to reassemble their clothes. Daniel slipped the vial of lubricant into his pocket. Then they went downstairs.

When they came into the kitchen, Mr. Hogue was lying on the floor, amid hundreds and hundreds of spilt threepenny nails, cupping his chin in his hands. Blood leaked out between his fingers and drizzled down his neck into the plaid of his madras jacket. The reclining brass pasha, the Ping-Pong paddle, Space Needle, and all the other things he had stolen lay scattered on the floor around him. A handsome woman with red spectacles, whom Daniel recognized as Mrs. Hogue, was kneeling beside him, tears on her face, wiping at the cut on his chin with a paper towel.

"Christy," she said. "Hello, Daniel."

She smiled ruefully and looked down at Mr. Hogue, moaning and whispering curses on the terra-cotta floor.

"Is he okay?" Daniel said, pointing to the realtor, who was, he saw now, no stranger to these troubled rooms.

"I certainly hope not. I hit him as hard as I could." Mrs. Hogue dabbed tenderly at the cut with the paper towel, then looked around at the kitchen she had renovated at such great expense. "So," she said, "what do you two think of the house?"

Daniel looked at Christy. She had lost her scarf sometime in the course of their struggle upstairs. Her face was a blur of smeared lipstick and streaked mascara and the radiant blood in her cheeks.

"It's perfect," he said.

A Daughter of Albion

ANTON CHEKHOV

A fine carriage with rubber tyres, a fat coachman, and velvet on the seats, rolled up to the house of a landowner called Gryabov. Fyodor Andreitch Otsov, the district Marshal of Nobility, jumped out of the carriage. A drowsy footman met him in the hall.

"Are the family at home?" asked the Marshal.

"No, sir. The mistress and the children are gone out paying visits, while the master and mademoiselle are catching fish. Fishing all the morning, sir."

Otsov stood a little, thought a little, and then went to the river to look for Gryabov. Going down to the river he found him a mile and a half from the house. Looking down from the steep bank and catching sight of Gryabov, Otsov gushed with laughter. . . . Gryabov a large stout man, with a very big head, was sitting on the sand, angling, with his legs tucked under him like a Turk. His hat was on the back of his head and his cravat had slipped on one side. Beside him stood a tall thin Englishwoman, with prominent eyes like a crab's, and a big bird-like nose more like a hook than a nose. She was dressed in a white muslin gown through which her scraggy yellow shoulders were very distinctly apparent. On her gold belt hung a little gold watch. She too was angling. The stillness of the grave reigned about them both. Both were motionless, as the river upon which their floats were swimming.

"A desperate passion, but deadly dull!" laughed Otsov. "Good-day, Ivan Kuzmitch."

"Ah . . . is that you?" asked Gryabov, not taking his eyes off the water. "Have you come?"

"As you see . . . And you are still taken up with your crazy nonsense! Not given it up yet?"

"The devil's in it. . . . I begin in the morning and fish all day. . . . The fishing is not up to much to-day. I've caught nothing and this dummy hasn't either. We sit on and on and not a devil of a fish! I could scream!"

"Well, chuck it up then. Let's go and have some vodka!"

"Wait a little, maybe we shall catch something. Towards evening the fish bite better . . . I've been sitting here, my boy, ever since the morning! I can't tell you how fearfully boring it is. It was the devil drove me to take to this fishing! I know that it is rotten idiocy for me to sit here. I sit here like some scoundrel, like a convict, and I stare at the water like a fool. I ought to go to the haymaking, but here I sit catching fish. Yesterday His Holiness held a service at Haponyevo, but I didn't go. I spent the day here with this . . . with this she-devil."

"But . . . have you taken leave of your senses?" asked Otsov, glancing in embarrassment at the Englishwoman. "Using such language before a lady and she . . ."

"Oh, confound her, it doesn't matter, she doesn't understand a syllable of Russian, whether you praise her or blame her, it is all the same to her! Just look at her nose! Her nose alone is enough to make one faint. We sit here for whole days together and not a single word! She stands like a stuffed image and rolls the whites of her eyes at the water."

The Englishwoman gave a yawn, put a new worm on, and dropped the hook into the water.

"I wonder at her not a little," Gryabov went on, "the great stupid has been living in Russia for ten years and not a word of Russian! . . . Any little aristocrat among us goes to them and learns to babble away in their lingo, while they . . . there's no making them out. Just look at her nose, do look at her nose!"

"Come, drop it . . . it's uncomfortable. Why attack a woman?"

"She's not a woman, but a maiden lady. . . . I bet she's dreaming of suitors. The ugly doll. And she smells of something decaying . . . I've got a loathing for her my boy! I can't look at her with indifference. When she turns her ugly eyes on me it sends a twinge all through me as though I had knocked my elbow on the parapet. She likes fishing too. Watch her: she fishes as though it were a holy rite! She looks upon everything with disdain . . . She stands there, the wretch, and is conscious that she is a human being, and that therefore she is the monarch of nature. And do you know what her name is? Wilka Charlesovna Fyce! Tfoo! There is no getting it out!"

The Englishwoman, hearing her name, deliberately turned her nose in Gryabov's direction and scanned him with a disdainful glance; she raised her eyes from Gryabov to Otsov and steeped him in disdain. And all this in silence, with dignity and deliberation.

"Did you see?" said Gryabov chuckling. "As though to say 'take that.' Ah, you monster! It's only for the children's sake that I keep that triton. If it weren't for the children, I wouldn't let her come within ten miles of my estate. . . . She has got a nose like a hawk's . . . and her figure! That doll makes me think of a long nail, so I could take her and knock her into the ground, you know. Stay, I believe I have got a bite. . . ."

Gryabov jumped up and raised his rod. The line drew taut. . . . Gryabov tugged again, but could not pull out the hook.

"It has caught," he said, frowning, "on a stone I expect . . . damnation take it . . ."

There was a look of distress on Gryabov's face. Sighing, moving uneasily, and muttering oaths, he began tugging at the line.

"What a pity, I shall have to go into the water."

"Oh, chuck it!"

"I can't. . . . There's always good fishing in the evening. . . . What a nuisance. Lord, forgive us, I shall have to wade into the water, I must! And if only you knew, I have no inclination to undress, I shall have to get rid of the Englishwoman. . . . It's awkward to undress before her. After all, she is a lady, you know!"

Gryabov flung off his hat, and his cravat.

"Meess . . . er, er . . ." he said, addressing the Englishwoman, "Meess Fyce, je voo pree. . . ? Well, what am I to say to her? How am I to tell you so that you can understand? I say . . . over there! Go away over there! Do you hear?"

Miss Fyce enveloped Gryabov in disdain, and uttered a nasal sound.

"What? Don't you understand? Go away from here, I tell you! I must undress, you devil's doll! Go over there! Over there!"

Gryabov pulled the lady by her sleeve, pointed her towards the bushes, and made as though he would sit down, as much as to say: Go behind the bushes and hide yourself there. . . . The Englishwoman, moving her eyebrows vigorously, uttered rapidly a long sentence in English. The gentlemen gushed with laughter.

"It's the first time in my life I've heard her voice. . . . There's no denying, it is a voice! She does not understand! Well, what am I to do with her?"

"Chuck it, let's go and have a drink of vodka!"

"I can't. Now's the time to fish, the evening. . . . It's evening . . . Come, what would you have me do? It is a nuisance! I shall have to undress before her. . . ."

Gryabov flung off his coat and his waistcoat and sat on the sand to take off his boots.

"I say, Ivan Kuzmitch," said the marshal, chuckling behind his hand. "It's really outrageous, an insult."

"Nobody asks her not to understand! It's a lesson for these foreigners!"

Gryabov took off his boots and his trousers, flung off his undergarments and remained in the costume of Adam. Otsov held his sides, he turned crimson both from laughter and embarrassment. The Englishwoman twitched her brows and blinked . . . A haughty disdainful smile passed over her yellow face.

"I must cool off," said Gryabov, slapping himself on the ribs. "Tell me if you please, Fyodor Andreitch, why I have a rash on my chest every summer."

"Oh, do get into the water quickly or cover yourself with something, you beast."

"And if only she were confused, the nasty thing," said Gryabov, crossing himself as he waded into the water. "Brrr . . . the water's cold. . . . Look how she moves her eyebrows! She doesn't go away . . . she is far above the crowd he, he, he . . . and she doesn't reckon us as human beings."

Wading knee deep in the water and drawing his huge figure up to its full height, he gave a wink and said:

"This isn't England, you see!"

Miss Fyce coolly put on another worm, gave a yawn, and dropped the hook in. Otsov turned away, Gryabov released his hook, ducked into the water and, spluttering, waded out. Two minutes later he was sitting on the sand and angling as before.

The Story of an Hour

KATE CHOPIN

Knowing that Mrs. Mallard was afflicted with a heart trouble, great care was taken to break to her as gently as possible the news of her husband's death.

It was her sister Josephine who told her, in broken sentences; veiled hints that revealed in half concealing. Her husband's friend Richards was there, too, near her. It was he who had been in the newspaper office when intelligence of the railroad disaster was received, with Brently Mallard's name leading the list of "killed." He had only taken the time to assure himself of its truth by a second telegram, and had hastened to forestall any less careful, less tender friend in bearing the sad message.

She did not hear the story as many women have heard the same, with a paralyzed inability to accept its significance. She wept at once, with sudden, wild abandonment, in her sister's arms. When the storm of grief had spent itself she went away to her room alone. She would have no one follow her.

There stood, facing the open window, a comfortable, roomy armchair. Into this she sank, pressed down by a physical exhaustion that haunted her body and seemed to reach into her soul.

She could see in the open square before her house the tops of trees that were all aquiver with the new spring life. The delicious breath of rain was in the air. In the street below a peddler was crying his wares. The notes of a distant song which some one was singing reached her faintly, and countless sparrows were twittering in the eaves.

There were patches of blue sky showing here and there through the clouds that had met and piled one above the other in the west facing her window.

She sat with her head thrown back upon the cushion of the chair, quite motionless, except when a sob came up into her throat and shook her, as a child who has cried itself to sleep continues to sob in its dreams.

She was young, with a fair, calm face, whose lines bespoke repression and even a certain strength. But now there was a dull stare in her eyes, whose gaze was fixed away off yonder on one of those patches of blue sky. It was not a glance of reflection, but rather indicated a suspension of intelligent thought.

There was something coming to her and she was waiting for it, fearfully. What was it? She did not know; it was too subtle and elusive to name. But she felt it, creeping out of the sky, reaching toward her through the sounds, the scents, the color that filled the air.

Now her bosom rose and fell tumultuously. She was beginning to recognize this thing that was approaching to possess her, and she was striving to beat it back with her will—as powerless as her two white slender hands would have been.

When she abandoned herself a little whispered word escaped her slightly parted lips. She said it over and over under her breath: "free, free, free!" The vacant stare and the look of terror that had followed it went from her eyes. They stayed keen and bright. Her pulses beat fast, and the coursing blood warmed and relaxed every inch of her body.

She did not stop to ask if it were or were not a monstrous joy that held her. A clear and exalted perception enabled her to dismiss the suggestion as trivial.

She knew that she would weep again when she saw the kind, tender hands folded in death; the face that had never looked save with love upon her, fixed and gray and dead. But she saw beyond that bitter moment a long procession of years to come that would belong to her absolutely. And she opened and spread her arms out to them in welcome.

There would be no one to live for her during those coming years; she would live for herself. There would be no powerful will bending hers in that blind persistence with which men and women believe they have a right to impose a private will upon a fellow-creature. A kind intention or a cruel intention made the act seem no less a crime as she looked upon it in that brief moment of illumination.

And yet she had loved him—sometimes. Often she had not. What did it matter! What could love, the unsolved mystery, count for in face of this possession of self-assertion which she suddenly recognized as the strongest impulse of her being!

"Free! Body and soul free!" she kept whispering.

Josephine was kneeling before the closed door with her lips to the keyhole, imploring for admission. "Louise, open the door! I beg; open the door—you will make yourself ill. What are you doing, Louise? For heaven's sake open the door."

"Go away. I am not making myself ill." No; she was drinking in a very elixir of life through that open window.

Her fancy was running riot along those days ahead of her. Spring days, and summer days, and all sorts of days that would be her own. She breathed a quick prayer that life might be long. It was only yesterday she had thought with a shudder that life might be long.

She arose at length and opened the door to her sister's importunities. There was a feverish triumph in her eyes, and she carried herself unwittingly like a goddess of Victory. She clasped her sister's waist, and together they descended the stairs. Richards stood waiting for them at the bottom.

Some one was opening the front door with a latchkey. It was Brently Mallard who entered, a little travel-stained, composedly carrying his gripsack and umbrella. He had been far from the scene of accident, and did not even know there had been one. He stood amazed at Josephine's piercing cry; at Richards' quick motion to screen him from the view of his wife.

But Richards was too late.

When the doctors came they said she had died of heart disease—of joy that kills.

The Other Wife

COLETTE

T able for two? This way, Monsieur, Madame there is still a table next to the window, if Madame and Monsieur would like a view of the bay."

Alice followed the maître d'.

"Oh, yes. Come on, Marc, it'll be like having lunch on a boat on the water . . ."

Her husband caught her by passing his arm under hers. "We'll be more comfortable over there."

"There? In the middle of all those people? I'd much rather . . ."

"Alice, please."

He tightened his grip in such a meaningful way that she turned around. "What's the matter?"

"Shh . . ." he said softly, looking at her intently, and led her toward the table in the middle.

"What is it, Marc?"

"I'll tell you, darling. Let me order lunch first. Would you like the shrimp? Or the eggs in aspic?"

"Whatever you like, you know that."

They smiled at one another, wasting the precious time of an overworked maître d', stricken with a kind of nervous dance, who was standing next to them, perspiring.

"The shrimp," said Marc. "Then the eggs and bacon. And the cold chicken with a romaine salad. *Fromage blanc?* The house specialty? We'll go with the specialty. Two strong coffees. My chauffeur will be having lunch also, we'll be leaving again at two o'clock. Some cider? No, I don't trust it . . . Dry champagne."

He sighed as if he had just moved an armoire, gazed at the colorless midday sea, at the pearly white sky, then at his wife, whom he found lovely in her little Mercury hat with its large, hanging veil.

"You're looking well, darling. And all this blue water makes your eyes look green, imagine that! And you've put on weight since you've been traveling . . . It's nice up to a point, but only up to a point!"

Her firm, round breasts rose proudly as she leaned over the table.

"Why did you keep me from taking that place next to the window?"

Marc Seguy never considered lying. "Because you were about to sit next to someone I know."

"Someone I don't know?"

"My ex-wife."

She couldn't think of anything to say and opened her blue eyes wider.

"So what, darling? It'll happen again. It's not important."

The words came back to Alice and she asked, in order, the inevitable questions. "Did she see you? Could she see that you saw her? Will you point her out to me?"

"Don't look now, please, she must be watching us . . . The lady with brown hair, no hat, she must be staying in this hotel. By herself, behind those children in red . . ."

"Yes. I see."

Hidden behind some broad-brimmed beach hats, Alice was able to look at the woman who, fifteen months ago, had still been her husband's wife.

"Incompatibility," Marc said. "Oh, I mean . . . total incompatibility! We divorced like well-bred people, almost like friends, quietly, quickly. And then I fell in love with you, and you really wanted to be happy with me. How lucky we are that our happiness doesn't involve any guilty parties or victims!"

The woman in white, whose smooth, lustrous hair reflected the light from the sea in azure patches, was smoking a cigarette with her eyes half closed. Alice turned back toward her husband, took some shrimp and butter, and ate calmly. After a moment's silence she asked: "Why didn't you ever tell me that she had blue eyes, too?"

"Well, I never thought about it!"

He kissed the hand she was extending toward the bread basket and she blushed with pleasure. Dusky and ample, she might have seemed somewhat coarse, but the changeable blue of her eyes and her wavy, golden hair made her look like a frail and sentimental blonde. She vowed overwhelming gratitude to her husband. Immodest without knowing it, everything about her bore the overly conspicuous marks of extreme happiness.

They ate and drank heartily, and each thought the other had forgotten the woman in white. Now and then, however, Alice laughed too loudly, and Marc was careful about his posture, holding his shoulders back, his head up. They waited quite a long time for their coffee, in silence. An incandescent river, the straggled reflection of the invisible sun overhead, shifted slowly across the sea and shone with a blinding brilliance.

"She's still there, you know," Alice whispered.

"Is she making you uncomfortable? Would you like to have coffee somewhere else?"

"No, not at all! She's the one who must be uncomfortable! Besides, she doesn't exactly seem to be having a wild time, if you could see her . . ."

"I don't have to. I know that look of hers."

"Oh, was she like that?"

He exhaled his cigarette smoke through his nostrils and knitted his eyebrows. "Like that? No. To tell you honestly, she wasn't happy with me."

"Oh, really now!"

"The way you indulge me is so charming, darling . . . It's crazy . . . You're an angel . . . You love me . . . I'm so proud when I see those eyes of yours. Yes, those eyes . . . She . . . I just didn't know how to make her happy, that's all. I didn't know how."

"She's just difficult!"

Alice fanned herself irritably, and cast brief glances at the woman in white, who was smoking, her head resting against the back of the cane chair, her eyes closed with an air of satisfied lassitude.

Marc shrugged his shoulders modestly.

"That's the right word," he admitted. "What can you do? You have to feel sorry for people who are never satisfied. But we're satisfied . . . Aren't we, darling?"

She did not answer. She was looking furtively, and closely, at her husband's face, ruddy and regular; at his thick hair, threaded here and there with white silk; at his short, well-cared-for hands; and doubtful for the first time, she asked herself, "What more did she want from him?"

And as they were leaving, while Marc was paying the bill and asking for the chauffeur and about the route, she kept looking, with envy and curiosity, at the woman in white, this dissatisfied, this difficult, this superior . . .

The Upturned Face

STEPHEN CRANE

W hat will we do now?" said the adjutant, troubled and excited.

"Bury him," said Timothy Lean.

The two officers looked down close to their toes where lay the body of their comrade. The face was chalk-blue; gleaming eyes stared at the sky. Over the two upright figures was a windy sound of bullets, and on the top of the hill Lean's prostrate company of Spitzbergen infantry was firing measured volleys.

"Don't you think it would be better—" began the adjutant. "We might leave him until to-morrow."

"No," said Lean. "I can't hold that post an hour longer. I've got to fall back, and we've got to bury old Bill."

"Of course," said the adjutant, at once. "Your men got entrenching tools?"

Lean shouted back to his little line, and two men came slowly, one with a pick, one with a shovel. They started in the direction of the Rostina sharp-shooters. Bullets cracked near their ears. "Dig here," said Lean gruffly. The men, thus caused to lower their glances to the turf, became hurried and frightened, merely because they could not look to see whence the bullets came. The dull beat of the pick striking the earth sounded amid the swift snap of close bullets. Presently the other private began to shovel.

"I suppose," said the adjutant, slowly, "we'd better search his clothes for—things."

Lean nodded. Together in curious abstraction they looked at the body. Then Lean stirred his shoulders suddenly, arousing himself.

"Yes," he said, "we'd better see what he' got." He dropped to his knees, and his hands approached the body of the dead officer. But his hands wavered over the buttons of the tunic. The first button was brick-red with drying blood, and he did not seem to dare touch it.

"Go on," said the adjutant, hoarsely.

Lean stretched his wooden hand, and his fingers fumbled the blood-stained buttons. At last he rose with ghastly face. He had gathered a watch, a whistle, a pipe, a tobacco-pouch, a handkerchief, a little case of cards and papers. He looked at the adjutant. There was a silence. The adjutant was feeling that he had been a coward to make Lean do all the grisly business.

"Well," said Lean, "that's all, I think. You have his sword and revolver?"

"Yes," said the adjutant, his face working, and then he burst out in a sudden strange fury at the two privates. "Why don't you hurry up with that grave? What are you doing, anyhow? Hurry, do you hear? I never saw such stupid—"

Even as he cried out in his passion the two men were labouring for their lives. Ever overhead the bullets were spitting.

The grave was finished. It was not a masterpiece—a poor little shallow thing. Lean and the adjutant again looked at each other in a curious silent communication.

Suddenly the adjutant croaked out a weird laugh. It was a terrible laugh, which had its origin in that part of the mind which is first moved by the singing of the nerves. "Well," he said humorously to Lean, "I suppose we had best tumble him in."

"Yes," said Lean. The two privates stood waiting, bent over their implements. "I suppose," said Lean, "it would be better if we laid him in ourselves."

"Yes," said the adjutant. Then, apparently remembering that he had made Lean search the body, he stooped with great fortitude and took hold of the dead officer's clothing. Lean joined him. Both were particular that their fingers should not feel the corpse. They tugged away; the corpse lifted, heaved, toppled, flopped into the grave, and the two officers, straightening, looked again at each other—they were always looking at each other. They sighed with relief.

The adjutant said, "I suppose we should—we should say something. Do you know the service, Tim?"

"They don't read the service until the grave is filled in," said Lean, pressing his lips to an academic expression.

"Don't they?" said the adjutant, shocked that he had made the mistake.

"Oh, well," he cried, suddenly, "let us—let us say something—while he can hear us."

"All right," said Lean. "Do you know the service?"

"I can't remember a line of it," said the adjutant.

Lean was extremely dubious. "I can repeat two lines, but—"

"Well, do it," said the adjutant. "Go as far as you can. That's better than nothing. And the beasts have got our range exactly."

Lean looked at his two men. "Attention," he barked. The privates came to attention with a click, looking much aggrieved The adjutant lowered his helmet to his knee. Lean, bareheaded, he stood over the grave. The Rostina sharpshooters fired briskly.

"O Father our friend has sunk in the deep waters of death but his spirit has leaped toward Thee as the bubble arises from the lips of the drowning. Perceive, we beseech, O Father, the little flying bubble, and—"

Lean, although husky and ashamed, had suffered no hesitation up to this point, but he stopped with a hopeless feeling and looked at the corpse

The adjutant moved uneasily. "And from Thy superb heights—" he began, and then he too came to an end.

"And from Thy superb heights," said Lean.

The adjutant suddenly remembered a phrase in the back of the Spitzbergen burial service, and he exploited it with the triumphant manner of a man who has recalled everything, and can go on.

"O God, have mercy—"

"O God, have mercy—" said Lean.

"Mercy," repeated the adjutant, in quick failure.

"Mercy," said Lean. And then he was moved by some violence of feeling, for he turned upon his two men and tigerishly said, "Throw the dirt in."

The fire of the Rostina sharpshooters was accurate and continuous.

One of the aggrieved privates came forward with his shovel. He lifted his first shovel-load of earth, and for a moment of inexplicable hesitation it was held poised above this corpse, which from its chalk-blue face looked keenly out from the grave. Then the soldier emptied his shovel on—on the feet.

Timothy Lean felt as if tons had been swiftly lifted from off his forehead. He had felt that perhaps the private might empty the shovel on—on the face. It had been emptied on the feet. There was a great point gained there—

ha, ha!—the first shovelful had been emptied on the feet. How satisfactory!

The adjutant began to babble. "Well, of course—a man we've messed with all these years—impossible— you can't, you know, leave your intimate friends rotting on the field. Go on, for God's sake, and shovel, you."

The man with the shovel suddenly ducked, grabbed his left arm with his right hand, and looked at his officer for orders. Lean picked the shovel from the ground. "Go to the rear," he said to the wounded man. He also addressed the other private. "You get under cover, too; I'll finish this business."

The wounded man scrambled hard still for the top of the ridge without devoting any glances to the direction from whence the bullets came, and the other man followed at an equal pace, but he was different, in that he looked back anxiously three times.

This is merely the way—often—of the hit and unhit.

Timothy Lean filled the shovel, hesitated, and then, in a movement which was like a gesture of abhorrence, he flung the dirt into the grave, and as it landed it made a sound—plop. Lean suddenly stopped and mopped his brow—a tired labourer.

"Perhaps we have been wrong," said the adjutant. His glance wavered stupidly. "It might have been better if we hadn't buried him just at this time. Of course, if we advance to-morrow the body would have been—"

"Damn you," said Lean, "shut your mouth." He was not the senior officer.

He again filled the shovel and flung the earth. Always the earth made that sound—plop. For a space Lean worked frantically, like a man digging himself out of danger.

Soon there was nothing to be seen but the chalk-blue face. Lean filled the shovel. "Good God," he cried to the adjutant. "Why didn't you turn him somehow when you put him in? This—" Then Lean began to stutter.

The adjutant understood. He was pale to the lips. "Go on, man," he cried, beseechingly, almost in a shout.

Lean swung back the shovel. It went forward in a pendulum curve. When the earth landed it made a sound—plop.

The Hypnotizer

CHARLOTTE PERKINS GILMAN

I don't know where the man came from. None of us did. He was a friend of a friend of Mat Newcome's—Mat brought him down for a week-end at the Belithorpe and he stayed.

He wasn't very big, but I admit he was a good-looker, and as graceful as a girl. He could play all the games well enough to be a good partner,—not well enough to beat all the time—ideal for the women. And he seemed to like to play with them.

He said he was a writer, but when the girls tried to find out what he had written he only said, "a lot of poor stuff," or something like that—never showed the goods.

Also he seemed to have plenty of money.

I don't know why I say "seemed" in that scornful way; maybe he did, maybe he earned it. If you don't like a fellow, nothing he does strikes you right, somehow.

All the girls liked him fast enough, including Sophie. You can call me jealous all you like—I'll admit it. I was jealous—who wouldn't have been?

Here I'd been working two years to get next to Sophie—two years, and most of it was uplift! I'd left off smoking—not that I ever smoked much—that wasn't much of a sacrifice; and drinking—which was less; and coffee—that, now, was a pull. But I'd have given up eating to please Sophie—if she'd have married me before I died!

And here comes this hypnotizer, Maurice Foster—a pussy-cattish sort of name, I call it—who smokes and drinks and takes coffee three times a day—and she falls for him at once.

When I taxed her with it, she said that she did not mind his habits because she took no personal interest in him—which sounded comforting.

We were practically engaged, though she wouldn't really promise yet, when he came; and then, whether it was personal interest or not, she spent far more time with him than she did with me.

The fellow certainly had "a winning way" with him. He made himself solid with the landlady in no time,—lean, fierce-looking, old thing she was, but soft-hearted for all that. He pleased all the mothers by praising their children—that didn't take long— he could do it between dances.

I noticed he didn't take any of the kids out sailing, or play games with 'em—too busy with the young ladies; but he got around the mothers all right. If they were mothers of the pretty girls he went with, then be gave more time to them, and would sit talking New Thought or Bergson or Brieux, or whatever their specialty was, till he had 'em hypnotized. We called him a hypnotizer before any of us knew he was one, but he was the real article all right.

Sophie had a cousin there; a poor little skate he was to look at, but a mighty nice boy for all that. I'd have liked him even if he hadn't been her cousin, and in spite of his money; but he was so rich a good many of us fellows rather shied off—and he spent most of his time in his boats. I use the plural advisedly—he had a regular fleet,—a sea-going yacht, a fine little nosy powerboat that was good for all inland waters, and a first rate racing catboat—to say nothing of rowboats and canoes. Oh, and one of those seasleds. That was a goer!

Well, this boy Maurice just laid for Hal Jerome, the cousin; it seemed to me that he gunned for him, as if he was an heiress he could marry—and he succeeded fast enough. He made Jerome feel that be didn't care for his money. How he managed it I don't know, but he did. Instead of toadying to him, he bossed him; instead of being respectful he talked about "the idle rich"—and took the boy to task for loafing around in those boats and all that.

Everybody was for him except the fellows whose girls he monopolized so much. We had our opinion of him—but much good that did us.

All this was going on, and Mat Newcome kicking himself that he ever brought the chap down, when the real hypnotizing began.

Now I'm studying medicine—about ready to start practise—and I know what the real thing is; how useful it is, how dangerous it is. I've been in Charcot's hospital and seen amazing things done. I knew of a case over here—one of a good many, of course, but vivid—where a woman had some nervous affection of the throat and couldn't swallow. She had money to burn, and all the doctors and surgeons and osteopaths could do was done—done pretty quick too, for she was missing her food and drink, and the woman was at death's door—with the door beginning to open—and still she couldn't swallow.

Then they brought in a hypnotist. He fixed her with his glittering eye all right; went through the motions—just told her that she could swallow—and lo, she did it. That's the good of hypnotism.

As to the harm it does—that I know about too, with good reason. From the mildest and most insidious "suggestion," and what the lawyers call "undue influence," up to these powerful rascals who make other people do their crimes for them—it's bad. Bad for the ones who do it, too; a degrading business, I call it, monkeying with another person's internal machinery like that.

I rather suspected this boy was that kind of a person, but didn't know how much, till they got him started in the hotel parlor one night; first just talking, and then doing tricks.

Everyone was interested of course—red hot—they always are. Some hung back and some wouldn't have anything to do with it, and some were eager to be "subjects," but all of 'em wanted to see the performance.

Foster was in his element. That dark pale face of his got rather set in its lines, his big eyes looked bigger; he was going to show what he could do.

Sophie was intensely interested. She drew closer and closer, and when he asked for subjects I could see she meant to offer—she was courageous, and had what she called "scientific curiosity" to a high degree.

I simply couldn't bear to think of her putting herself in that fellow's grip even for a few moments in that hotel parlor.

"Sophie! Sophie!" I urged softly. "Please step out here a moment—I want very much to speak to you." She was annoyed, but came—not a very favorable opportunity.

"What is it?" she asked in that cold impersonal sort of way that takes all the ginger out of you.

"Don't let that fellow try his tricks on you!" I said. "It's not safe—really."

Its always a mistake to try to scare that kind of a girl.

"Thank you for your interest," she said, "but I am not in the least afraid of anything Mr. Foster can do."

"I know more about this thing than you do," I urged. "I've studied it abroad—it is really a serious matter. I hate to see it played with in this way—there's no knowing what mischief it may lead to—please, Sophie—I beg of you."

I guess that was a mistake, too; perhaps anything I said then would have been wrong. Anyway she wouldn't agree to keep out.

He'd got three people to come forward,—one of the boys, about twelve or thirteen, a sturdy little fellow with a round cheerful face and a nice grin—I wasn't worried about him; Miss Meakins, a maiden lady, very plump and emotional, and Jerome.

"Your cousin oughtn't to be in it either," I insisted. He's not at all strong—he's in no condition for such experimenting—can't you persuade him not to try it?"

"Perhaps you can persuade him yourself, Jack," she said sweetly. "Better try!" And she stepped back into the parlor—we'd been just outside a long window on the verandah—and marched up to those other three and said she'd like to try too.

He was tremendously pleased. I could see he'd been wanting her—even before I spoke, and he'd had his eye on that window for some time.

I was mad clear through, personally and professionally—too mad to be reasonable, but I wanted to see everything that was done, so I came in and got a good position.

He fell to work, and I could see at once that he knew the game and was good at it. The boy was too much for him. He was willing, even eager, and did everything Foster told him, in the way of fixing his eyes on this and taking his mind off that; but when he was solemnly told: "You cannot remember your name," he only grinned and said "Yes, I can."

Foster went on with his treatment a bit, and then solemnly repeated: "You—can—NOT—remember your name. You can—NOT—tell me what your name is when I ask you!" And then while we all waited and young Norton grinned, he solemnly asked: "What is your name?"

"Parr Norton," said the youngster without the least hesitation. I wondered why on earth he had picked out such an unlikely subject to begin with, but I thought afterward he did it on purpose—to show good faith and reassure the spectators.

He smiled it off. "Failure!!" he said easily. "Complete failure! We cannot always succeed. I congratulate you Master Norton—you need never fear the hypnotist."

Norton was mightily pleased with himself.

Then Foster concentrated on Miss Meakins. She was a pretty easy mark. It didn't take any time to get her reduced to a jelly. He was perfectly polite of

course, didn't lay a hand on her, or make her do anything the others could really object to, but I thought it was abominable. He made the poor lady recite:
"Jack be nimble, Jack be quick,
Jack jump over the candle-stick,"
and say that in her opinion it was the most beautiful poem ever written. He made her say her name was Pollyoodle, and Mary Janey and a dozen absurdities—each time passionately asserting that it was hers. He made her chew her own handkerchief under the profound conviction that it was a peach. It was pitiful, and, to me, highly offensive, to see that harmless woman made a monkey of by this fellow from goodness knows where.

Sophie watched it all, and I did hope she would change her mind—she's quite capable of that at times. But she saw me looking on, my arms folded and my face pretty black, I dare say, and her mouth tightened a little—I know the look. Perhaps she thought she could stick it out like young Norton. Anyhow she was next.

He was mighty careful, I'll say that for him, just as cautious and respectful as could be. And I will say it was quite masterly, the subtle steady way he worked. But it was all I could do to keep my hands off him when I saw she was abdicating her own mind—letting that chap run it, if only for a moment.

I thought I saw a special look of triumph come across him, but he hid it. And he didn't make her ridiculous in any way—not a bit; just some nonsense about matches being flowers—enough to show him he could do it—and let her off—said she was not a good subject—that her will was too strong.

But I had got closer to her than he noticed, and my ears are hypersensitive anyway. I heard him whisper to her: "You will meet me at moonrise to-morrow by the old boathouse," before he let her go.

And the moon past the full!

But the sport of the evening, for the lookers-on, was poor young Jerome. Foster certainly did play cat-and-fiddle with him. If the boy had been well I'm sure he couldn't have done it, but he was in a low nervous condition, and he had a serious breakdown afterward—took him a year or more to get over it.

He had been watching all this with feverish eagerness, getting more and more excited, and it didn't take three minutes to put his intellect and will out of commission. He was a reed in Foster's hands. Foster did anything he liked with him. He made him ridiculous. He made him pathetic. He set him to doing silly stunts, or to not doing them, rather. He laid a walking-stick down on the floor and told the boy he couldn't jump over it. And he couldn't all right. He'd start and totter, and nearly fall on his nose; but cross that stick he couldn't.

Then he straightened his arm down by his side, stroked it carefully down.

"You cannot bend your arm," he told him. "It is as stiff as a log of wood. Nobody else can bend it."

Sure enough—Jerome couldn't, and the men who tried to, couldn't. They laid him, head and heels, stretched between two chairs—and told him he was a log—and couldn't bend—and he didn't, though they sat a boy on his stomach.

Then finally he stood him up there, all white and tired, and arranged the closing scene. "I am going out in the hall," he told him, "and will call you to me. You must come. Nothing can prevent you. You must come. I will set three men here to hold you back and they cannot do it."

Then he picked out three of us, two rather light weights, who had been looking on, over-awed, and myself. "Try your best," he said, "you cannot do it."

Success had gone to his head a little, I think, or he would have noticed my—state of mind.

Mad? I don't think I'd ever been so mad in my life. But my folks are English; when we're mad we're cold—and hard.

I stood up there in front of that pale sweating, exhausted boy and con-centrated all the power I had, all the method I had ever learned.

Foster, out in the hall, they told me afterward, was a sight. He was pret-ty well exhausted too, the perspiration rolled down his face; he couldn't see us inside, but stood at the foot of the stairs and beckoned steadily, with a drawing clutching motion. "Come!" he was commanding softly. "Come!"

And I stood there, big and healthy and so full of rage I was equal to any ten of them, and I put my hands up against Jerome—didn't touch him, you know, but sort of pushed the air, and said: "Stay here! Stay here! You shall not go!" Silently, of course.

Well—Jerome wavered like a grass stalk He leaned forward, swayed backward, that poor body of his was a mere rag between those opposing wills. But I was fresher to the game, and, I fancy, little as I use the power, that I've really got a lot of it. It was all there that night, and red hot.

"Go and sit on that sofa," I inwardly commanded Jerome. He did.

Then I turned on Foster, still frantically pulling, and made him come into the room, paying no attention to me and apologize to Jerome—and to the company in general—for his cruel and silly performance.

He was terribly upset; didn't really know what had got hold of him. I said to him—inside: "You will leave here tomorrow morning before breakfast. But first—state your business, now, to us."

He did—owned that he was a professional hypnotizer—and left, as directed—was glad to.

* * * *

Sophie seemed dazed. I suggested a turn in the moonlight, to relax our minds before sleeping, and she came cheerfully.

I was still pretty well keyed up—but she didn't know it. We were silent for a bit, and all the time I was turning on all the power that was in me, saying to my darling: "You will not go to the old boathouse at moonrise to-morrow night. You will never think of that man again, nor see him, without contempt and loathing. You will never again submit yourself to any such foolish experiment as this!"

And she never did. I don't really think she would have anyhow. She is a very sensible girl.

I had the job of fixing up young Jerome—went off on a trip with him, and it helped me much in starting my practice. So much so that Sophie and I got married next year.

Hills Like White Elephants

ERNEST HEMINGWAY

The hills across the valley of the Ebro were long and white. On this side there was no shade and no trees and the station was between two lines of rails in the sun. Close against the side of the station there was the warm shadow of the building and a curtain, made of strings of bamboo beads, hung across the open door into the bar, to keep out flies. The American and the girl with him sat at a table in the shade, outside the building. It was very hot and the express from Barcelona would come in forty minutes. It stopped at this junction for two minutes and went on to Madrid.

"What should we drink?" the girl asked. She had taken off her hat and put it on the table.

"It's pretty hot," the man said.

"Let's drink beer."

"Dos cervezas," the man said into the curtain.

"Big ones?" a woman asked from the doorway.

"Yes. Two big ones."

The woman brought two glasses of beer and two felt pads. She put the felt pads and the beer glasses on the table and looked at the man and the girl. The girl was looking off at the line of hills. They were white in the sun and the country was brown and dry.

"They look like white elephants," she said.

"I've never seen one," the man drank his beer.

"No, you wouldn't have."

"I might have," the man said. "Just because you say I wouldn't have doesn't prove anything."

The girl looked at the bead curtain. "They've painted something on it," she said. "What does it say?"

"Anis del Toro. It's a drink."

"Could we try it?"

The man called "Listen" through the curtain. The woman came out from the bar.

"Four reales."

"We want two Anis del Toro."

"With water?"

"Do you want it with water?"

"I don't know," the girl said. "Is it good with water?"

"It's all right."

"You want them with water?" asked the woman.

"Yes, with water."

"It tastes like licorice," the girl said and put the glass down.

"That's the way with everything."

"Yes," said the girl. "Everything tastes of licorice. Especially all the things you've waited so long for, like absinthe."

"Oh, cut it out."

"You started it," the girl said. "I was being amused. I was having a fine time."

"Well, let's try and have a fine time."

"All right. I was trying. I said the mountains looked like white elephants. Wasn't that bright?"

"That was bright."

"I wanted to try this new drink. That's all we do, isn't it—look at things and try new drinks?"

"I guess so."

The girl looked across at the hills.

"They're lovely hills," she said. "They don't really look like white elephants. I just meant the coloring of their skin through the trees."

"Should we have another drink?"

"All right."

The warm wind blew the bead curtain against the table.

"The beer's nice and cool," the man said.

"It's lovely," the girl said.

"It's really an awfully simple operation, Jig," the man said. "It's not really an operation at all."

The girl looked at the ground the table legs rested on.

"I know you wouldn't mind it, Jig. It's really not anything. It's just to let the air in."

The girl did not say anything.

"I'll go with you and I'll stay with you all the time. They just let the air in and then it's all perfectly natural."

"Then what will we do afterward?"

"We'll be fine afterward. Just like we were before."

"What makes you think so?"

"That's the only thing that bothers us. It's the only thing that's made us unhappy."

The girl looked at the bead curtain, put her hand out and took hold of two of the strings of beads.

"And you think then we'll be all right and be happy."

"I know we will. You don't have to be afraid. I've known lots of people that have done it."

"So have I," said the girl. "And afterward they were all so happy."

"Well," the man said, "if you don't want to you don't have to. I wouldn't have you do it if you didn't want to. But I know it's perfectly simple."

"And you really want to?"

"I think it's the best thing to do. But I don't want you to do it if you don't really want to."

"And if I do it you'll be happy and things will be like they were and you'll love me?"

"I love you now. You know I love you."

"I know. But if I do it, then it will be nice again if I say things are like white elephants, and you'll like it?"

"I'll love it. I love it now but I just can't think about it. You know how I get when I worry."

"If I do it you won't ever worry?"

"I won't worry about that because it's perfectly simple."

"Then I'll do it. Because I don't care about me."

"What do you mean?"

"I don't care about me."

"Well, I care about you."

"Oh, yes. But I don't care about me. And I'll do it and then everything will be fine."

"I don't want you to do it if you feel that way."

The girl stood up and walked to the end of the station. Across, on the other side, were fields of grain and trees along the banks of the Ebro. Far away, beyond the river, were mountains. The shadow of a cloud moved across the field of grain and she saw the river through the trees.

"And we could have all this," she said. "And we could have everything and every day we make it more impossible."

"What did you say?"

"I said we could have everything."

"We can have everything."

"No, we can't."

"We can have the whole world."

"No, we can't."

"We can go everywhere."

"No, we can't. It isn't ours any more."

"It's ours."

"No, it isn't. And once they take it away, you never get it back."

"But they haven't taken it away."

"We'll wait and see."

"Come on back in the shade," he said. "You mustn't feel that way."

"I don't feel any way," the girl said. "I just know things."

"I don't want you to do anything that you don't want to do—"

"Nor that isn't good for me," she said. "I know. Could we have another beer?"

"All right. But you've got to realize—"

"I realize," the girl said. "Can't we maybe stop talking?"

They sat down at the table and the girl looked across at the hills on the dry side of the valley and the man looked at her and at the table.

"You've got to realize," he said, "that I don't want you to do it if you don't want to. I'm perfectly willing to go through with it if it means anything to you."

"Doesn't it mean anything to you? We could get along."

"Of course it does. But I don't want anybody but you. I don't want any one else. And I know it's perfectly simple."

"Yes, you know it's perfectly simple."

"It's all right for you to say that, but I do know it."

"Would you do something for me now?"

"I'd do anything for you."

"Would you please please please please please please please stop talking?" He did not say anything but looked at the bags against the wall of the station. There were labels on them from all the hotels where they had spent nights.

"But I don't want you to," he said, "I don't care anything about it."

"I'll scream," the girl said.

The woman came out through the curtains with two glasses of beer and put them down on the damp felt pads. "The train comes in five minutes," she said.

"What did she say?" asked the girl.

"That the train is coming in five minutes."

The girl smiled brightly at the woman, to thank her.

"I'd better take the bags over to the other side of the station," the man said. She smiled at him.

"All right. Then come back and we'll finish the beer."

He picked up the two heavy bags and carried them around the station to the other tracks. He looked up the tracks but could not see the train. Coming back, he walked through the barroom, where people waiting for the train were drinking. He drank an Anis at the bar and looked at the people. They were all waiting reasonably for the train. He went out through the bead curtain. She was sitting at the table and smiled at him.

"Do you feel better?" he asked.

"I feel fine," she said. "There's nothing wrong with me. I feel fine."

San Francisco

AMY HEMPEL

D o you know what I think?

I think it was the tremors. That's what must have done it. The way the floor rolled like bongo boards under our feet? Remember it was you and Daddy and me having lunch? "I guess that's not an earthquake," you said. "I guess you're shaking the table?"

That's when it must have happened. A watch on a dresser, a small thing like that—it must have been shaken right off, onto the floor.

And how would Maidy know? Maidy at the doctor's office? All those years on a psychiatrist's couch and suddenly the couch is *moving*.

Good God, she is on that couch when the big one hits.

Maidy didn't tell you, but you know what her doctor said? When she sprang from the couch and said, "My God, was that an earthquake?"

The doctor said this: "Did it *feel* like an earthquake to you?"

I think we are agreed, you have to look on the light side.

So that's when I think it must have happened. Not that it matters to me. Maidy is the one who wants to know. She thinks she has it coming, being the older daughter. Although where was the older daughter when it happened? Which daughter was it that found you?

When Maidy started asking about your watch, I felt I had to say it. I said, "With the body barely cold?"

Maidy said the body is not the person, that the *essence* is the person, and that the essence leaves the body behind it, along with the body's possessions —for example, its watch?

"Time flies," I said. "Like an arrow.

"*Fruit* flies," I said, and Maidy said, "What?"

"Fruit flies," I said again. "Fruit flies like a banana."

That's how easy it is to play a joke on Maidy.

Remember how easy?

Now Maidy thinks I took your watch. She thinks because I got there first, my first thought was to take it. Maidy keeps asking, "Who took Mama's watch?" She says, "Did *you* take Mama's watch?"

Eveline

JAMES JOYCE

She sat at the window watching the evening invade the avenue. Her head was leaned against the window curtains and in her nostrils was the odour of dusty cretonne. She was tired.

Few people passed. The man out of the last house passed on his way home; she heard his footsteps clacking along the concrete pavement and afterwards crunching on the cinder path before the new red houses. One time there used to be a field there in which they used to play every evening with other people's children. Then a man from Belfast bought the field and built houses in it—not like their little brown houses but bright brick houses with shining roofs. The children of the avenue used to play together in that field— the Devines, the Waters, the Dunns, little Keogh the cripple, she and her brothers and sisters. Ernest, however, never played: he was too grown up. Her father used often to hunt them in out of the field with his blackthorn stick; but usually little Keogh used to keep *nix* and call out when he saw her father coming. Still they seemed to have been rather happy then. Her father was not so bad then; and besides, her mother was alive. That was a long time ago; she and her brothers and sisters were all grown up; her mother was dead. Tizzie Dunn was dead, too, and the Waters had gone back to England. Everything changes. Now she was going to go away like the others, to leave her home.

Home! She looked round the room, reviewing all its familiar objects which she had dusted once a week for so many years, wondering where on earth all the dust came from. Perhaps she would never see again those familiar objects from which she had never dreamed of being divided and yet during all those years she had never found out the name of the priest whose yellowing photograph hung on the wall above the broken harmonium beside the coloured print of the promises made to Blessed Margaret Mary Alacoque. He had been a school friend of her father. Whenever he showed the photograph to a visitor her father used to pass it with a casual word:

—He is in Melbourne now.

She had consented to go away, to leave her home. Was that wise? She tried to weigh each side of the question. In her home anyway she had shelter and food; she had those whom she had known all her life about her. Of course she had to work hard both in the house and at business. What would they say of her in the Stores when they found out that she had run away with a fellow? Say she was a fool, perhaps, and her place would be filled up by advertisement. Miss Gavan would be glad. She had always had an edge on her, especially whenever there were people listening.

—Miss Hill, don't you see these ladies are waiting?

—Look lively, Miss Hill, please.

She would not cry many tears at leaving the Stores.

But in her new home, in a distant unknown country, it would not be like that. Then she would be married—she, Eveline. People would treat her with respect then. She would not be treated as her mother had been. Even now, though she was over nineteen, she sometimes felt herself in danger of her father's violence. She knew it was that that had given her the palpitations. When they were growing up he had never gone for her, like he used to go for Harry and Ernest, because she was a girl; but latterly he had begun to threaten her and say what he would do to her only for her dead mother's sake. And now she had nobody to protect her. Ernest was dead and Harry, who was in the church decorating business, was nearly always down somewhere in the country. Besides, the invariable squabble for money on Saturday nights had begun to weary her unspeakably. She always gave her entire wages—seven shillings—and Harry always sent up what he could but the trouble was to get any money from her father. He said she used to squander the money, that she had no head, that he wasn't going to give her his hard-earned money to throw about the streets, and much more, for he was usually fairly bad of a Saturday night. In the end he would give her the money and ask her had she any intention of buying Sunday's dinner. Then she had to rush out as quickly as she could and do her marketing, holding her black leather purse tightly in her hand as she elbowed her way through the crowds and returning home late under her load of provisions. She had hard work to keep the house together and to see that the two young children who had been left to her charge went to school regularly and got their meals regularly. It was hard work—a hard life—but now that she was about to leave it she did not find it a wholly undesirable life.

She was about to explore another life with Frank. Frank was very kind, manly, open-hearted. She was to go away with him by the night-boat to be his wife and to live with him in Buenos Ayres where he had a home waiting for her. How well she remembered the first time she had seen him; he was lodging in a house on the main road where she used to visit. It seemed a few weeks ago. He was standing at the gate, his peaked cap pushed back on his head and his hair tumbled forward over a face of bronze. Then they had come to know each other. He used to meet her outside the Stores every evening and see her home. He took her to see *The Bohemian Girl* and she felt elated as she sat in an unaccustomed part of the theatre with him. He was awfully fond of music and sang a little. People knew that they were courting and, when he sang about the lass that loves a sailor, she always felt pleasantly confused. He used to call her Poppens out of fun. First of all it had been an excitement for her to have a fellow and then she had begun to like him. He had tales of distant countries. He had started as a deck boy at a pound a month on a ship of the Allan Line going out to Canada. He told her the names of the ships he had been on and the names of the different services. He had sailed through the Straits of Magellan and he told her stories of the terrible Patagonians. He had fallen on his feet in Buenos Ayres, he said, and had come over to the old country just for a holiday. Of course, her father had found out the affair and had forbidden her to have anything to say to him.

—I know these sailor chaps, he said.

One day he had quarrelled with Frank and after that she had to meet her lover secretly.

The evening deepened in the avenue. The white of two letters in her lap grew indistinct. One was to Harry; the other was to her father. Ernest had been her favourite but she liked Harry too. Her father was becoming old lately, she noticed; he would miss her. Sometimes he could be very nice. Not long before, when she had been laid up for a day, he had read her out a ghost story and made toast for her at the fire. Another day, when their mother was alive, they had all gone for a picnic to the Hill of Howth. She remembered her father putting on her mother's bonnet to make the children laugh.

Her time was running out but she continued to sit by the window, leaning her head against the window curtain, inhaling the odour of dusty cretonne. Down far in the avenue she could hear a street organ playing. She knew the air. Strange that it should come that very night to remind her of the promise to her mother, her promise to keep the home together as long as she could. She remembered the last night of her mother's illness; she was again in the close dark room at the other side of the hall and outside she heard a melancholy air of Italy. The organ-player had been ordered to go away and given sixpence. She remembered her father strutting back into the sickroom saying:

—Damned Italians! coming over here!

As she mused the pitiful vision of her mother's life laid its spell on the very quick of her being—that life of commonplace sacrifices closing in final craziness. She trembled as she heard again her mother's voice saying constantly with foolish insistence:

—Derevaun Seraun Derevaun Seraun!

She stood up in a sudden impulse of terror. Escape! She must escape! Frank would save her. He would give her life, perhaps love, too. But she wanted to live. Why should she be unhappy? She had a right to happiness. Frank would take her in his arms, fold her in his arms. He would save her.

* * * *

She stood among the swaying crowd in the station at the North Wall. He held her hand and she knew that he was speaking to her, saying something about the passage over and over again. The station was full of soldiers with brown baggages. Through the wide doors of the sheds she caught a glimpse of the black mass of the boat, lying in beside the quay wall, with illumined portholes. She answered nothing. She felt her cheek pale and cold and, out of a maze of distress, she prayed to God to direct her, to show her what was her duty. The boat blew a long mournful whistle into the mist. If she went, to-morrow she would be on the sea with Frank, steaming towards Buenos Ayres. Their passage had been booked. Could she still draw back after all he had done for her? Her distress awoke a nausea in her body and she kept moving her lips in silent fervent prayer.

A bell clanged upon her heart. She felt him seize her hand:

—Come!

All the seas of the world tumbled about her heart. He was drawing her into them: he would drown her. She gripped with both hands at the iron railing.

—Come!

No! No! No! It was impossible. Her hands clutched the iron in frenzy. Amid the seas she sent a cry of anguish

—Eveline! Evvy!

He rushed beyond the barrier and called to her to follow. He was shouted at to go on but he still called to her. She set her white face to him, passive, like a helpless animal. Her eyes gave him no sign of love or farewell or recognition.

Wine

DORIS LESSING

A man and woman walked toward the boulevard from a little hotel in a side street.

The trees were still leafless, black, cold; but the fine twigs were swelling toward spring, so that looking upward it was with an expectation of the first glimmering greenness. Yet everything was calm, and the sky was a calm, classic blue.

The couple drifted slowly along. Effort, after days of laziness, seemed impossible; and almost at once they turned into a café and sank down, as if exhausted, in the glass-walled space that was thrust forward into the street.

The place was empty. People were seeking the midday meal in the restaurants. Not all: that morning crowds had been demonstrating, a procession had just passed, and its straggling end could still be seen. The sounds of violence, shouted slogans and singing, no longer absorbed the din of Paris traffic; but it was these sounds that had roused the couple from sleep.

A waiter leaned at the door, looking after the crowds, and he reluctantly took an order for coffee.

The man yawned; the woman caught the infection; and they laughed with an affectation of guilt and exchanged glances before their eyes, without regret, parted. When the coffee came, it remained untouched. Neither spoke. After some time the woman yawned again; and this time the man turned and looked at her critically, and she looked back. Desire asleep, they looked. This remained: that while everything which drove them slept, they accepted from each other a sad irony; they could look at each other without illusion, steady-eyed.

And then, inevitably, the sadness deepened in her till she consciously resisted it; and into him came the flicker of cruelty.

"Your nose needs powdering," he said.

"You need a whipping boy."

But always he refused to feel sad. She shrugged, and, leaving him to it, turned to look out. So did he. At the far end of the boulevard there was a faint agitation, like stirred ants, and she heard him mutter, "Yes, and it still goes on. . . ."

Mocking, she said, "Nothing changes, everything always the same. . . .

But he had flushed. "I remember," he began, in a different voice. He stopped, and she did not press him, for he was gazing at the distant demonstrators with a bitterly nostalgic face.

Outside drifted the lovers, the married couples, the students, the old people. There the stark trees; there the blue, quiet sky. In a month the trees would be vivid green; the sun would pour down heat; the people would be brown, laughing, bare-limbed. No, no, she said to herself, at this vision of activity. Better the static sadness. And, all at once, unhappiness welled up in her, catching her throat, and she was back fifteen years in another country. She stood in blazing tropical moonlight, stretching her arms to a landscape that offered her nothing but silence; and then she was running down a path where small stones glinted sharp underfoot, till at last she fell spent in a swathe of glistening grass. Fifteen years.

It was at this moment that the man turned abruptly and called the waiter and ordered wine.

"What," she said humorously, "already?"

"Why not?"

For the moment she loved him completely and maternally, till she suppressed the counterfeit and watched him wait, fidgeting, for the wine, pour it, and then set the two glasses before them beside the still-brimming coffee cups. But she was again remembering that night, envying the girl ecstatic with moonlight, who ran crazily through the trees in an unsharable desire for—but that was the point.

"What are you thinking of?" he asked, still a little cruel.

"Ohhh," she protested humorously.

"That's the trouble, that's the trouble." He lifted his glass, glanced at her, and set it down. "Don't you want to drink?"

"Not yet."

He left his glass untouched and began to smoke.

These moments demanded some kind of gesture—something slight, even casual, but still an acknowledgment of the separateness of those two people in each of them; the one seen, perhaps, as a soft-staring never-closing eye, observing, always observing, with a tired compassion; the other, a shape of violence that struggled on in the cycle of desire and rest, creation and achievement.

He gave it her. Again their eyes met in the grave irony, before he turned away, flicking his fingers irritably against the table; and she turned also, to note the black branches where the sap was tingling.

"I remember," he began; and again she said, in protest, "Ohhh "

He checked himself. "Darling," he said drily, "you're the only woman I've ever loved." They laughed.

"It must have been this street. Perhaps this café—only they change so. When I went back yesterday to see the place where I came every summer, it was a *pâtisserie*, and the woman had forgotten me. There was a whole crowd of us—we used to go around together—and I met a girl here, I think, for the first time. There were recognized places for contacts; people coming from Vienna or Prague, or wherever it was, knew the places—it couldn't be this café, unless they've smartened it up. We didn't have the money for all this leather and chromium."

"Well, go on."

"I keep remembering her, for some reason. Haven't thought of her for years. She was about sixteen, I suppose. Very pretty—no, you're quite wrong. We used to study together. She used to bring her books to my room. I liked her, but I had my own girl, only she was studying something else, I forget what." He paused again, and again his face was twisted with nostalgia, and involuntarily she glanced over her shoulder down the street. The procession had completely disappeared, not even the sounds of singing and shouting remained.

"I remember her because. . . ." And, after a preoccupied silence: "Perhaps it is always the fate of the virgin who comes and offers herself, naked, to be refused."

"What!" she exclaimed, startled. Also, anger stirred in her. She noted it, and sighed. "Go on."

"I never made love to her. We studied together all that summer. Then, one weekend, we all went off in a bunch. None of us had any money, of course, and we used to stand on the pavements and beg lifts, and meet up again in some village. I was with my own girl, but that night we were help-ing the farmer get in his fruit, in payment for using his barn to sleep in, and I found this girl Marie was beside me. It was moonlight, a lovely night, and we were all singing and making love. I kissed her, but that was all. That night she came to me. I was sleeping up in the loft with another lad. He was asleep. I sent her back down to the others. They were all together down in the hay. I told her she was too young. But she was no younger than my own girl." He stopped; and after all these years his face was rueful and puzzled. "I don't know," he said. "I don't know why I sent her back." Then he laughed. "Not that it matters, I suppose."

"Shameless hussy," she said. The anger was strong now. "You had kissed her, hadn't you?"

He shrugged. "But we were all playing the fool. It was a glorious night—gathering apples, the farmer shouting and swearing at us because we were making love more than working, and singing and drinking wine. Besides, it was that time: the youth movement. We regarded faithfulness and jealousy and all that sort of thing as remnants of bourgeois morality." He laughed again, rather painfully. "I kissed her. There she was, beside me, and she knew my girl was with me that weekend."

"You kissed her," she said accusingly.

He fingered the stem of his wineglass, looking over at her and grinning. "Yes, darling," he almost crooned at her. "I kissed her."

She snapped over into anger. "There's a girl all ready for love. You make use of her for working. Then you kiss her. You know quite well. . . ."

"What do I know quite well?"

"It was a cruel thing to do."

"I was a kid myself. . . ."

"Doesn't matter." She noted, with discomfort, that she was almost cry-ing. "Working with her! Working with a girl of sixteen, all summer!"

"But we all studied very seriously. She was a doctor afterward, in Vienna. She managed to get out when the Nazis came in, but. . . ."

She said impatiently, "Then you kissed her, on *that* night. Imagine her, waiting till the others were asleep, then she climbed up the ladder to the loft, terrified the other man might wake up, then she stood watching you sleep, and she slowly took off her dress and. . . ."

"Oh, I wasn't asleep. I pretended to be. She came up dressed. Shorts and sweater—our girls didn't wear dresses and lipstick—more bourgeois morality.

I watched her strip. The loft was full of moonlight. She put her hand over my mouth and came down beside me." Again, his face was filled with rueful amazement. "God knows, I can't understand it myself. She was a beautiful creature. I don't know why I remember it. It's been coming into my mind the last few days." After a pause, slowly twirling the wineglass: "I've been a failure in many things, but not with. . . ." He quickly lifted her hand, kissed it, and said sincerely: "I don't know why I remember it now, when. . . . " Their eyes met, and they sighed.

She said slowly, her hand lying in his: "And so you turned her away."

He laughed. "Next morning she wouldn't speak to me. She started a love affair with my best friend—the man who'd been beside me that night in the loft, as a matter of fact. She hated my guts, and I suppose she was right."

"Think of her. Think of her at that moment. She picked up her clothes, hardly daring to look at you. . . ."

"As a matter of fact, she was furious. She called me all the names she could think of; I had to keep telling her to shut up, she'd wake the whole crowd."

"She climbed down the ladder and dressed again, in the dark. Then she went out of the barn, unable to go back to the others. She went into the orchard. It was still brilliant moonlight. Everything was silent and deserted, and she remembered how you'd all been singing and laughing and making love. She went to the tree where you'd kissed her. The moon was shining on the apples. She'll never forget it, never, never!"

He looked at her curiously. The tears were pouring down her face.

"It's terrible," she said. "Terrible. Nothing could ever make up to her for that. Nothing, as long as she lived. Just when everything was most perfect, all her life, she'd suddenly remember that night, standing alone, not a soul anywhere, miles of damned empty moonlight. . . ."

He looked at her shrewdly. Then, with a sort of humorous, deprecating grimace, he bent over and kissed her and said: "Darling, it's not my fault; it just isn't my fault."

"No," she said.

He put the wineglass into her hands; and she lifted it, looked at the small crimson globule of warming liquid, and drank with him.

To Build a Fire

JACK LONDON

Day had broken cold and gray, exceedingly cold and gray, when the man turned aside from the main Yukon trail and climbed the high earth-bank, where a dim and little-travelled trail led eastward through the fat spruce timberland. It was a steep bank, and he paused for breath at the top, excusing the act to himself by looking at his watch. It was nine o'clock. There was no sun nor hint of sun, though there was not a cloud in the sky. It was a clear day, and yet there seemed an intangible pall over the face of things, a subtle gloom that made the day dark, and that was due to the absence of sun. This fact did not worry the man. He was used to the lack of sun. It had been days since he had seen the sun, and he knew that a few more days must pass before that cheerful orb, due south, would just peep above the sky-line and dip immediately from view.

The man flung a look back along the way he had come. The Yukon lay a mile wide and hidden under three feet of ice. On top of this ice were as many feet of snow. It was all pure white, rolling in gentle undulations where the ice-jams of the freeze-up had formed. North and south, as far as his eye could see, it was unbroken white, save for a dark hair-line that curved and twisted from around the spruce-covered island to the south, and that curved and twisted away into the north, where it disappeared behind another spruce-covered island. This dark hair-line was the trail—the main trail—that led south five hundred miles to the Chilcoot Pass, Dyea, and salt water; and that led north seventy miles to Dawson, and still on to the north a thousand miles to Nulato, and finally to St. Michael on Bering Sea, a thousand miles and half a thousand more.

But all this—the mysterious, far-reaching hair-line trail, the absence of sun from the sky, the tremendous cold, and the strangeness and weirdness of it all—made no impression on the man. It was not because he was long used to it. He was a newcomer in the land, a *chechaquo*, and this was his first winter. The trouble with him was that he was without imagination. He was quick and alert in the things of life, but only in the things, and not in the significances. Fifty degrees below zero meant eighty-odd degrees of frost. Such fact impressed him as being cold and uncomfortable, and that was all. It did not lead him to meditate upon his frailty as a creature of temperature, and upon man's frailty in general, able only to live within certain narrow limits of heat and cold; and from there on it did not lead him to the conjectural field of immortality and man's place in the universe. Fifty degrees below zero stood for a bite of frost that hurt and that must be guarded against by the use of mittens, ear-flaps, warm moccasins, and thick socks. Fifty degrees below zero was to him just precisely fifty degrees below zero. That there should be anything more to it than that was a thought that never entered his head.

As he turned to go on, he spat speculatively. There was a sharp, explosive crackle that startled him. He spat again. And again, in the air, before it could fall to the snow, the spittle crackled. He knew that at fifty below spittle crackled on the snow, but this spittle had crackled in the air. Undoubtedly it was colder than fifty below—how much colder he did not know. But the temperature did not matter. He was bound for the old claim on the left fork of Henderson Creek, where the boys were already. They had come over across the divide from the Indian Creek country, while he had come the roundabout way to take a look at the possibilities of getting out logs in the spring from the islands in the Yukon. He would be in to camp by six o'clock; a bit after dark, it was true, but the boys would be there, a fire would be going, and a hot supper would be ready. As for lunch, he pressed his hand against the protruding bundle under his jacket. It was also under his shirt, wrapped up in a handkerchief and lying against the naked skin. It was the only way to keep the biscuits from freezing. He smiled agreeably to himself as he thought of those biscuits, each cut open and sopped in bacon grease, and each enclosing a generous slice of fried bacon.

He plunged in among the big spruce trees. The trail was faint. A foot of snow had fallen since the last sled had passed over, and he was glad he was without a sled, travelling light. In fact, he carried nothing but the lunch wrapped in the handkerchief. He was surprised, however, at the cold. It certainly was cold, he concluded, as he rubbed his numb nose and cheek-bones with his mittened hand. He was a warm-whiskered man, but the hair on his face did not protect the high cheek-bones and the eager nose that thrust itself aggressively into the frosty air.

At the man's heels trotted a dog, a big native husky, the proper wolf-dog, gray-coated and without any visible or temperamental difference from its brother, the wild wolf. The animal was depressed by the tremendous cold. It knew that it was no time for travelling. Its instinct told it a truer tale than was told to the man by the man's judgment. In reality, it was not merely colder than fifty below zero; it was colder than sixty below, than seventy below. It was seventy-five below zero. Since the freezing-point is thirty-two above zero, it meant that one hundred and seven degrees of frost obtained. The dog did not know anything about thermometers. Possibly in its brain there was no sharp consciousness of a condition of very cold such as was in the man's brain. But the brute had its instinct. It experienced a vague but menacing apprehension that subdued it and made it slink along at the man's heels, and that made it question eagerly every unwonted movement of the man as if expecting him to go into camp or to seek shelter somewhere and build a fire. The dog had learned fire, and it wanted fire, or else to burrow under the snow and cuddle its warmth away from the air.

The frozen moisture of its breathing had settled on its fur in a fine powder of frost, and especially were its jowls, muzzle, and eyelashes whitened by its crystalled breath. The man's red beard and mustache were likewise frosted, but more solidly, the deposit taking the form of ice and increasing with every warm, moist breath he exhaled. Also, the man was chewing tobacco, and the muzzle of ice held his lips so rigidly that he was unable to clear his chin when he expelled the juice. The result was that a crystal beard of the color and solidity of amber was increasing its length on his chin. If he fell down it would shatter itself, like glass, into brittle fragments. But he did not mind the appendage. It was the penalty all tobacco-chewers paid in that country, and he had been out before in two cold snaps. They had not been so cold as this, he knew, but by the spirit thermometer at Sixty Mile he knew they had been registered at fifty below and at fifty-five.

He held on through the level stretch of woods for several miles, crossed a wide flat of niggerheads, and dropped down a bank to the frozen bed of a small stream. This was Henderson Creek, and he knew he was ten miles from the forks. He looked at his watch. It was ten o'clock. He was making four miles an hour, and he calculated that he would arrive at the forks at half-past twelve. He decided to celebrate that event by eating his lunch there.

The dog dropped in again at his heels, with a tail drooping discouragement, as the man swung along the creek-bed. The furrow of the old sled-trail was plainly visible, but a dozen inches of snow covered the marks of the last runners. In a month no man had come up or down that silent creek. The man held steadily on. He was not much given to thinking, and just then particularly he had nothing to think about save that he would eat lunch at the forks and that at six o'clock he would be in camp with the boys. There was nobody to talk to; and, had there been, speech would have been impossible because of the ice-muzzle on his mouth. So he continued monotonously to chew tobacco and to increase the length of his amber beard.

Once in a while the thought reiterated itself that it was very cold and that he had never experienced such cold. As he walked along he rubbed his cheek-bones and nose with the back of his mittened hand. He did this automatically, now and again changing hands. But rub as he would, the instant he stopped his cheek-bones went numb, and the following instant the end of his nose went numb. He was sure to frost his cheeks; he knew that, and experienced a pang of regret that he had not devised a nose-strap of the sort Bud wore in cold snaps. Such a strap passed across the cheeks, as well, and saved them. But it didn't matter much, after all. What were frosted cheeks? A bit painful, that was all; they were never serious.

Empty as the man's mind was of thoughts, he was keenly observant, and he noticed the changes in the creek, the curves and bends and timber-jams, and always he sharply noted where he placed his feet. Once, coming around a bend, he shied abruptly, like a startled horse, curved away from the place where he had been walking, and retreated several paces back along the trail. The creek he knew was frozen clear to the bottom,—no creek could contain water in that arctic winter,—but he knew also that there were springs that bubbled out from the hillsides and ran along under the snow and on top the ice of the creek. He knew that the coldest snaps never froze these springs, and he knew likewise their danger. They were traps. They hid pools of water under the snow that might be three inches deep, or three feet. Sometimes a skin of ice half an inch thick covered them, and in turn was covered by the snow. Sometimes there were alternate layers of water and ice-skin, so that when one broke through he kept on breaking through for a while, sometimes wetting himself to the waist.

That was why he had shied in such panic. He had felt the give under his feet and heard the crackle of a snow-hidden ice-skin. And to get his feet wet in such a temperature meant trouble and danger. At the very least it meant delay, for he would be forced to stop and build a fire, and under its protection to bare his feet while he dried his socks and moccasins. He stood and studied the creek-bed and its banks, and decided that the flow of water came from the right. He reflected awhile, rubbing his nose and cheeks, then skirted to the left, stepping gingerly and testing the footing for each step. Once clear of the danger, he took a fresh chew of tobacco and swung along at his four-mile gait. In the course of the next two hours he came upon several similar traps. Usually the snow above the hidden pools had a sunken, candied appearance that advertised the danger. Once again, however, he had a close call; and once, suspecting danger, he compelled the dog to go on in front. The dog did not want to go. It hung back until the man shoved it forward, and then it went quickly across the white, unbroken surface. Suddenly it broke through, floundered to one side, and got away to firmer footing. It had wet its forefeet and legs, and almost immediately the water that clung to it turned to ice. It made quick efforts to lick the ice off its legs, then dropped down in the snow and began to bite out the ice that had formed between the toes. This was a matter of instinct. To permit the ice to remain would mean sore feet. It did not know this. It merely obeyed the mysterious prompting that arose from the deep crypts of its being. But the man knew, having achieved a judgment on the subject, and he removed the mitten from his right hand and helped tear out the ice-particles. He did not expose his fingers more than a minute, and was astonished at the swift numbness that smote them. It certainly was cold. He pulled on the mitten hastily, and beat the hand savagely across his chest.

At twelve o'clock the day was at its brightest. Yet the sun was too far south on its winter journey to clear the horizon. The bulge of the earth intervened between it and Henderson Creek, where the man walked under a clear sky at noon and cast no shadow. At half-past twelve, to the minute, he arrived at the forks of the creek. He was pleased at the speed he had made. If he kept it up, he would certainly be with the boys by six. He unbuttoned his jacket and shirt and drew forth his lunch. The action consumed no more than a quarter of a minute, yet in that brief moment the numbness laid hold of the exposed fingers. He did not put the mitten on, but, instead, struck the fingers a dozen sharp smashes against his leg. Then he sat down on a snow-covered log to eat. The sting that followed upon the striking of his fingers against his leg ceased so quickly that he was startled. He had had no chance to take a bite of biscuit. He struck the fingers repeatedly and returned them to the mitten, baring the other hand for the purpose of eating. He tried to take a mouthful, but the ice-muzzle prevented. He had forgotten to build a fire and thaw out. He chuckled at his foolishness, and as he chuckled he noted the numbness creeping into the exposed fingers. Also, he noted that the stinging which had first come to his toes when he sat down was already passing away. He wondered whether the toes were warm or numb. He moved them inside the moccasins and decided that they were numb.

He pulled the mitten on hurriedly and stood up. He was a bit frightened. He stamped up and down until the stinging returned into the feet. It certainly was cold, was his thought. That man from Sulphur Creek had spoken the truth when telling how cold it sometimes got in the country. And he had laughed at him at the time! That showed one must not be too sure of things. There was no mistake about it, it *was* cold. He strode up and down, stamping his feet and threshing his arms, until reassured by the returning warmth. Then he got out matches and proceeded to make a fire. From the undergrowth, where high water of the previous spring had lodged a supply of seasoned twigs, he got his fire-wood. Working carefully from a small beginning, he soon had a roaring fire, over which he thawed the ice from his face and in the protection of which he ate his biscuits. For the moment the cold of space was outwitted. The dog took satisfaction in the fire, stretching out close enough for warmth and far enough away to escape being singed.

When the man had finished, he filled his pipe and took his comfortable time over a smoke. Then he pulled on his mittens, settled the ear-flaps of his cap firmly about his ears, and took the creek trail up the left fork. The dog was disappointed and yearned back toward the fire. This man did not know cold. Possibly all the generations of his ancestry had been ignorant of cold, of real cold, of cold one hundred and seven degrees below freezing-point. But the dog knew; all its ancestry knew, and it had inherited the knowledge. And it knew that it was not good to walk abroad in such fearful cold. It was the time to lie snug in a hole in the snow and wait for a curtain of cloud to be drawn across the face of outer space whence this cold came. On the other hand, there was no keen intimacy between the dog and the man. The one was the toil-slave of the other, and the only caresses it had ever received were the caresses of the whip-lash and of harsh and menacing throat-sounds that threatened the whip-lash. So the dog made no effort to communicate its apprehension to the man. It was not concerned in the welfare of the man; it was for its own sake that it yearned back toward the fire. But the man whistled, and spoke to it with the sound of whip-lashes, and the dog swung in at the man's heels and followed after.

The man took a chew of tobacco and proceeded to start a new amber beard. Also, his moist breath quickly powdered with white his mustache, eyebrows, and lashes. There did not seem to be so many springs on the left fork of the Henderson, and for half an hour the man saw no signs of any. And then it happened. At a place where there were no signs, where the soft, unbroken snow seemed to advertise solidity beneath, the man broke through. It was not deep. He wet himself halfway to the knees before he floundered out to the firm crust.

He was angry, and cursed his luck aloud. He had hoped to get into camp with the boys at six o'clock, and this would delay him an hour, for he would have to build a fire and dry out his foot-gear. This was imperative at that low temperature—he knew that much; and he turned aside to the bank, which he climbed. On top, tangled in the underbrush about the trunks of several small spruce trees, was a high-water deposit of dry fire-wood—sticks and twigs, principally, but also larger portions of seasoned branches and fine, dry, last-year's grasses. He threw down several large pieces on top of the snow. This served for a foundation and prevented the young flame from drowning itself in the snow it otherwise would melt. The flame he got by touching a match to a small shred of birch-bark that he took from his pocket. This burned even more readily than paper. Placing it on the foundation, he fed the young flame with wisps of dry grass and with the tiniest dry twigs.

He worked slowly and carefully, keenly aware of his danger. Gradually, as the flame grew stronger, he increased the size of the twigs with which he fed it. He squatted in the snow, pulling the twigs out from their entanglement in the brush and feeding directly to the flame. He knew there must be no failure. When it is seventy-five below zero, a man must not fail in his first attempt to build a fire—that is, if his feet are wet. If his feet are dry, and he fails, he can run along the trail for half a mile and restore his circulation. But the circulation of wet and freezing feet cannot be restored by running when it is seventy-five below. No matter how fast he runs, the wet feet will freeze the harder.

All this the man knew. The old-timer on Sulphur Creek had told him about it the previous fall, and now he was appreciating the advice. Already all sensation had gone out of his feet. To build the fire he had been forced to remove his mittens, and the fingers had quickly gone numb. His pace of four miles an hour had kept his heart pumping blood to the surface of his body and to all the extremities. But the instant he stopped, the action of the pump eased down. The cold of space smote the unprotected tip of the planet, and he, being on that unprotected tip, received the full force of the blow. The blood of his body recoiled before it. The blood was alive, like the dog, and like the dog it wanted to hide away and cover itself up from the fearful cold. So long as he walked four miles an hour, he pumped that blood, willy-nilly, to the surface; but now it ebbed away and sank down into the recesses of his body. The extremities were the first to feel its absence. His wet feet froze the faster, and his exposed fingers numbed the faster, though they had not yet begun to freeze. Nose and cheeks were already freezing, while the skin of all his body chilled as it lost its blood.

But he was safe. Toes and nose and cheeks would be only touched by the frost, for the fire was beginning to burn with strength. He was feeding it with twigs the size of his finger. In another minute he would be able to feed it with branches the size of his wrist, and then he could remove his wet foot-gear, and, while it dried, he could keep his naked feet warm by the fire, rubbing them at first, of course, with snow. The fire was a success. He was safe. He remembered the advice of the old-timer on Sulphur Creek, and smiled. The old-timer had been very serious in laying down the law that no man must travel alone in the Klondike after fifty below. Well, here he was; he had had the accident; he was alone; and he had saved himself. Those old-timers were rather womanish, some of them, he thought. All a man had to do was to keep his head, and he was all right. Any man who was a man could travel alone. But it was surprising, the rapidity with which his cheeks and nose were freezing. And he had not thought his fingers could go life-less in so short a time. Lifeless they were, for he could scarcely make them move together to grip a twig, and they seemed remote from his body and from him. When he touched a twig, he had to look and see whether or not he had hold of it. The wires were pretty well down between him and his finger-ends.

All of which counted for little. There was the fire, snapping and crackling and promising life with every dancing flame. He started to untie his moc-casins. They were coated with ice; the thick German socks were like sheaths of iron halfway to the knees; and the moccasin strings were like rods of steel all twisted and knotted as by some conflagration. For a moment he tugged with his numb fingers, then, realizing the folly of it, he drew his sheath-knife.

But before he could cut the strings, it happened. It was his own fault or, rather, his mistake. He should not have built the fire under the spruce tree. He should have built it in the open. But it had been easier to pull the twigs from the brush and drop them directly on the fire. Now the tree under which he had done this carried a weight of snow on its boughs. No wind had blown for weeks, and each bough was fully freighted. Each time he had pulled a twig he had communicated a slight agitation to the tree—an imper-ceptible agitation, so far as he was concerned, but an agitation sufficient to bring about the disaster. High up in the tree one bough capsized its load of snow. This fell on the boughs beneath, capsizing them. This process contin-ued, spreading out and involving the whole tree. It grew like an avalanche, and it descended without warning upon the man and the fire, and the fire was blotted out!

Where it had burned was a mantle of fresh and disordered snow.

The man was shocked. It was as though he had just heard his own sentence of death. For a moment he sat and stared at the spot where the fire had been. Then he grew very calm. Perhaps the old-timer on Sulphur Creek was right. If he had only had a trail-mate he would have been in no danger now. The trail-mate could have built the fire. Well, it was up to him to build the fire over again, and this second time there must be no failure. Even if he succeeded, he would most likely lose some toes. His feet must be badly frozen by now, and there would be some time before the second fire was ready.

Such were his thoughts, but he did not sit and think them. He was busy all the time they were passing through his mind. He made a new foundation for a fire, this time in the open, where no treacherous tree could blot it out. Next, he gathered dry grasses and tiny twigs from the high-water flotsam. He could not bring his fingers together to pull them out, but he was able to gather them by the handful. In this way he got many rotten twigs and bits of green moss that were undesirable, but it was the best he could do. He worked methodically, even collecting an armful of the larger branches to be used later when the fire gathered strength. And all the while the dog sat and watched him, a certain yearning wistfulness in its eyes, for it looked upon him as the fire-provider, and the fire was slow in coming.

When all was ready, the man reached in his pocket for a second piece of birch-bark. He knew the bark was there, and, though he could not feel it with his fingers, he could hear its crisp rustling as he fumbled for it. Try as he would, he could not clutch hold of it. And all the time, in his consciousness, was the knowledge that each instant his feet were freezing. This thought tended to put him in a panic, but he fought against it and kept calm. He pulled on his mittens with his teeth, and threshed his arms back and forth, beating his hands with all his might against his sides. He did this sitting down, and he stood up to do it; and all the while the dog sat in the snow, its wolf-brush of a tail curled around warmly over its forefeet, its sharp wolf-ears pricked forward intently as it watched the man. And the man, as he beat and threshed with his arms and hands, felt a great surge of envy as he regarded the creature that was warm and secure in its natural covering.

After a time he was aware of the first faraway signals of sensation in his beaten fingers. The faint tingling grew stronger till it evolved into a stinging ache that was excruciating, but which the man hailed with satisfaction. He stripped the mitten from his right hand and fetched forth the birch-bark. The exposed fingers were quickly going numb again. Next he brought out his bunch of sulphur matches. But the tremendous cold had already driven the life out of his fingers. In his effort to separate one match from the others, the whole bunch fell in the snow. He tried to pick it out of the snow, but failed. The dead fingers could neither touch nor clutch. He was very careful. He drove the thought of his freezing feet, and nose, and cheeks, out of his mind, devoting his whole soul to the matches. He watched, using the sense of vision in place of that of touch, and when he saw his fingers on each side the bunch, he closed them—that is, he willed to close them, for the wires were down, and the fingers did not obey. He pulled the mitten on the right hand, and beat it fiercely against his knee. Then, with both mittened hands, he scooped the bunch of matches, along with much snow, into his lap. Yet he was no better off.

After some manipulation he managed to get the bunch between the heels of his mittened hands. In this fashion he carried it to his mouth. The ice crackled and snapped when by a violent effort he opened his mouth. He drew the lower jaw in, curled the upper lip out of the way, and scraped the bunch with his upper teeth in order to separate a match. He succeeded in getting one, which he dropped on his lap. He was no better off. He could not pick it up. Then he devised a way. He picked it up in his teeth and scratched it on his leg. Twenty times he scratched before he succeeded in lighting it. As it flamed he held it with his teeth to the birch-bark. But the burning brimstone went up his nostrils and into his lungs, causing him to cough spasmodically. The match fell into the snow and went out.

The old-timer on Sulphur Creek was right, he thought in the moment of controlled despair that ensued: after fifty below, a man should travel with a partner. He beat his hands, but failed in exciting any sensation. Suddenly he bared both hands, removing the mittens with his teeth. He caught the whole bunch between the heels of his hands. His arm-muscles not being frozen enabled him to press the hand-heels tightly against the matches. Then he scratched the bunch along his leg. It flared into flame, seventy sulphur matches at once! There was no wind to blow them out. He kept his head to one side to escape the strangling fumes, and held the blazing bunch to the birch-bark. As he so held it, he became aware of sensation in his hand. His flesh was burning. He could smell it. Deep down below the surface he could feel it. The sensation developed into pain that grew acute. And still he endured it, holding the flame of the matches clumsily to the bark that would not light readily because his own burning hands were in the way, absorbing most of the flame.

At last, when he could endure no more, he jerked his hands apart. The blazing matches fell sizzling into the snow, but the birch-bark was alight. He began laying dry grasses and the tiniest twigs on the flame. He could not pick and choose, for he had to lift the fuel between the heels of his hands. Small pieces of rotten wood and green moss clung to the twigs, and he bit them off as well as he could with his teeth. He cherished the flame carefully and awkwardly. It meant life, and it must not perish. The withdrawal of blood from the surface of his body now made him begin to shiver, and he grew more awkward. A large piece of green moss fell squarely on the little fire. He tried to poke it out with his fingers, but his shivering frame made him poke too far, and he disrupted the nucleus of the little fire, the burning grasses and tiny twigs separating and scattering. He tried to poke them together again, but in spite of the tenseness of the effort, his shivering got away with him, and the twigs were hopelessly scattered. Each twig gushed a puff of smoke and went out. The fire-provider had failed. As he looked apathetically about him, his eyes chanced on the dog, sitting across the ruins of the fire from him, in the snow, making restless, hunching movements, slightly lifting one forefoot and then the other, shifting its weight back and forth on them with wistful eagerness.

The sight of the dog put a wild idea into his head. He remembered the tale of the man, caught in a blizzard, who killed a steer and crawled inside the carcass, and so was saved. He would kill the dog and bury his hands in the warm body until the numbness went out of them. Then he could build another fire. He spoke to the dog, calling it to him; but in his voice was a strange note of fear that frightened the animal, who had never known the man to speak in such way before. Something was the matter, and its suspicious nature sensed danger—it knew not what danger, but somewhere, somehow, in its brain arose an apprehension of the man. It flattened its ears down at the sound of the man's voice, and its restless, hunching movements and the liftings and shiftings of its forefeet became more pronounced; but it would not come to the man. He got on his hands and knees and crawled toward the dog. This unusual posture again excited suspicion, and the animal sidled mincingly away.

The man sat up in the snow for a moment and struggled for calmness. Then he pulled on his mittens, by means of his teeth, and got upon his feet. He glanced down at first in order to assure himself that he was really standing up, for the absence of sensation in his feet left him unrelated to the earth. His erect position in itself started to drive the webs of suspicion from the dog's mind; and when he spoke peremptorily, with the sound of whip-lashes in his voice, the dog rendered its customary allegiance and came to him. As it came within reaching distance, the man lost his control. His arms flashed out to the dog, and he experienced genuine surprise when he discovered that his hands could not clutch, that there was neither bend nor feeling in the fingers. He had forgotten for the moment that they were frozen and that they were freezing more and more. All this happened quickly, and before the animal could get away, he encircled its body with his arms. He sat down in the snow, and in this fashion held the dog, while it snarled and whined and struggled.

But it was all he could do, hold its body encircled in his arms and sit there. He realized that he could not kill the dog. There was no way to do it. With his helpless hands he could neither draw nor hold his sheath-knife nor throttle the animal. He released it, and it plunged wildly away, with tail between its legs, and still snarling. It halted forty feet away and surveyed him curiously, with ears sharply pricked forward. The man looked down at his hands in order to locate them, and found them hanging on the ends of his arms. It struck him as curious that one should have to use his eyes in order to find out where his hands were. He began threshing his arms back and forth, beating the mittened hands against his sides. He did this for five minutes, violently, and his heart pumped enough blood up to the surface to put a stop to his shivering. But no sensation was aroused in the hands. He had an impression that they hung like weights on the ends of his arms, but when he tried to run the impression down, he could not find it.

A certain fear of death, dull and oppressive, came to him. This fear quickly became poignant as he realized that it was no longer a mere matter of freezing his fingers and toes, or of losing his hands and feet, but that it was a matter of life and death with the chances against him. This threw him into a panic, and he turned and ran up the creek-bed along the old, dim trail. The dog joined in behind and kept up with him. He ran blindly, without intention, in fear such as he had never known in his life. Slowly, as he ploughed and floundered through the snow, he began to see things again,— the banks of the creek, the old timber-jams, the leafless aspens, and the sky. The running made him feel better. He did not shiver. Maybe, if he ran on, his feet would thaw out; and, anyway, if he ran far enough, he would reach camp and the boys. Without doubt he would lose some fingers and toes and some of his face; but the boys would take care of him, and save the rest of him when he got there. And at the same time there was another thought in his mind that said he would never get to the camp and the boys; that it was too many miles away, that the freezing had too great a start on him, and that he would soon be stiff and dead. This thought he kept in the background and refused to consider. Sometimes it pushed itself forward and demanded to be heard, but he thrust it back and strove to think of other things.

It struck him as curious that he could run at all on feet so frozen that he could not feel them when they struck the earth and took the weight of his body. He seemed to himself to skim along above the surface, and to have no connection with the earth. Somewhere he had once seen a winged Mercury, and he wondered if Mercury felt as he felt when skimming over the earth.

His theory of running until he reached camp and the boys had one flaw in it: he lacked the endurance. Several times he stumbled, and finally he tottered, crumpled up, and fell. When he tried to rise, he failed. He must sit and rest, he decided, and next time he would merely walk and keep on going. As he sat and regained his breath, he noted that he was feeling quite warm and comfortable. He was not shivering, and it even seemed that a warm glow had come to his chest and trunk. And yet, when he touched his nose or cheeks, there was no sensation. Running would not thaw them out.

Nor would it thaw out his hands and feet. Then the thought came to him that the frozen portions of his body must be extending. He tried to keep this thought down, to forget it, to think of something else; he was aware of the panicky feeling that it caused, and he was afraid of the panic. But the thought asserted itself, and persisted, until it produced a vision of his body totally frozen. This was too much, and he made another wild run along the trail. Once he slowed down to a walk, but the thought of the freezing extending itself made him run again.

And all the time the dog ran with him, at his heels. When he fell down a second time, it curled its tail over its forefeet and sat in front of him, facing him, curiously eager and intent. The warmth and security of the animal angered him, and he cursed it till it flattened down its ears appeasingly. This time the shivering came more quickly upon the man. He was losing in his battle with the frost. It was creeping into his body from all sides. The thought of it drove him on, but he ran no more than a hundred feet, when he staggered and pitched headlong. It was his last panic. When he had recovered his breath and control, he sat up and entertained in his mind the conception of meeting death with dignity. However, the conception did not come to him in such terms. His idea of it was that he had been making a fool of himself, running around like a chicken with its head cut off—such was the simile that occurred to him. Well, he was bound to freeze anyway, and he might as well take it decently. With this new-found peace of mind came the first glimmerings of drowsiness. A good idea, he thought, to sleep off to death. It was like taking an anaesthetic. Freezing was not so bad as people thought. There were lots worse ways to die.

He pictured the boys finding his body next day. Suddenly he found himself with them, coming along the trail and looking for himself. And, still with them, he came around a turn in the trail and found himself lying in the snow. He did not belong with himself any more, for even then he was out of himself, standing with the boys and looking at himself in the snow. It certainly was cold, was his thought. When he got back to the States he could tell the folks what real cold was. He drifted on from this to a vision of the old-timer on Sulphur Creek. He could see him quite clearly, warm and comfortable, and smoking a pipe.

"You were right, old hoss; you were right," the man mumbled to the old-timer of Sulphur Creek.

Then the man drowsed off into what seemed to him the most comfortable and satisfying sleep he had ever known. The dog sat facing him and waiting. The brief day drew to a close in a long, slow twilight. There were no signs of a fire to be made, and, besides, never in the dog's experience had it known a man to sit like that in the snow and make no fire. As the twilight drew on, its eager yearning for the fire mastered it, and with a great lifting and shifting of forefeet, it whined softly, then flattened its ears down in anticipation of being chidden by the man. But the man remained silent. Later, the dog whined loudly. And still later it crept close to the man and caught the scent of death. This made the animal bristle and back away. A little longer it delayed, howling under the stars that leaped and danced and shone brightly in the cold sky. Then it turned and trotted up the trail in the direction of the camp it knew, where were the other food-providers and fire-providers.

Psychology

KATHERINE MANSFIELD

When she opened the door and saw him standing there she was more pleased than ever before, and he, too, as he followed her into the studio, seemed very very happy to have come.

"Not busy?"

"No. Just going to have tea."

"And you are not expecting anybody?"

"Nobody at all."

"Ah! That's good."

He laid aside his coat and hat gently, lingeringly, as though he had time and to spare for everything, or as though he were taking leave of them for ever, and came over to the fire and held out his hands to the quick, leaping flame.

Just for a moment both of them stood silent in that leaping light. Still, as it were, they tasted on their smiling lips the sweet shock of their greeting. Their secret selves whispered:

"Why should we speak? Isn't this enough?"

"More than enough. I never realized until this moment . . ."

"How good it is just to be with you . . ."

"Like this. . . ."

"It's more than enough."

But suddenly he turned and looked at her and she moved quickly away.

"Have a cigarette? I'll put the kettle on. Are you longing for tea?"

"No. Not longing."

"Well, I am."

"Oh, you." He thumped the Armenian cushion and flung on to the *sommier*. "You're a perfect little Chinee."

"Yes, I am," she laughed. "I long for tea as strong men long for wine."

She lighted the lamp under its broad orange shade, pulled the curtains and drew up the tea table. Two birds sang in the kettle; the fire fluttered. He sat up clasping his knees. It was delightful—this business of having tea—and she always had delicious things to eat—little sharp sandwiches, short sweet almond fingers, and a dark, rich cake tasting of rum—but it was an interruption. He wanted it over, the table pushed away, their two chairs drawn up to the light, and the moment came when he took out his pipe, filled it, and said, pressing the tobacco tight into the bowl: "I have been thinking over what you said last time and it seems to me . . ."

Yes, that was what he waited for and so did she. Yes, while she shook the teapot hot and dry over the spirit flame she saw those other two, him, leaning back, taking his ease among the cushions, and her, curled up *en escargot* in the blue shell armchair. The picture was so clear and so minute it might have been painted on the blue teapot lid. And yet she couldn't hurry. She could almost have cried: "Give me time." She must have time in which to grow calm. She wanted time in which to free herself from all these familiar things with which she lived so vividly. For all these gay things round her were part of her—her offspring—and they knew it and made the largest, most vehement claims. But now they must go. They must be swept away, shooed away—like children, sent up the shadowy stairs, packed into bed and commanded to go to sleep—at once—without a murmur!

For the special thrilling quality of their friendship was in their complete surrender. Like two open cities in the midst of some vast plain their two minds lay open to each other. And it wasn't as if he rode into hers like a conqueror, armed to the eyebrows and seeing nothing but a gay silken flutter—nor did she enter his like a queen walking soft on petals. No, they were eager, serious travellers, absorbed in understanding what was to be seen and discovering what was hidden—making the most of this extraordinary absolute chance which made it possible for him to be utterly truthful to her and for her to be utterly sincere with him.

And the best of it was they were both of them old enough to enjoy their adventure to the full without any stupid emotional complication. Passion would have ruined everything; they quite saw that. Besides, all that sort of thing was over and done with for both of them—he was thirty-one, she was thirty—they had had their experiences, and very rich and varied they had been, but now was the time for harvest—harvest. Weren't his novels to be very big novels indeed? And her plays. Who else had her exquisite sense of real English Comedy? . . .

Carefully she cut the cake into thick little wads and he reached across for a piece.

"Do you realize how good it is," she implored. "Eat it imaginatively. Roll your eyes if you can and taste it on the breath. It's not a sandwich from the hatter's bag—it's the kind of cake that might have been mentioned in the Book of Genesis. . . . And God said: 'Let there be cake. And there was cake. And God saw that it was good.'"

"You needn't entreat me," said he. "Really you needn't. It's a queer thing but I always do notice what I eat here and never anywhere else. I suppose it comes of living alone so long and always reading while I feed . . . my habit of looking upon food as just food . . . something that's there, at certain times . . . to be devoured . . . to be . . . not there." He laughed. "That shocks you. Doesn't it?"

"To the bone," she said.

"But—look here—" He pushed away his cup and began to speak very fast. "I simply haven't got any external life at all. I don't know the names of things a bit—trees and so on—and I never notice places or furniture or what people look like. One room is just like another to me—a place to sit and read or talk in—except," and here he paused, smiled in a strange naive way, and said, "except this studio." He looked round him and then at her; he laughed in his astonishment and pleasure. He was like a man who wakes up in a train to find that he has arrived, already, at the journey's end.

"Here's another queer thing. If I shut my eyes I can see this place down to every detail—every detail. . . . Now I come to think of it—I've never realized this consciously before. Often when I am away from here I revisit it in spirit—wander about among your red chairs, stare at the bowl of fruit on the black table—and just touch, very lightly, that marvel of a sleeping boy's head."

He looked at it as he spoke. It stood on the corner of the mantelpiece; the head to one side down-drooping, the lips parted, as though in his sleep the little boy listened to some sweet sound. . . .

"I love that little boy," he murmured. And then they both were silent.

A new silence came between them. Nothing in the least like the satisfactory pause that had followed their greetings—the "Well, here we are together again, and there's no reason why we shouldn't go on from just where we left off last time." That silence could be contained in the circle of warm, delightful fire and lamplight. How many times hadn't they flung something into it just for the fun of watching the ripples break on the easy shores. But into this unfamiliar pool the head of the little boy sleeping his timeless sleep dropped and the ripples flowed away, away—boundlessly far—into deep glittering darkness.

And then both of them broke it. She said: "I must make up the fire," and he said: "I have been trying a new . . ." Both of them escaped. She made up the fire and put the table back, the blue chair was wheeled forward, she curled up and he lay back among the cushions. Quickly! Quickly! They must stop it from happening again.

"Well I read the book you left last time."

"Oh, what do you think of it?"

They were off and all was as usual. But was it? Weren't they just a little too quick, too prompt with their replies, too ready to take each other up? Was this really anything more than a wonderfully good imitation of other occasions? His heart beat; her cheek burned and the stupid thing was she could not discover where exactly they were or what exactly was happening. She hadn't time to glance back. And just as she had got so far it happened again. They faltered, wavered, broke down, were silent. Again they were conscious of the boundless, questioning dark. Again, there they were—two hunters, bending over their fire, but hearing suddenly from the jungle beyond a shake of wind and a loud, questioning cry. . . .

She lifted her head. "It's raining," she murmured. And her voice was like his when he had said "I love that little boy."

Well. Why didn't they just give way to it—yield—and see what will happen then? But no. Vague and troubled though they were, they knew enough to realize their precious friendship was in danger. She was the one who would be destroyed—not they—and they'd be no party to that.

He got up, knocked out his pipe, ran his hand through his hair and said: "I have been wondering very much lately whether the novel of the future will be a psychological novel or not. How sure are you that psychology *qua* psychology has got anything to do with literature at all?"

"Do you mean you feel there's quite a chance that the mysterious non-existent creatures—the young writers of to-day—are trying simply to jump the psycho-analyst's claim?"

"Yes, I do. And I think it's because this generation is just wise enough to know that it is sick and to realize that its only chance of recovery is by going into its symptoms—making an exhaustive study of them—tracking them down—trying to get at the root of the trouble."

"But oh," she wailed. "What a dreadfully dismal outlook."

"Not at all," said he. "Look here . . ." On the talk went. And now it seemed they really had succeeded. She turned in her chair to look at him while she answered. Her smile said: "We have won." And he smiled back, confident: "Absolutely."

But the smile undid them. It lasted too long; it became a grin. They saw themselves as two little grinning puppets jigging away in nothingness.

"What have we been talking about?" thought he. He was so utterly bored he almost groaned.

"What a spectacle we have made of ourselves," thought she. And she saw him laboriously—oh, laboriously—laying out the grounds and herself running after, putting here a tree and there a flowery shrub and here a hand-ful of glittering fish in a pool. They were silent this time from sheer dismay.

The clock struck six merry little pings and the fire made a soft flutter. What fools they were—heavy, stodgy, elderly—with positively upholstered minds.

And now the silence put a spell upon them like solemn music. It was anguish—anguish for her to bear it and he would die—he'd die if it were broken. . . . And yet he longed to break it. Not by speech. At any rate not by their ordinary maddening chatter. There was another way for them to speak to each other, and in the new way he wanted to murmur: "Do you feel this too? Do you understand it at all?" . . .

Instead, to his horror, he heard himself say: "I must be off; I'm meeting Brand at six."

What devil made him say that instead of the other? She jumped—simply jumped out of her chair, and he heard her crying: "You must rush, then. He's so punctual. Why didn't you say so before?"

"You've hurt me; you've hurt me! We've failed!" said her secret self while she handed him his hat and stick, smiling gaily. She wouldn't give him a moment for another word, but ran along the passage and opened the big outer door.

Could they leave each other like this? How could they? He stood on the step and she just inside holding the door. It was not raining now.

"You've hurt me—hurt me," said her heart. "Why don't you go? No, don't go. Stay. No—go!" And she looked out upon the night.

She saw the beautiful fall of the steps, the dark garden ringed with glittering ivy, on the other side of the road the huge bare willows and above them the sky big and bright with stars. But of course he would see nothing of all this. He was superior to it all. He—with his wonderful "spiritual" vision!

She was right. He did see nothing at all. Misery! He'd missed it. It was too late to do anything now. Was it too late? Yes, it was. A cold snatch of hateful wind blew into the garden. Curse life! He heard her cry "au revoir" and the door slammed.

Running back into the studio she behaved so strangely. She ran up and down lifting her arms and crying: "Oh! Oh! How stupid! How imbecile! How stupid!" And then she flung herself down on the *sommier* thinking of nothing—just lying there in her rage. All was over. What was over? Oh—something was. And she'd never see him again—never. After a long long time (or perhaps ten minutes) had passed in that black gulf her bell rang a sharp quick jingle. It was he, of course. And equally, of course, she oughtn't to have paid the slightest attention to it but just let it go on ringing and ringing. She flew to answer.

On the doorstep there stood an elderly virgin, a pathetic creature who simply idolized her (heaven knows why) and had this habit of turning up and ringing the bell and then saying, when she opened the door: "My dear, send me away!" She never did. As a rule she asked her in and let her admire everything and accepted the bunch of slightly soiled looking flowers—more than graciously. But to-day . . .

"Oh, I am so sorry," she cried. "But I've got someone with me. We are working on some wood-cuts. I'm hopelessly busy all evening."

"It doesn't matter. It doesn't matter at all, darling," said the good friend. "I was just passing and I thought I'd leave you some violets." She fumbled down among the ribs of a large old umbrella. "I put them down here. Such a good place to keep flowers out of the wind. Here they are," she said, shaking out a little dead bunch.

For a moment she did not take the violets. But while she stood just inside, holding the door, a strange thing happened. . . . Again she saw the beautiful fall of the steps, the dark garden tinged with glittering ivy, the willows, the big bright sky. Again she felt the silence that was like a question. But this time she did not hesitate. She moved forward. Very softly and gently, as though fearful of making a ripple in that boundless pool of quiet she put her arms round her friend.

"My dear," murmured her happy friend, quite overcome by this gratitude. "They are really nothing. Just the simplest little thrippeny bunch."

But as she spoke she was enfolded—more tenderly, more beautifully embraced, held by such a sweet pressure and for so long that the poor dear's mind positively reeled and she just had the strength to quaver: "Then you really don't mind me too much?"

"Good night, my friend," whispered the other. "Come again soon."

"Oh, I will. I will."

This time she walked back to the studio slowly, and standing in the middle of the room with half-shut eyes she felt so light, so rested, as if she had woken up out of a childish sleep. Even the act of breathing was a joy.

The *sommier* was very untidy. All the cushions "like furious mountains" as she said; she put them in order before going over to the writing-table.

"I have been thinking over our talk about the psychological novel," she dashed off, "it really is intensely interesting.". . . And so on and so on.

At the end she wrote: "Good night, my friend. Come again soon."

A Ruse

GUY DE MAUPASSANT

The old doctor and his young patient were chatting by the fire. She was not really ill, but merely suffering from one of those feminine ailments which often afflict pretty women: a touch of nerves, a little anaemia, and a hint of fatigue, that fatigue which a newly married couple normally experience at the end of their first month of married life, when they have made a love match.

She was lying on her couch and talking.

'No, Doctor,' she said, 'I shall never be able to understand a woman deceiving her husband. Even supposing that she doesn't love him, that she takes no notice of her promises and vows, how can she bear to give herself to another man? How can she conceal what she is doing from other people's eyes? How can she find it possible to love in the midst of lies and treachery?'

The doctor smiled.

'Oh, that's easy. I can assure you that a woman doesn't think about all those little niceties when she takes it into her head to stray off the straight and narrow path. I would go further and say that no woman is ripe for true love until she has gone through all the promiscuities and disappointments of married life, which, according to a famous man, is nothing but an exchange of bad tempers during the day and bad smells during the night. Nobody ever spoke a truer word, for no woman can love passionately until she has been married. If I might compare her to a house, she's uninhabitable until a husband has dried out the plaster.

'As for dissimulation, every woman can provide plenty of that on such occasions. The simplest of women are wonderful liars and can extricate themselves from the most difficult dilemmas with a skill bordering on genius.'

The young woman seemed reluctant to believe him.

'No, Doctor,' she said, 'nobody ever thinks of what he ought to have done in a dangerous situation until after it is over, and women are certainly more liable than men to lose their heads in such circumstances.'

The doctor threw up his hands.

'After it is over, you say! We men only get our inspirations after the event, that's true. But you women! . . . Look here, let me tell you something that happened to one of my patients whom I had always regarded as a woman of unimpeachable virtue.

'It happened in a provincial town. One night when I was fast asleep, in that deep first sleep which it is so difficult to disturb, I had the impression, in my dreams, that all the bells in the town were sounding the fire alarm. Suddenly I woke up: it was my own door-bell which was ringing wildly. As my manservant didn't seem to be answering it, I in my turn pulled the bell at the head of my bed, and soon the sound of banging doors and hurrying footsteps disturbed the silence of the sleeping house. Then Jean appeared and handed me a letter which said: "Madame Lelièvre begs Doctor Siméon to come to her house at once."

'I thought for a few moments, and then said to myself: "Nerves, a fit of hysterics, something of that sort: I'm too tired." So I replied: "Doctor Siméon is ill and asks Madame Lelièvre to be good enough to send for his colleague Monsieur Bonnet."

'I sent this note off in an envelope and went back to sleep. Half an hour later the doorbell went again and Jean came to tell me: "There is somebody downstairs—I don't know whether it's a man or a woman, he's so well wrapped up—who would like to see you straight away. He says it's a matter of life and death for two people."

'I sat up in bed, told Jean to show the caller in, and waited.

'A sort of black phantom appeared who raised her veil as soon as Jean had left the room. It was Madame Berthe Lelièvre, a young woman who had been married for three years to a large shopkeeper in the town and was considered the prettiest girl in the province.

'She was terribly pale, her face twitching with panic and her hands trembling violently. Twice she tried to speak without being able to utter a sound. At last she managed to stammer: "Quick . . . quick . . . quick, Doctor. . . . Come quick. My . . . my lover has just died in my bedroom." She stopped, choking with emotion, then went on: "My husband will be . . .

will be coming home from the club soon . . ."

'I jumped out of bed without even thinking that I was in my nightshirt and got dressed in a few seconds. Then I said: "Was it you who came a little while ago?"

"No," she murmured, standing there like a statue, petrified with fear. "That was my maid. . . . She knows . . ." Then after a pause she went on: "I stayed . . . by his side." A sort of terrible cry of horror came from her lips and after a fit of choking which made her gasp for breath she burst into tears, weeping helplessly and shaking with sobs for a minute or two. Then her tears suddenly stopped, as if dried up by an inner fire, and resuming her air of tragic calm she said: "Let's hurry."

'I was ready, but I exclaimed: "Heavens, I forgot to order my carriage!"

"'I have one," she said; "it's his carriage, which was waiting for him."

'She wrapped herself up, covering her face completely, and we set off.

'When she was beside me in the darkness of the carriage she suddenly seized my hand and crushing it in her delicate fingers she said quaveringly in a voice which came from a broken heart: "Oh, if you only knew, if you only knew how I'm suffering! I've been in love with him, madly in love with him, for the past six months."

"'Is anybody up at your house?" I asked.

"'No," she replied. "Nobody except Rose, who knows everything."

'We stopped in front of the door. As she had said, everybody was obviously asleep. We let ourselves in with a latchkey without making any noise and tiptoed upstairs. The frightened maid was sitting on the floor at the top of the stairs with a lighted candle beside her, as she had not dared to stay with the dead man.

'I went into the bedroom which was turned upside down as if there had been a struggle in it. The bed was crumpled and open and seemed to be waiting for somebody. One of the sheets was hanging down to the carpet and wet towels with which they had bathed the young man's temples were lying on the floor beside a basin and a glass. A peculiar smell of kitchen vinegar mingled with whiffs of perfume filled the room.

'The corpse was lying full length on its back in the middle of the room. I went up to it, looked at it, touched it. I opened the eyes and felt the hands, and then, turning to the two women who were shivering as if they were freezing, I said: "Help me to lift him on to the bed." After we had laid him out gently, I listened to his heart and held a mirror to his lips. Then I murmured:

"It's all over; let's dress him quickly."

'It was a terrible business. I took his limbs one by one, like those of an enormous doll, and held them out to the clothes the women brought. Like that we put on his socks, underpants, trousers and waistcoat; and finally we managed to put on his coat, although we had a great deal of trouble getting his arms into the sleeves.

'When it came to buttoning his boots, the two women knelt down, while I held the light. His feet were slightly swollen, so this was extremely difficult; and as they were unable to find a buttonhook they had to use their hairpins.

'As soon as the horrible business of dressing the corpse was over, I inspected our handiwork and said: "You ought to tidy up his hair." The maid went and fetched her mistress's brush and comb, but as she was trembling and kept pulling out the long, tangled hairs without meaning to, Madame Lelièvre snatched the comb out of her hand and arranged the dead man's hair as if she were caressing it. She made a fresh parting, brushed the beard, and slowly rolled the ends of the moustache round her fingers, as she had probably been used to doing in the familiarities of love.

'All of a sudden, letting go of his hair, she grasped her lover's inert head and gazed for a long time in despair at the dead face which could no longer smile at her. Then throwing herself on to him she clasped him in her arms and kissed him passionately. Her kisses fell like blows on the closed lips, on the dead eyes, on the temples and the forehead. And then, putting her lips to his ear, as if he could still hear her and she were about to whisper something to make their embraces still more ardent, she repeated several times in a heartrending voice: "Good-bye darling."

'Just then the clock struck midnight and I gave a start. "Good Lord," I said, "twelve o'clock. That's the time the club closes. Come, Madame, we've no time to lose!"

'She got to her feet, and I said: "Let's carry him into the drawing-room." The three of us carried him there and I sat him on a sofa and lit the candelabra.

'The front door opened and shut with a bang. The husband was already back. I said: "Rose, quick, bring me the towels and basin and tidy up the bedroom. Hurry, for God's sake! Monsieur Lelièvre has just come home."

'I heard his steps coming upstairs and along the corridor. His hands were feeling the walls in the dark. "Come in here, my dear fellow," I called out; "we have had an accident."

'And the astonished husband appeared in the doorway with a cigar in his mouth. "What's the matter?" he asked. "What's the meaning of this?"

'"My dear chap," I said, going up to him, "you find us in something of a spot. I had stayed here late, chatting with your wife and our friend, who had brought me in his carriage. All of a sudden he collapsed, and in spite of all our efforts he has remained unconscious for the last two hours. I didn't want to call in any strangers, and if you'll help me to get him downstairs I'll be able to attend to him better in his own house."

'The husband, who was surprised but completely unsuspecting, took off his hat. Then he took hold of his henceforth inoffensive rival under the armpits, I got between the legs like a horse between the shafts, and we went downstairs, with the wife now holding the light.

'When we got outside I held the corpse up and spoke to it encouragingly so as to deceive the coachman. "Come now, old fellow," I said, "it's nothing; you feel better already, don't you? Buck up, now, and make an effort, and it'll soon be over."

'As I could feel that the body was on the point of collapsing and slipping out of my hands, I gave it a shove which sent it tumbling into the carriage. Then I got in after it.

'Monsieur Lelièvre asked me anxiously: "Do you think it's anything serious?" I replied: "No," with a smile, and looked at his wife. She had put her arm into that of her lawful husband and was staring into the dark interior of the carriage.

'I shook hands with them and told the coachman to start. During the whole journey the dead man kept falling against my right side. When we got to his house I said that he had lost consciousness on the way and helped to carry him upstairs. There I certified that he was dead and acted another comedy for the benefit of the distracted family. At last I got back to bed, not without cursing all lovers.'

The doctor stopped, still smiling, and the young woman asked him with a shudder: 'Why did you tell me that horrible story?'

He gave her a gallant bow and answered: 'So as to offer you my services in case of need.'

Charades

LORRIE MOORE

t's fitting that Christmas should degenerate to this, its barest bones. The family has begun to seem to Therese like a pack of thespians anyway; everyone arrives, performs for one another, catches early flights out, to Logan or O'Hare. Probably it's appropriate that a party game should literally appear and insert itself in the guise of a holiday tradition (which it isn't). Usually, no one in Therese's family expresses much genuine feeling anyway; everyone aims instead—though gamely!—for enactments.

Each year now, the stage is a new one—their aging parents, in their restless old age, buying and selling town houses, moving steadily southward from Maine. The real estate is Therese's mother's idea. Since he's retired, Therese's father has focused more on bird feeders; he is learning how to build them. "Who knows what he'll do next?" Her mother sighs. "He'll probably start carving designs into the side of the house."

This year, they are in Bethesda, Maryland, near where Andrew, Therese's brother, lives. Andrew works as an electrical engineer and is married to a sweet, pretty, part-time private detective named Pam. Pam is pixie-haired and smiley. Who would ever suspect her of discreetly gathering confidences and facts for one's adversaries? She freezes hams. She makes Jell-O salad days in advance. She and Andrew are the parents of a one-and-a-half-year-old named Winnie, who already reads.

Reads the reading videos on TV, but reads.

Everyone has divided into teams, four and four, and written the names of famous people, songs, films, plays, books on scraps of wrapping paper torn off the gifts hours earlier. It is another few hours until Therese and her husband Ray's flight, at 4:30, from National Airport. "Yes," says Therese, "I guess we'll have to forgo the 'Averell Harriman: Statesman for All Seasons' exhibit."

"I don't know why you couldn't catch a later flight," says Therese's sister, Ann. She is scowling. Ann is the youngest, and ten years younger than Therese, who is the oldest, but lately Ann's voice has taken up a prissy and matronly scolding that startles Therese. "Four-thirty," says Ann, pursing her lips and propping her feet up on the chair next to her. "That's a little ridiculous. You're missing dinner." Her shoes are pointy and Victorian-looking. They are green suede—a cross between a courtesan's and Peter Pan's.

The teams are divided in such a way that Therese and Ray and her parents are on one team, Andrew and Pam, Ann and Tad, Ann's fiancé, on the other. Tad is slender and red-haired, a marketing rep for Neutrogena. He and Ann have just become engaged. After nearly a decade of casting about in love and work, Ann is now going to law school and planning her summer wedding. Since Therese worked for years as a public defender and is currently, through a fluky political appointment, a county circuit court judge, she has assumed that Ann's decision to be a lawyer is a kind of sororal affirmation, that it will somehow mean the two of them will have new things in common, that Ann will have questions for her, observations, forensic things to say. But this seems not to be so. Ann appears instead to be preoccupied with trying to hire bands and caterers, and to rent a large room in a restaurant. "Ugh," said Therese sympathetically. "Doesn't it make you want to elope?" Therese and Ray were married at the courthouse, with the file clerks as witnesses.

Ann shrugged. "I'm trying to figure out how to get everybody from the church to the restaurant in a way that won't wrinkle their outfits and spoil the pictures."

"Really?" asked Therese. "You are?"

The titles are put in two big salad bowls, each team receiving the other's bowl of titles. Therese's father goes first. "All right! Everyone ready!" He has always been witty, competitive, tense; games have usually brought out the best and worst in him. These days, however, he seems anxious and elderly. There is a pain in his eyes, something sad and unfocused that sometimes stabs at them—the fear of a misspent life, or an uncertainty as to where he's left the keys. He signals that his assigned name is a famous person. No one could remember how to signal that and so the family has invented one: a quick pompous posture, hands on hips, chin in air. Mustering up a sense of drama, Therese's father does this well.

"Famous person!" Everyone shouts it, though of course there is someone who shouts "Idiot" to be witty. This time, it is Therese's mother.

"Idiot!" she shouts. "Village idiot!"

But Therese's father has continued signaling the syllables, ignoring his wife, slapping the fingers of his right hand hard on his left sleeve. The famous person has three names. He is doing the first name, first syllable. He takes out a dollar bill and points to it.

"George Washington," shouts Ray.

"George Washington Carver!" shouts Therese. Therese's father shakes his head angrily, turning the dollar around and pointing at it violently. It bothers him not to be able to control the discourse.

"Dollar bill," says Therese's mother.

"Bill!" says Therese. At this, her father begins nodding and pointing at her psychotically. *Yes, yes, yes.* Now he makes stretching motions with his hands. "Bill, Billy, William," says Therese, and her father points wildly at her again. "William," she says. "William Kennedy Smith."

"Yes!" shouts her father, clapping his hands and throwing his head back as if to praise the ceiling.

"William Kennedy Smith?" Ann is scowling again. "How did you get that from just William?"

"He's been in the news." Therese shrugs. She does not know how to explain Ann's sourness. Perhaps it has something to do with Ann's struggles in law school, or with Therese's being a circuit court judge, or with the diamond on Ann's finger, which is so huge that it seems, to Therese, unkind to wear it around their mother's, which is, when one gets right down to it, a chip. Earlier this morning, Ann told Therese that she is going to take Tad's name, as well. "You're going to call yourself Tad?" Therese asked, but Ann was not amused. Ann's sense of humor was never that flexible, though she used to like a good sight gag.

Ann officiously explained the name change: "Because I believe a family is like a team, and everyone on the team should have the same name, like a color. I believe a spouse should be a team player."

Therese no longer has any idea who Ann is. She liked her better when Ann was eight, with her blue pencil case, and a strange, loping run that came from having one leg a quarter of an inch longer than the other. Ann was more attractive as a child. She was awkward and inquiring. She was cute. Or so she seemed to Therese, who was mostly in high school and college, slightly depressed and studying too much, destroying her already-bad eyes, so that now she wore glasses so thick her eyes swam in a cloudy way behind them.

This morning, when she'd stood listening to Ann talk about team players, Therese had smiled and nodded, but she felt preached at, as if she were a messy, wayward hippie. She wanted to grab her sister, throw herself upon her, embrace her, shut her up. She tried to understand Ann's dark and worried nuptial words, but instead she found herself recalling the pratfalls she used to perform for Ann—Therese could take a fall straight on the face—in order to make Ann laugh.

Ann's voice was going on now. "When you sit too long, the bodices bunch up. . . ."

Therese mentally measured the length of her body in front of her and wondered if she could do it. Of course she could. Of course. But *would* she? And then suddenly, she knew she would. She let her hip twist and fell straight forward, her arm at an angle, her mouth in a whoop. She had learned to do this in drama club when she was fifteen. She hadn't been pretty, and it was a means of getting the boys' attention. She landed with a thud.

"You still do that?" asked Ann with incredulity and disgust. "You're a judge and you still *do* that?"

"Sort of." said Therese from the floor. She felt around for her glasses.

Now it is the team player herself standing up to give clues to her team. She looks at the name on her scrap of paper and makes a slight face. "I need a consultation," she says in a vaguely repelled way that perhaps she imagines is sophisticated. She takes the scrap of wrapping paper over to Therese's team. "What is this?" Ann asks. There in Ray's handwriting is a misspelled *Arachnophobia*.

"It's a movie," says Ray apologetically. "Did I spell it wrong?"

"I think you did, honey," says Therese, leaning in to look at it. "You got some of the *o*'s and *a*'s mixed up." Ray is dyslexic. When the roofing business slows in the winter months, instead of staying in with a book, or going to psychotherapy, he drives to cheap matinees of bad movies—"flicks," he calls them, or "cliffs" when he's making fun of himself. Ray misspells everything. Is it *input* or *imput*? Is it *averse*, *adverse*, or *adversed*? *Stock* or *stalk*? *Carrot* or *karate*? His roofing business has a reputation for being reasonable, but a bit slipshod and second-rate. Nonetheless, Therese thinks he is great. He is never condescending. He cooks infinite dishes with chicken. He is ardent and capable and claims almost every night in his husbandly way to find Therese the sexiest woman he's ever known. Therese likes that. She is also having an affair with a young assistant DA in the prosecutor's office, but it is a limited thing like taking her gloves off, clapping her hands, and putting the gloves back on again. It is quiet and undiscoverable. It is nothing, except that it is sex with a man who is not dyslexic, and once in a while, Jesus Christ, she needs that.

Ann is acting out *Arachnophobia*, the whole concept, rather than working syllable by syllable. She stares into her fiancé's eyes, wiggling her fingers about and then jumping away in a fright, but Tad doesn't get it, though he does look a little alarmed. Ann waves her Christmas-manicured nails at him more furiously. One of the nails has a little Santa Claus painted on it. Ann's black hair is cut severely in sharp, expensive lines, and her long, drapey clothes hang from her shoulders, as if still on a hanger. She looks starved and rich and enraged. Everything seems struggled toward and forced, a little cartoonish, like the green shoes, which may be why her fiancé suddenly shouts out, "Little Miss Muffett!" Ann turns now instead to Andrew, motioning at him encouragingly, as if to punish Tad. The awkward lope of her childhood has taken on a chiropracticed slink. Therese turns back toward her own team, toward her father, who is still muttering something about William Kennedy Smith. "A woman shouldn't be in a bar at three o'clock in the morning, that's all there is to it."

"Dad, that's ludicrous," whispers Therese, not wanting to interrupt the game. "Bars are open to everyone. Public Accommodations Law."

"I'm not talking about the cold legalities," he says chastisingly. He has never liked lawyers, and is baffled by his daughters. "I'm talking about a long-understood *moral code*." Her father is of that Victorian sensibility that deep down respects prostitutes more than it does women in general.

"'Long-understood moral code'?" Therese looks at him gently. "Dad, you're seventy-five years old. Things change."

"*Arachnophobia!*" Andrew shouts, and he and Ann rush together and do high fives.

Therese's father makes a quick little spitting sound, then crosses his legs and looks the other way. Therese looks over at her mother and her mother is smiling at her conspiratorially, behind Therese's father's back, making little donkey ears with her fingers, her sign for when she thinks he's being a jackass.

"All right, forget the William Kennedy Smith. Doll, your turn," says Therese's father to her mother. Therese's mother gets up slowly but bends gleefully to pick up the scrap of paper. She looks at it, walks to the center of the room, and shoves the paper scrap in her pocket. She faces the other team and makes the sign for a famous person.

"Wrong team, Mom," says Therese, and her mother says "Oops," and turns around. She repeats the famous person stance.

"Famous person," says Ray encouragingly. Therese's mother nods. She pauses for a bit to think. Then she spins around, throws her arms up into the air, collapses forward onto the floor, then backward, hitting her head on the stereo.

"Marjorie, what are you doing?" asks Therese's father. Her mother is lying there on the floor, laughing.

"Are you okay?" Therese asks. Her mother nods, still laughing quietly.

"Fall," says Ray. "Dizziness. Dizzy Gillespie."

Therese's mother shakes her head.

"Epilepsy," says Therese.

"Explode," says her father, and her mother nods. "Explosion. Bomb. Robert Oppenheimer!"

"That's it." Her mother sighs. She has a little trouble getting back up. She is seventy and her knees are jammed with arthritis.

"You need help, Mom?" Therese asks.

"Yeah, Mom, you need help?" asks Ann, who has risen and walked toward the center of the room, to take charge.

"I'm okay." Therese's mother sighs, with a quiet, slightly faked giggle, and walks stiffly back to her seat.

"That was great, Ma," says Therese.

Her mother smiles proudly. "Well, thank you!"

After that, there are many rounds, and every time Therese's mother gets anything like Dom De Luise or Tom Jones, she does her bomb imitation again, whipping herself into a spastic frenzy and falling, then rising stiffly again to great applause. Pam brings Winnie in from her nap and everyone oohs and aahs at the child's sweet sleep-streaked face. "There she is," coos Aunt Therese. "You want to come see Grandma be a bomb?"

"It's your turn," says Andrew impatiently.

"Mine?" asks Therese.

"I think that's right," says her father.

She gets up, digs into the bowl, unfolds the scrap of wrapping paper. It says "Jekylls Street." "I need a consultation here. Andrew, I think this is your writing."

"Okay," he says, rising, and together they step into the foyer.

"Is this a TV show?" whispers Therese. "I don't watch much TV."

"No," says Andrew with a vague smile.

"What is it?"

He shifts his weight, reluctant to tell her. Perhaps it is because he is married to a detective. Or, more likely, it is because he himself works with Top Secret documents from the Defense Department; he was recently promoted from the just plain Secret ones. As an engineer, he consults, reviews, approves. His eyes are suppressed, annoyed. "It's the name of a street two blocks from here." There's a surly and defensive curve to his mouth.

"But that's not the title of anything famous."

"It's a place. I thought we could do names of places."

"It's not a famous place."

"So?"

"I mean, we all could write down the names of streets in our neighborhoods, near where we work, a road we walked down once on the way to a store—"

"You're the one who said we could do places."

"I did? Well, all right, then, what did I say was the sign for a place? We don't have a sign for places."

"I don't know. You figure it out," he says. A saucy rage is all over him now. Is this from childhood? Is this from hair loss? Once, she and Andrew were close. But now, as with Ann, she has no idea who he is anymore. She has only a theory: an electrical engineer worked over years ago by high school guidance counselors paid by the Pentagon to recruit, train, and militarize all the boys with high math SAT scores. "From M.I.T. to MIA," Andrew once put it himself. "A military-industrial asshole." But she can't find that satirical place in him anymore. Last year, at least, they had joked about their upbringing. "I scarcely remember Dad reading to us," she'd said.

"Sure he read to us," said Andrew. "You don't remember him reading to us? You don't remember him reading to us silently from the *Wall Street Journal*?"

Now she scans his hardening face for a joke, a glimmer, a bit of love. Andrew and Ann have seemed close, and Therese feels a bit wistful, wondering when and how that happened. She is a little jealous. The only expression she can get from Andrew is a derisive one. He is a traffic cop. She is the speeding flower child.

Don't you know I'm a *judge*? she wants to ask. A judge via a fluke political appointment, sure. A judge with a reputation around the courthouse for light sentencing, true. A judge who is having an affair that mildly tarnishes her character—okay. A softy; an easy touch: but a judge nonetheless.

Instead, she says, "Do you mind if I just pick another one?"

"Fine by me," he says, and strides brusquely back into the living room.

Oh, well, Therese thinks. It is her new mantra. It usually calms her better than *ohm*, which she also tries. *Ohm* is where the heart is. *Ohm* is not here. *Oh, well. Oh, well.* When she was first practicing law, to combat her courtroom stage fright, she would chant to herself, *Everybody loves me. Everybody loves me*, and when that didn't work, she'd switch to *Kill! Kill! Kill!*

"We're doing another one," announces Andrew, and Therese picks another one.

A book and a movie. She opens her palms, prayerlike for a book. She cranks one hand in the air for a movie. She pulls on her ear and points at a lamp. "Sounds like *light*," Ray says. His expression is open and helpful. "Bite, kite, dite, fight, night—"

Therese signals yes, that's it.

"Night," repeats Ray.

"*Tender Is the Night*," says her mother.

"Yes!" says Therese, and bends to kiss her mother on the cheek. Her mother smiles exuberantly, her face in a kind of burst; she loves affection, is hungry and grateful for it. When she was younger, she was a frustrated, mean mother, and so she is pleased when her children act as if they don't remember.

It is Andrew's turn. He stands before his own team, staring at the red scrap in his hand. He ponders it, shakes his head, then looks back toward Therese. "This must be yours," he says with a smirk that maybe is a good-natured smirk. Is there such a thing? Therese hopes.

"You need a consultation?" She gets up to look at the writing; it reads, "The Surrey with the Fringe on Top." "Yup, that's mine," she says.

"Come here," he says, and the two of them go back down the corridor toward the foyer again. This time, Therese notices the photographs her parents have hung there. Photographs of their children, of weddings and Winnie, though all the ones of Therese seem to her to be aggressively unflattering, advertising an asymmetry in her expression, or the magnified haziness of her eyes, her hair in a dry, peppery frizz. Vanity surges in her:

surely there must have been better pictures! The ones of Andrew, of Ann, of Tad, of Pam and Winnie are sunlit, posed, wholesome, pretty. But the ones of Therese seem slightly disturbed, as if her parents were convinced she is insane.

"We'll stand here by the demented-looking pictures of me," says Therese.

"Ann sent her those," says Andrew.

"Really?" says Therese.

He studies her hair. "Didn't your hair used to be a different color? I don't remember it ever being quite that color. What *is* that color?"

"Why, whatever do you mean?"

"Look," he says, getting back to the game. "I've never heard of this," and he waves the scrap of paper as if it were a gum wrapper.

"You haven't? It's a song: 'Geese and chicks and ducks better scurry, when I take you out in the surrey . . .'"

"No."

"No?" She keeps going. She looks up at him romantically, yearningly. "'When I take you out in my surrey, when I take you out in my surrey with the fringe on—'"

"No," Andrew interrupts emphatically.

"Hmm. Well, don't worry. Everyone on your team will know it."

The righteous indignation is returning to his face. "If *I* don't know it, what makes you think *they'll* know it?" Perhaps this is because of his work, the technosecrecy of it. *He* knows; *they* don't.

"They'll know it," Therese says. "I guarantee." She turns to leave.

"Whoa, whoa, whoa," says Andrew. The gray-pink of rage is back in his skin. What has he become? She hasn't a clue. He is successfully top secret. He is classified information. "I'm not doing this," he says. "I refuse."

Therese stares at him. This is the assertiveness he can't exercise on the job. Perhaps here, where he is no longer a cog-though-a-prized cog, he can insist on certain things. The Cold War is over, she wants to say. But what has replaced it is this: children who have turned on one another, now that the gods—or were they only guards?—have fled. "Okay, fine," she says. "I'll make up another."

"We're doing another one," announces Andrew triumphantly as they go back into the living room. He waves the paper scrap. "Have any of you ever even heard of a song called 'The Surrey with the Fringe on Top'?"

"Sure," says Pam, looking at him in a puzzled way. No doubt he seems different to her around the holidays.

"You have?" He seems a bit flummoxed. He looks at Ann. "Have you?"

Ann looks reluctant to break ranks with him but says, quietly, "Yeah."

"Tad, how about you?" he asks.

Tad has been napping off and on, his head thrown back against the sofa, but now he jerks awake. "Uh, yeah," he says.

"Tad's not feeling that well," says Ann.

In desperation, Andrew turns toward the other team. "And you all know it, too?"

"I don't know it," says Ray. He is the only one. He doesn't know a show tune from a chauffeur. In a way, that's what Therese likes about him.

Andrew sits back down, refusing to admit defeat. "Ray didn't know it," he says.

Therese can't think of a song, so she writes "Clarence Thomas" and hands the slip back to Andrew. As he ponders his claim options, Therese's mother gets up and comes back holding and Dixie cups and a bottle of cranberry drink. "Who would like some cranberry juice?" she says, and starts pouring. She hands the cups out carefully to everyone. We don't have the wine glasses unpacked, so we'll have to make do."

"We'll have to make do" is one of their mother's favorite expressions, acquired during the Depression and made indelible during the war. When they were little, Therese and Andrew used to look at each other and say, "We'll have to make do-do," but when Therese glances over at Andrew now, nothing registers. He has forgotten. He is thinking only of the charade.

Ray sips his a little sloppily, and a drop spills on the chair. Therese hands him a napkin and he dabs at the upholstery with it, but it is Ann who is swiftly up, out to the kitchen, and back with a cold, wet cloth, wiping at Ray's chair in a kind of rebuke.

"Oh, don't worry," her mother is saying.

"I think I've got it," says Ann solemnly.

"I'm doing my clues now," says Andrew impatiently.

Therese looks over at Winnie, who, calm and observant in her mother's arms, a pink incontinent Buddha who knows all her letters, seems like the sanest person in the room.

Andrew is making a sweeping gesture with his arm, something meant to include everyone in the room.

"People," says Tad.

"Family," says Pam.

Ann has come back from the kitchen and sits down on the sofa. "Us," she says.

Andrew smiles and nods.

"Us. Thom-us," says Ann. "Clarence Thomas."

"Yes," says Andrew with a clap. "What was the time on that?"

"Thirty seconds," says Tad.

"Well, I guess he's on the tip of everyone's tongue," says Therese's mother.

"I guess so," says Therese.

"It was interesting to see all those black people from Yale," says Therese's mother. "All sitting there in the Senate caucus room. I'll bet their parents were proud."

Ann did not get in to Yale. "What I don't like," she says, "is all these black people who don't like whites. They're so hostile. I see it all the time in law school. Most white people are more than willing to sit down, be friendly and integrated. But it's the blacks who are too angry."

"Imagine that," says Ray.

"Yes. Imagine," says Therese. "Why would they be angry? You know what else I don't like? I don't like all these gay men who have gotten just a little too somber and butch. You know what I mean? They're so funereal and upset these days! Where is the mincing and *high-spiritedness* of yesteryear? Where is the *gayness* in *gay*? It's all so confusing and inconvenient! You can't tell who's who without a goddamn *Playbill!*" She stands up and looks at Ray. It is time to go. She has lost her judicial temperament hours ago. She fears she is going to do another pratfall, only this time she will break something. Already she sees herself carted out on a stretcher, taken toward the airport, and toward home, saying the final words she has to say to her family, has always had to say to her family. Sounds like *could cry*.

"Good-bye!"

"Good-bye!"

"Good-bye!"

"Good-bye!"

"Good-bye!"

"Good-bye!"

"Good-bye!"

But first Ray must do his charade, which is Confucius. "Okay. I'm ready," he says, and begins to wander around the living room in a wild-eyed daze, looking as confused as possible, groping at the bookcases, placing his palm to his brow. And in that moment, Therese thinks how good-looking he is and how kind and strong and how she loves nobody else in the world even half as much.

In the Warehouse

JOYCE CAROL OATES

W hy does your mother do that to her hair? Does she think it looks nice or something?"

"Do what to her hair?"

"Frizz it up or whatever that is—she's such an ugly old bag. If I looked like that I'd stick my head in the oven"

The two girls are standing out on the sidewalk before a house, at twilight. The taller one makes vast good-humored gestures in the air as she talks, and the other stands silently, her lips pursed. She has a small, dark, patient face; her brown hair falls in thick puffy bangs across her forehead. The taller girl has hair that is in no style at all—just messy, not very clean, pulled back from her big face, and fixed with black bobby pins, which are the wrong color for her dark blond hair. She has a lot to talk about. She is talking now about Nancy, who lives a few houses away. Nancy is eighteen and works uptown in a store; she thinks she's too good for everyone—"I could show her a thing or two, just give me a match and let me at that dyed hair of hers"—and her mother is grumpy and ugly, like everyone's mother, "just an old bitch that might as well be dead."

It is autumn. Down the street kids are playing after supper, running along between houses or all the way down to the open area that is blocked off because of an expressway nearby. "You don't want to go in already, do you?" the taller girl whines. "Why d'ya always want to go in, you think your house is so hot? Your goddam mother is so hot? We could walk down by the warehouse, see if anybody's around. Just for something to do."

"I better go in."

"Your mother isn't calling you, is she? What's so hot about going in that dump of a house?"

I am the short, dark girl, and my friend Ronnie is laughing into my face as she always does. Ronnie lives two houses away. Her mother has five children and no husband—he died or ran away—and Ronnie is the middle child, thirteen years old. She is big for her age. I am twelve, skinny and meek and incredulous as she jumps to another subject: how Nancy's boyfriend slapped her around and burned her with his cigar just the other night. "Don't you believe me? You think I'm lying?" she challenges me.

"I never heard about that."

"So what? Nobody'd tell you anything. You'd tell the cops or something."

"No I wouldn't."

"Some cop comes to see your father, don't he?"

"He's just somebody—some old friend. I don't know who he is," I tell her, but it's too late. My whining voice gives Ronnie what she needs. It's like an opening for a wedge or the toe of her worn-out old "Indian" moccasins. She pinches my arm and I say feebly, "Don't. That hurts."

"Oh, does it hurt?"

She pinches me again.

"I said don't—"

She laughs and forgets about it. She's a big strong girl. Her legs are thick. Her face is round and her teeth are a little crooked, so that she looks as if she is always smiling. In school she sits at the back and makes trouble, hiding her yellowish teeth behind her hand when she laughs. One day she said to our teacher—our teacher is Mrs. Gunderson—"There was a man out by the front door who did something bad. He opened up his pants and everything." Mrs. Gunderson was always nervous. She told Ronnie to come out into the hall with her, and everyone tried to listen, and in a minute she called me out too Ronnie said to me, "Wasn't that Mr. Whalen out by the front door? Wasn't it, Sarah?" "When?" I said. "You know when, you were right there," Ronnie said. She was very excited and her face had a pleasant, high color. "You know what he did." "I didn't see anything," I said. Mrs. Gunderson wore ugly black shoes and her stockings were so thick you couldn't see her skin through them. Ronnie wore her moccasin loafers and no socks and her legs were pale and lumpy, covered with fine blond hairs. "Mr. Whalen stood *right out there* and Sarah saw him but she's too afraid to say. She's just a damn dirty coward," Ronnie said. Mr. Whalen was the fifth-grade teacher. Nobody liked him, but I had to say, "There wasn't any man out there." So Mrs. Gunderson let us go. Ronnie whispered, "You dirty goddam teacher's pet."

That day at noon hour she rubbed my face in the dirt by the swings, and when I began crying she let me up. "Oh, don't cry, you big baby," she said. She rubbed my head playfully. She always did this to her little brother, her favorite brother. "I didn't mean to hurt you, but you had it coming. Right? You got to do what I say. If we're friends you got to obey me, don't you?"

"Yes."

Now she talks faster and faster. I know her mother isn't home and that's why she doesn't want to go in yet—her mother is always out somewhere. No one dares to ask Ronnie about her mother. In our house my mother is waiting somewhere, or maybe not waiting at all but upstairs doing something, listening to the radio. The supper dishes are put away. My father is working the night shift. When he comes home he will sleep downstairs on the sofa and when I come down for school in the morning there he'll be, stretched out and snoring. When my father and mother are together there are two currents of air, like invisible clouds, that move with them and will not overlap. These clouds keep them separate even when they are together; they seem to be calling across a deep ditch.

"Okay, let's walk down by the warehouse."

"Why do you want to go down there?"

"Just for the hell of it."

"I got a lot of homework to do—"

"Are you trying to make me mad?"

The first day I met Ronnie was the first day they had moved into their house, about two months ago. Ronnie strolled up and down the street, looking around, and she saw me right away sitting up on our veranda, reading. She was wearing soiled white shorts that came down to her knees and a baggy pullover shirt that was her brother's. Her hands were shoved in her pockets as she walked. She said to me on that first day: "Hey, what are you doing? Are you busy or can I come up?"

Now she is my best friend and I do everything she says, almost everything. She keeps talking. She likes to touch people when she talks, tap them on the arm or nudge them. "Come on. You don't have nothing to do inside," she says, whining, wheedling, and I give in. We stroll down the block. Nobody sits outside anymore at night, because it is too cold now. I am wearing a jacket and blue jeans, and Ronnie is wearing the same coat she wears to school: it used to be her mother's coat. It is made of shiny material, with black and fluorescent green splotches and tiny white umbrellas because it is a raincoat. As we walk down the street she points out houses we pass, telling me who the people are. "In there lives a fat old bastard, he goes to the bathroom in the sink," she says, her voice loud and helpful like a teacher's voice. "His name is Chanock or Chanick or some crappy name like that."

"How do you know about him?"

"I know lots of things, stupid. You think I'm lying?"

"No."

We walk on idly. We cross the street over toward Don's Drugstore. A few boys are standing around outside, leaning on their bicycles. When they see us coming they say, "Here comes that fat old cow Lay-zer," and they all laugh. Ronnie sticks out her tongue and says what she always says: a short loud nasty word that makes them laugh louder. When she does this I feel like laughing or running away, I feel as if something had opened in the ground before me—a great gaping crack in the sidewalk. The boys don't bother with me but keep on teasing Ronnie until we're past.

This street is darker. The houses are older, set back from the sidewalk with little plots of grass that are like mounds of graves in front of them. There are "boarders" in these houses. "Dirty old perverts," Ronnie calls them if we ever see them. One of the houses is vacant and kids come from all over to break windows and fool around, even though the police have chased them away. "In this next house is a man who does nasty things with a dog. I saw him out in the alley once," Ronnie says, snickering.

I have to take big steps to keep up with her. We're headed out toward the warehouse, which is boarded up, but everyone goes in there to play. I am afraid of the warehouse at night, because bums sometimes sleep there, but if I tell Ronnie, she'll snort with laughter and pinch me. Walking along fast, she says, "I sure don't want to miss that show on Saturday. You and me can go early," and then, whistling through her teeth, "One of these days that big dumpy warehouse is going to burn down. Wait and see."

Ronnie once lit a little fire in someone's garage, but it must have gone out because nothing happened. She wanted to get back at the people because she didn't like the girl who lived there, a girl ahead of us in school. At noon hour Ronnie and I sat alone to eat our lunches. If she was angry about some-thing she could stare me down with her cold blue eyes that were like plastic caps; but other times she has to wipe at her eyes, saying, "This bastard who came home with her last night, he—He—" Or she talks bitterly of the other girls and how they all hate her because they're afraid of her. She has dirty hair, a dirty neck, and her dresses are just . . . just old baggy things passed down from someone else. At noon she often whispers to me about kids in the cafeteria, naming them one by one, telling me what she'll do to them when she gets around to it: certain acts with shears, razors, ice picks, butcher knives, acts described so vividly and with such passion that I feel sick.

Even when I'm not with Ronnie I feel a little sick, but not just in my stomach. It's all through my body. Ma always says, "Why do you run out when that big cow calls you? What do you see in her?" and I answer miserably, frightened, "I like her all right." But I have never thought about liking Ronnie. I have no choice. She has never given me the privilege of liking or disliking her, and if she knew I was thinking such a thought she would yank my hair out of my head.

Light from the street lamp falls onto the front and part of the side of the old warehouse. There is a basement entrance I am afraid of because of spiders and rats. Junk is stored in the warehouse, things we don't recognize and never bother to wonder about, parts from machines, rails, strange wheels that are solid metal and must weigh hundreds of pounds. "Let's climb in the window," I say to Ronnie. "The cellar way's faster," she says. "Please, let's go in the window," I beg. I have begun to tremble and don't know why. It seems to me that something terrible is waiting inside the warehouse.

Ronnie looks at me contemptuously. She is grave and large in the moonlight, her mother's shiny coat wrinkled tight across her broad shoulders. The way her eyes are in shadow makes me think suddenly of a person falling backwards, falling down—onto something hard and sharp. That could happen. Inside the warehouse there are all kinds of strange, sharp things half hidden in the junk, rusty edges and broken glass from the windows that have been smashed. "Please, Ron, let's climb in the window," I beg.

She laughs and we go around to the window. There is an important board pulled out that makes a place for your foot. Then you jump up and put one knee on the window ledge, then you slide inside. The boards crisscrossing the window have been torn down a long time ago. Ronnie goes first and then helps me up. She says, "What if I let you go right now? You'd fall down and split your dumb head open!"

But she helps me crawl inside. Why do we like the warehouse so much? During the day I like to explore in it; we never get tired of all the junk and the places to hide and the view from the upstairs windows. Machines—nails and nuts and bolts underfoot—big crates torn apart and left behind, with mysterious black markings on their sides. The moonlight is strong enough for us to see things dimly. I am nervous, even though I know where everything is. I know this place. In my bed at night I can climb up into the warehouse and envision everything, remember it clearly, every part of it—it is our secret place, no grownups come here—I can remember the big sliver of glass that is like a quarter moon, a beautiful shape, lying at the foot of the steps, and the thing we call the "tractor," and a great long dusty machine that is beside the stairs. When you touch it you feel first dust, then oil, beneath the dust there is a coating of oil. Three prongs rise out of one end like dull knives.

Ronnie bumps into something and says, "Oh Christ!" She is always bumping into things. One time when she hurt herself—fooling around with some bricks—she got angry at me for no reason and slapped me She was always poking or pinching or slapping. . . . It occurs to me that I should kill her. She is like a big hulking dead body tied to me, the mouth fixed up for a grin and always ready to laugh, and we are sinking together into the water, and I will have to slash out at her to get free—I want to get free. So I say, beginning to shiver, "Should we go upstairs?"

"What's upstairs but pigeon crap?"

"We can look out the window."

"You and your goddam windows—"

She laughs because I like to look out of the windows; she likes to grub around instead in corners, prying things loose, looking under things for "treasure." She told me once that she'd found a silver dollar in the warehouse. But now I go ahead of her to the stairs, a strange keen sensation in my bowels, and she grumbles but comes along behind me. These old steps are filthy with dust and some of the boards sag. I know exactly where to step. Behind me, Ronnie is like a horse. The stairs are shaking. I wait for her at the top and in that second I can see out a window and over to the street light—but past that nothing, there is nothing to see at night The street light has a cloudy halo about it, something that isn't real but seems real to my eye. Ronnie bounds up the stairs and I wait for her, sick with being so afraid, my heart pounding in a jerky, bouncy way as if it wanted to burst—but suddenly my heart is like another person inside me, nudging me and saying, "Do it! Do it!" When Ronnie is about two steps from the top I reach down and push her.

She falls at once. She falls over the side, her voice a screech that is yanked out into the air above her, and then her body hits the edge of that machine hard. She is screaming. I stand at the top, listening to her. Everything is dry and clear and pounding. She falls again, from the edge of the machine onto the floor, and now her scream is muffled as if someone had put his hand over her mouth.

I come down the stairs slowly. The air is hard and dry, like acid that burns my mouth, and I can't look anywhere except at Ronnie's twisting body. I wait for it to stop twisting. What if she doesn't die? At the base of the stairs I make a wide circle around her, brushing up against something and getting grease on my jeans.

There is this big girl half in the moonlight from the shattered window and half in the dark. Dust rolls in startled balls about her, aroused by her moans. She is bleeding. A dark stain explodes out from her and pushes the dust along before it, everything speeded up by her violent squirming, and I feel as if I must walk on tiptoe to keep from being seen by her. . . . Blood, all that blood!—is like an animal crawling out from under her, like the shadows we drag around with us, broken loose now and given its own life, twisting out from under her and grabbing her, big as she is. She cries out, "Sarah! Ma!" but I don't hear her. I am at the window already. "Ma!" she says. "Ma!" It does not seem that I am moving or hearing anything, but still my feet take me to the window and those words come to me from a distance, "Ma, help me!" and I think to myself that I will have to get to where those words won't reach.

At home our house is warm and my head aches because I am sleepy. I fall asleep on my bed without undressing, and the next day we all hear about Ronnie. "Fooling around in that old dump, I knew it was going to happen to somebody," my mother says grimly. "You stay the hell out of that place from now on. You hear?"

I tell her yes, yes. I will never go there again.

There is a great shadowy space about me, filled with waiting: waiting to cry, to feel sorry. I myself am waiting, my body is waiting the way it waited that night at the top of the steps. But nothing happens. Do you know that twenty years have gone by? I am still dark but not so skinny, I have grown into a body that is approved of by people who glance at me in the street, I have grown out of the skinny little body that knocked that clumsy body down—and I have never felt sorry. Never felt any guilt. I live in what is called a "colonial" house, on a lane of colonial houses called Meadowbrook Lane. Ours is the sixth house on the right. . . . Our mailboxes are down at the intersection with a larger road. I am married and have children and I am still waiting to feel guilty, to feel some of Ronnie's pain, to feel the shock of that impact again as I felt it when she struck the prongs of the machine—but nothing happens. In my quiet, pleasant life, when my two boys are at school, I write stories I hope may be put on television someday—why not, why couldn't that miracle happen?

My stories are more real than my childhood; my childhood is just another story, but one written by someone else.

Wants

GRACE PALEY

saw my ex-husband in the street. I was sitting on the steps of the new library.

Hello, my life, I said. We had once been married for twenty-seven years, so I felt justified.

He said, What? What life? No life of mine.

I said, O.K. I don't argue when there's real disagreement. I got up and went into the library to see how much I owed them.

The librarian said $32 even and you've owed it for eighteen years. I didn't deny anything. Because I don't understand how time passes. I have had those books. I have often thought of them. The library is only two blocks away.

My ex-husband followed me to the Books Returned desk. He interrupted the librarian, who had more to tell. In many ways, he said, as I look back, I attribute the dissolution of our marriage to the fact that you never invited the Bertrams to dinner.

That's possible, I said. But really, if you remember: first, my father was sick that Friday, then the children were born, then I had those Tuesday-night meetings, then the war began. Then we didn't seem to know them anymore. But you're right. I should have had them to dinner.

I gave the librarian a check for $32. Immediately she trusted me, put my past behind her, wiped the record clean, which is just what most other municipal and/or state bureaucracies will not do.

I checked out the two Edith Wharton books I had just returned because I'd read them so long ago and they are more apropos now than ever. They were *The House of Mirth* and *The Children*, which is about how life in the United States in New York changed in twenty-seven years fifty years ago.

A nice thing I do remember is breakfast, my ex-husband said. I was surprised. All we ever had was coffee. Then I remembered there was a hole in the back of the kitchen closet which opened into the apartment next door. There, they always ate sugar-cured smoked bacon. It gave us a very grand feeling about breakfast, but we never got stuffed and sluggish.

That was when we were poor, I said.

When were we ever rich? he asked.

Oh, as time went on, as our responsibilities increased, we didn't go in need. You took adequate financial care, I reminded him. The children went to camp four weeks a year and in decent ponchos with sleeping bags and boots, just like everyone else. They looked very nice. Our place was warm in winter, and we had nice red pillows and things.

I wanted a sailboat, he said. But you didn't want anything.

Don't be bitter, I said. It's never too late.

No, he said with a great deal of bitterness. I may get a sailboat. As a matter of fact I have money down on an eighteen-foot two-rigger. I'm doing well this year and can look forward to better. But as for you, it's too late. You'll always want nothing.

He had had a habit throughout the twenty-seven years of making a narrow remark which, like a plumber's snake, could work its way through the ear down the throat, halfway to my heart. He would then disappear, leaving me choking with equipment. What I mean is, I sat down on the library steps and he went away.

I looked through *The House of Mirth*, but lost interest. I felt extremely accused. Now, it's true, I'm short of requests and absolute requirements. But I do want *something*.

I want, for instance, to be a different person. I want to be the woman who brings these two books back in two weeks. I want to be the effective citizen who changes the school system and addresses the Board of Estimate on the troubles of this dear urban center.

I *had* promised my children to end the war before they grew up. I wanted to have been married forever to one person, my ex-husband or my present one. Either has enough character for a whole life, which as it turns out is really not such a long time. You couldn't exhaust either man's qualities or get under the rock of his reasons in one short life.

Just this morning I looked out the window to watch the street for a while and saw that the little sycamores the city had dreamily planted a couple of years before the kids were born had come that day to the prime of their lives.

Well! I decided to bring those two books back to the library. Which proves that when a person or an event comes along to jolt or appraise me I *can* take some appropriate action, although I am better known for my hospitable remarks.

Mrs. Carrington and Mrs. Crane

DOROTHY PARKER

My dear," Mrs. Carrington said, and she flicked a bead or two of caviar from her little fringed napkin, "I've got so I simply can't stand another minute of them. Not one single other minute."

"I know," Mrs. Crane said. She sighed and looked softly upon her friend. "Oh, don't I know. That's the way I feel all the time."

"Honestly," Mrs. Carrington said, "if I hadn't just simply dashed away from Angela's bridge and literally torn over here this afternoon, I—well, I don't know what I would have done."

"You don't have to tell me," Mrs. Crane said. "I know so well. You don't need to tell me."

"The emptiness," Mrs. Carrington needed to tell her. "And the silliness. And the eternal gossip, gossip, gossip. And all the talk about the clothes they have and the clothes they're going to get, and what they do to keep thin. Well, I'm fed up with it, that's all. No, thanks, dear, I don't dare take another sandwich; I'll have to roll all day tomorrow as it is."

"Rolling doesn't do a thing for me," Mrs. Crane said. "What I do is put my feet over my head thirty-five times every morning, and then, if I'm at home during the day, I don't have any lunch."

"That would simply kill me," Mrs. Carrington said. "That would be literally death to me. If I go without lunch, I simply lose control at dinner. Potatoes and everything. Angela's got a new diet; you know, one of those things where it doesn't matter so much how much you eat, it's what you eat with what. She's lost eight pounds."

"How does she look?" Mrs. Crane said.

"Oh, all right, I suppose," Mrs. Carrington said. "Honestly, I've got to the state where they all look alike to me. And talk alike. All those silly, empty women. Never a thought about anything except clothes and parties, never a discussion of anything really worth while. It isn't so bad in the winter. You can get away from them, a little bit, in New York. You can get off by yourself and do something really worth while—picture galleries, and the Philharmonic, and, oh, exhibitions of paintings, and concerts, and things like that. But in the summer, down here in the country—well, there's literally no getting away from them. That's all."

"I know," Mrs. Crane said. "You don't have to say it."

"Nothing but parties, parties, parties," Mrs. Carrington had to say. "Yes, and drinking, drinking, drinking. No, dear, please don't give me any more. After the way they all behaved at the Weldons' party last night, I feel as if I never wanted to see anything to drink again."

"Oh, please—it's really nothing but fruit juice," Mrs. Crane said. She refilled first her own glass, for she was a cozy hostess who shared rather than merely gave, and then her guest's, with a suave blending of gin, vermouth, and zest of lemon. "Oh, you went to the Weldons' last night? Was it any fun?"

"Fun!" Mrs. Carrington said. "The same old thing over again. Backgammon and gossip and diets and clothes. Oh, I nearly forgot to tell you, Betty had on that Florelle model, you know the one with the coat with little tails, only she had it in blue. I sort of thought I'd order it in black. What do you think? Don't you think it would be useful in black?"

"Oh, yes, lovely," Mrs. Crane said. "Was Betty tight?"

"Oh, of course," Mrs. Carrington said. "Blind."

"She's really getting tiresome," Mrs. Crane said. "I don't see how Jack stands her. Well, he's always so drunk himself, I suppose he doesn't notice. It's sickening, isn't it? Oh, my dear, just let me fill it up—it's really nothing but melted ice, anyway."

"No, don't, please don't," Mrs. Carrington said. "Well. Well, just that much, then. Oh, not all that, really. Well. Well, I literally need it, after that bridge party. And last night. What did you do last night?"

"We went to the Lockwoods'," Mrs. Crane said. "I don't have to tell you what it was like. I was so bored, I thought I couldn't last through the evening. But, my dear, it really was awfully amusing. Cynthia had on that white Cygnette model with the two little capes, and Maggie Chase had on the same model in green, and then Dorette came in later on with it in bright yellow."

"Oh, Lord," Mrs. Carrington said. "Now isn't that typical? Isn't that just the way their minds work? Never an original idea; even have to have clothes like one another's. I really don't see how I'm going to stand it until the end of the summer. I said as much to Freddy, coming home last night. 'Freddy,' I said, as we were coming home, 'Freddy,' I said, 'I literally cannot stand that silly, empty, drunken crowd any longer.'"

"I've said the same thing to Jim," Mrs. Crane said, "many a time. Many and many a time. What are you and Freddy doing tonight?"

"We're going to the Grays'," Mrs. Carrington said. "And it will be the same old thing. The same old silly talk. Never a new idea, never a moment's thought of worth-while things."

"Why, we're going, too," Mrs. Crane said. "Well, that will save my life, that you're going. We might get a moment to talk."

"If we don't," Mrs. Carrington said, "I'll never be able to get through it. Honestly, dear, you don't know how much you do for me. No, really no more—please. Well, if you're going to have another one, too. Oh, that's plenty, honestly. No, but what I was going to say is, a person of any intelligence at all simply has to have a certain amount of stimulation. You can't exist entirely on emptiness and silliness and clothes, day in, day out. Well, those people can, I suppose, but people like us—well, we die, that's all, we literally die."

"I know," Mrs. Crane said. "Oh, I know so well."

"I wish it were time to go back to New York," Mrs. Carrington said. "I want to make something of this winter; something worth while. I think I'll take some sort of course or other at Columbia. Hester Coles did, last year. Well, of course, she's a silly little fool, like all the rest of them. But I thought I might do it, too."

"I want to do something this winter," Mrs. Crane said. "If I can only find the time. What I'd really like to do is take up tap-dancing. Mary Morton did, last year, and she lost twelve pounds."

"Is that how she did it?" Mrs. Carrington said. "Did she really? Didn't she have to diet besides?"

"No," Mrs. Crane said. "She just gave up sweets and starches and she couldn't have any meat, except chicken once or twice a week. Twelve pounds, she lost."

"That's wonderful," Mrs. Carrington said. "That's just about what I'd like to lose."

"And it stays lost, when you do it that way," Mrs. Crane said.

"Well, I'm going to take tap-dancing the minute I go back," Mrs. Carrington said. "My dear, let's do it together. You will, really? You literally will? Oh, I think that will be wonderful. You see what you do for me—I never talk to you without being stimulated. Well, now I can really get through the rest of the summer, as long as I have something to look forward to, as long as I know I'm going to get something real out of the winter. Lord, the way the time drags, down here, doesn't it? Good heavens, is it honestly as late as that? Oh, I've got to literally tear home and get dressed. I'm whole hours late. What are you going to wear?"

"Oh, I haven't even given it a thought," Mrs. Crane said. "I did sort of think of the black net, but I don't know. Probably the dusty-pink Valerie model. You know. Betty has it in beige."

"Oh, yes, it's adorable," Mrs. Carrington said. "I suppose Betty'll be there tonight. She's probably tight already."

She rose and moved toward the door. For a moment, it seemed as if the fruit juice and melted ice that she had consumed were about to have their way with her. She stumbled slightly. "Oops!" she said, and had her balance again. Gently she smiled upon her hostess.

"Well, you don't know what this has done for me," she said. "I feel all lifted up. If I hadn't talked to you this afternoon, I could not have faced all the silliness again tonight. I just simply couldn't."

Mrs. Crane swayed delicately toward her friend.

"I know," she said. "It's such a comfort to know that there's somebody, even here in the country, who isn't like all the others. You don't have to tell me."

Affectionately they kissed, and, for a little time, they parted.

The Jilting of Granny Weatherall

KATHERINE ANNE PORTER

She flicked her wrist neatly out of Doctor Harry's pudgy careful fingers and pulled the sheet up to her chin. The brat ought to be in knee breeches. Doctoring around the country with spectacles on his nose! "Get along now, take your schoolbooks and go. There's nothing wrong with me."

Doctor Harry spread a warm paw like a cushion on her forehead where the forked green vein danced and made her eyelids twitch. "Now, now, be a good girl, and we'll have you up in no time."

"That's no way to speak to a woman nearly eighty years old just because she's down. I'd have you respect your elders, young man."

"Well, Missy, excuse me." Doctor Harry patted her cheek. "But I've got to warn you, haven't I? You're a marvel, but you must be careful or you're going to be good and sorry."

"Don't tell me what I'm going to be. I'm on my feet now, morally speaking. It's Cornelia. I had to go to bed to get rid of her."

Her bones felt loose, and floated around in her skin, and Doctor Harry floated like a balloon around the foot of the bed. He floated and pulled down his waistcoat and swung his glasses on a cord. "Well, stay where you are, it certainly can't hurt you."

"Get along and doctor your sick," said Granny Weatherall. "Leave a well woman alone. I'll call for you when I want you. . . . Where were you forty years ago when I pulled through milk-leg and double pneumonia? You weren't even born. Don't let Cornelia lead you on," she shouted, because Doctor Harry appeared to float up to the ceiling and out. "I pay my own bills, and I don't throw my money away on nonsense!"

She meant to wave good-by, but it was too much trouble. Her eyes closed of themselves, it was like a dark curtain drawn around the bed. The pillow rose and floated under her, pleasant as a hammock in a light wind. She listened to the leaves rustling outside the window. No, somebody was swishing newspapers: no, Cornelia and Doctor Harry were whispering together. She leaped broad awake, thinking they whispered in her ear.

"She was never like this, *never* like this!" "Well, what can we expect?" "Yes, eighty years old. . . ."

Well, and what if she was? She still had ears. It was like Cornelia to whisper around doors. She always kept things secret in such a public way. She was always being tactful and kind. Cornelia was dutiful; that was the trouble with her. Dutiful and good: "So good and dutiful," said Granny, "that I'd like to spank her." She saw herself spanking Cornelia and making a fine job of it.

"What'd you say, Mother?"

Granny felt her face tying up in hard knots.

"Can't a body think, I'd like to know?"

"I thought you might want something."

"I do. I want a lot of things. First off, go away and don't whisper."

She lay and drowsed, hoping in her sleep that the children would keep out and let her rest a minute. It had been a long day. Not that she was tired. It was always pleasant to snatch a minute now and then. There was always so much to be done, let me see: tomorrow.

Tomorrow was far away and there was nothing to trouble about. Things were finished somehow when the time came; thank God there was always a little margin over for peace: then a person could spread out the plan of life and tuck in the edges orderly. It was good to have everything clean and folded away, with the hair brushes and tonic bottles sitting straight on the white embroidered linen: the day started without fuss and the pantry shelves laid out with rows of jelly glasses and brown jugs and white stone-china jars with blue whirligigs and words painted on them: coffee, tea, sugar, ginger, cinnamon, allspice: and the bronze clock with the lion on top nicely dusted off. The dust that lion could collect in twenty-four hours! The box in the attic with all those letters tied up, well, she'd have to go through that tomorrow. All those letters—George's letters and John's letters and her letters to them both—lying around for the children to find afterwards made her uneasy. Yes, that would be tomorrow's business. No use to let them know how silly she had been once.

While she was rummaging around she found death in her mind and it felt clammy and unfamiliar. She had spent so much time preparing for death there was no need for bringing it up again. Let it take care of itself now. When she was sixty she had felt very old, finished, and went around making farewell trips to see her children and grandchildren, with a secret in her mind: This is the very last of your mother, children! Then she made her will and came down with a long fever. That was all just a notion like a lot of other things, but it was lucky too, for she had once for all got over the idea of dying for a long time. Now she couldn't be worried. She hoped she had better sense now. Her father had lived to be one hundred and two years old and had drunk a noggin of strong hot toddy on his last birthday. He told the reporters it was his daily habit, and he owed his long life to that. He had made quite a scandal and was very pleased about it. She believed she'd just plague Cornelia a little.

"Cornelia! Cornelia!" No footsteps, but a sudden hand on her cheek. "Bless you, where have you been?"

"Here, Mother."

"Well, Cornelia, I want a noggin of hot toddy."

"Are you cold, darling?"

"I'm chilly, Cornelia. Lying in bed stops the circulation. I must have told you that a thousand times."

Well, she could just hear Cornelia telling her husband that Mother was getting a little childish and they'd have to humor her. The thing that most annoyed her was that Cornelia thought she was deaf, dumb, and blind. Little hasty glances and tiny gestures tossed around her and over her head saying, "Don't cross her, let her have her way, she's eighty years old," and she sitting there as if she lived in a thin glass cage. Sometimes Granny almost made up her mind to pack up and move back to her own house where nobody could remind her every minute that she was old. Wait, wait, Cornelia, till your own children whisper behind your back!

In her day she had kept a better house and had got more work done. She wasn't too old yet for Lydia to be driving eighty miles for advice when one of the children jumped the track, and Jimmy still dropped in and talked things over: "Now, Mammy, you've a good business head, I want to know what you think of this? . . ." Old. Cornelia couldn't change the furniture around without asking. Little things, little things! They had been so sweet when they were little. Granny wished the old days were back again with the children young and everything to be done over. It had been a hard pull, but not too much for her. When she thought of all the food she had cooked, and all the clothes she had cut and sewed, and all the gardens she had made— well, the children showed it. There they were, made out of her, and they couldn't get away from that. Sometimes she wanted to see John again and point to them and say, Well, I didn't do so badly, did I? But that would have to wait. That was for tomorrow. She used to think of him as a man, but now all the children were older than their father, and he would be a child beside her if she saw him now. It seemed strange and there was something wrong in the idea. Why, he couldn't possibly recognize her. She had fenced in a hundred acres once, digging the post holes herself and clamping the wires with just a negro boy to help. That changed a woman. John would be look- ing for a young woman with the peaked Spanish comb in her hair and the painted fan. Digging post holes changed a woman. Riding country roads in the winter when women had their babies was another thing: sitting up nights with sick horses and sick negroes and sick children and hardly ever losing one. John, I hardly ever lost one of them! John would see that in a minute, that would be something he could understand, she wouldn't have to explain anything!

It made her feel like rolling up her sleeves and putting the whole place to rights again. No matter if Cornelia was determined to be everywhere at once, there were a great many things left undone on this place. She would start tomorrow and do them. It was good to be strong enough for everything, even if all you made melted and changed and slipped under your hands, so that by the time you finished you almost forgot what you were working for. What was it I set out to do? she asked herself intently, but she could not remember. A fog rose over the valley, she saw it marching across the creek swallowing the trees and moving up the hill like an army of ghosts. Soon it would be at the near edge of the orchard, and then it was time to go in and light the lamps. Come in, children, don't stay out in the night air.

Lighting the lamps had been beautiful. The children huddled up to her and breathed like little calves waiting at the bars in the twilight. Their eyes followed the match and watched the flame rise and settle in a blue curve, then they moved away from her. The lamp was lit, they didn't have to be scared and hang on to mother any more. Never, never, never more. God, for all my life I thank Thee. Without Thee, my God, I could never have done it. Hail, Mary, full of grace.

I want you to pick all the fruit this year and see that nothing is wasted. There's always someone who can use it. Don't let good things rot for want of using. You waste life when you waste good food. Don't let things get lost. It's bitter to lose things. Now, don't let me get to thinking, not when I am tired and taking a little nap before supper. . . .

The pillow rose about her shoulders and pressed against her heart and the memory was being squeezed out of it: oh, push down the pillow, some-body: it would smother her if she tried to hold it. Such a fresh breeze blowing and such a green day with no threats in it. But he had not come, just the same. What does a woman do when she has put on the white veil and set out the white cake for a man and he doesn't come? She tried to remember. No, I swear he never harmed me but in that. He never harmed me but in that . . . and what if he did? There was the day, the day, but a whirl of dark smoke rose and covered it, crept up and over into the bright field where everything was planted so carefully in orderly rows. That was hell, she knew hell when she saw it. For sixty years she had prayed against remem-bering him and against losing her soul in the deep pit of hell, and now the two things were mingled in one and the thought of him was a smoky cloud from hell that moved and crept in her head when she had just got rid of Doctor Harry and was trying to rest a minute. Wounded vanity, Ellen, said a sharp voice in the top of her mind. Don't let your wounded vanity get the upper hand of you. Plenty of girls get jilted. You were jilted, weren't you? Then stand up to it. Her eyelids wavered and let in streamers of blue-gray light like tissue paper over her eyes. She must get up and pull the shades down or she'd never sleep. She was in bed again and the shades were not down. How could that happen? Better turn over, hide from the light, sleep-ing in the light gave you nightmares. "Mother, how do you feel now?" and a stinging wetness on her forehead. But I don't like having my face washed in cold water!

Hapsy? George? Lydia? Jimmy? No, Cornelia, and her features were swollen and full of little puddles. "They're coming, darling, they'll all be here soon." Go wash your face, child, you look funny.

Instead of obeying, Cornelia knelt down and put her head on the pil-low. She seemed to be talking but there was no sound. "Well, are you tongue-tied? Whose birthday is it? Are you going to give a party?"

Cornelia's mouth moved urgently in strange shapes. "Don't do that, you bother me, daughter."

"Oh, no, Mother. Oh, no. . . ."

Nonsense. It was strange about children. They disputed your every word. "No what, Cornelia?"

"Here's Doctor Harry."

"I won't see that boy again. He just left five minutes ago."

"That was this morning, Mother. It's night now. Here's the nurse."

"This is Doctor Harry, Mrs. Weatherall. I never saw you look so young and happy "

"Ah, I'll never be young again—but I'd be happy if they'd let me lie in peace and get rested."

She thought she spoke up loudly, but no one answered. A warm weight on her forehead, a warm bracelet on her wrist, and a breeze went on whispering, trying to tell her something. A shuffle of leaves in the everlasting hand of God, He blew on them and they danced and rattled. "Mother, don't mind, we're going to give you a little hypodermic." "Look here, daughter, how do ants get in this bed? I saw sugar ants yesterday." Did you send for Hapsy too?

It was Hapsy she really wanted. She had to go a long way back through a great many rooms to find Hapsy standing with a baby on her arm. She seemed to herself to be Hapsy also, and the baby on Hapsy's arm was Hapsy and himself and herself, all at once, and there was no surprise in the meeting. Then Hapsy melted from within and turned flimsy as gray gauze and the baby was a gauzy shadow, and Hapsy came up close and said, "I thought you'd never come," and looked at her very searchingly and said, "You haven't changed a bit!" They leaned forward to kiss, when Cornelia began whispering from a long way off, "Oh, is there anything you want to tell me? Is there anything I can do for you?"

Yes, she had changed her mind after sixty years and she would like to see George. I want you to find George. Find him and be sure to tell him I forgot him. I want him to know I had my husband just the same and my children and my house like any other woman. A good house too and a good husband that I loved and fine children out of him. Better than I hoped for even. Tell him I was given back everything he took away and more. Oh, no, oh, God, no, there was something else besides the house and the man and the children. Oh, surely they were not all? What was it? Something not given back. . . . Her breath crowded down under her ribs and grew into a monstrous frightening shape with cutting edges; it bored up into her head, and the agony was unbelievable: Yes, John, get the Doctor now, no more talk, my time has come.

When this one was born it should be the last. The last. It should have been born first, for it was the one she had truly wanted. Everything came in good time. Nothing left out, left over. She was strong, in three days she would be as well as ever. Better. A woman needed milk in her to have her full health.

"Mother, do you hear me?"

"I've been telling you—"

"Mother, Father Connolly's here."

"I went to Holy Communion only last week. Tell him I'm not so sinful as all that."

"Father just wants to speak to you."

He could speak as much as he pleased. It was like him to drop in and inquire about her soul as if it were a teething baby, and then stay on for a cup of tea and a round of cards and gossip. He always had a funny story of some sort, usually about an Irishman who made his little mistakes and confessed them, and the point lay in some absurd thing he would blurt out in the confessional showing his struggles between native piety and original sin. Granny felt easy about her soul. Cornelia, where are your manners? Give Father Connolly a chair. She had her secret comfortable understanding with a few favorite saints who cleared a straight road to God for her. All as surely signed and sealed as the papers for the new Forty Acres. Forever . . . heirs and assigns forever. Since the day the wedding cake was not cut, but thrown out and wasted. The whole bottom dropped out of the world, and there she was blind and sweating with nothing under her feet and the walls falling away. His hand had caught her under the breast, she had not fallen, there was the freshly polished floor with the green rug on it, just as before. He had cursed like a sailor's parrot and said, "I'll kill him for you." Don't lay a hand on him, for my sake leave something to God. "Now, Ellen, you must believe what I tell you. . . ."

So there was nothing, nothing to worry about any more, except sometimes in the night one of the children screamed in a nightmare, and they both hustled out shaking and hunting for the matches and calling, "There, wait a minute, here we are!" John, get the doctor now, Hapsy's time has come. But there was Hapsy standing by the bed in a white cap. "Cornelia, tell Hapsy to take off her cap. I can't see her plain."

Her eyes opened very wide and the room stood out like a picture she had seen somewhere. Dark colors with the shadows rising towards the ceiling in long angles. The tall black dresser gleamed with nothing on it but John's picture, enlarged from a little one, with John's eyes very black when they should have been blue. You never saw him, so how do you know how he looked? But the man insisted the copy was perfect, it was very rich and handsome. For a picture, yes, but it's not my husband. The table by the bed had a linen cover and a candle and a crucifix. The light was blue from Cornelia's silk lampshades. No sort of light at all, just frippery. You had to live forty years with kerosene lamps to appreciate honest electricity. She felt very strong and she saw Doctor Harry with a rosy nimbus around him.

"You look like a saint, Doctor Harry, and I vow that's as near as you'll ever come to it."

"She's saying something."

"I heard you, Cornelia. What's all this carrying-on?"

"Father Connolly's saying—"

Cornelia's voice staggered and bumped like a cart in a bad road. It rounded corners and turned back again and arrived nowhere. Granny stepped up in the cart very lightly and reached for the reins, but a man sat beside her and she knew him by his hands, driving the cart. She did not look in his face, for she knew without seeing, but looked instead down the road where the trees leaned over and bowed to each other and a thousand birds were singing a Mass. She felt like singing too, but she put her hand in the bosom of her dress and pulled out a rosary, and Father Connolly murmured Latin in a very solemn voice and tickled her feet. My God, will you stop that nonsense? I'm a married woman. What if he did run away and leave me to face the priest by myself? I found another a whole world better. I wouldn't have exchanged my husband for anybody except St. Michael himself, and you may tell him that for me with a thank you in the bargain.

Light flashed on her closed eyelids, and a deep roaring shook her. Cornelia, is that lightning? I hear thunder. There's going to be a storm. Close all the windows. Call the children in. . . . "Mother, here we are, all of us." "Is that you, Hapsy?" "Oh, no, I'm Lydia. We drove as fast as we could." Their faces drifted above her, drifted away. The rosary fell out of her hands and Lydia put it back. Jimmy tried to help, their hands fumbled together, and Granny closed two fingers around Jimmy's thumb. Beads wouldn't do, it must be something alive. She was so amazed her thoughts ran round and round. So, my dear Lord, this is my death and I wasn't even thinking about it. My children have come to see me die. But I can't, it's not time. Oh, I always hated surprises. I wanted to give Cornelia the amethyst set— Cornelia, you're to have the amethyst set, but Hapsy's to wear it when she wants, and, Doctor Harry, do shut up. Nobody sent for you. Oh, my dear Lord, do wait a minute. I meant to do something about the Forty Acres, Jimmy doesn't need it and Lydia will later on, with that worthless husband of hers. I meant to finish the altar cloth and send six bottles of wine to Sister Borgia for her dyspepsia. I want to send six bottles of wine to Sister Borgia, Father Connolly, now don't let me forget.

Cornelia's voice made short turns and tilted over and crashed. "Oh, Mother, oh, Mother, oh, Mother. . . ."

"I'm not going, Cornelia. I'm taken by surprise. I can't go."

You'll see Hapsy again. What about her? "I thought you'd never come." Granny made a long journey outward, looking for Hapsy. What if I don't find her? What then? Her heart sank down and down, there was no bottom to death, she couldn't come to the end of it. The blue light from Cornelia's lampshade drew into a tiny point in the center of her brain, it flickered and winked like an eye, quietly it fluttered and dwindled. Granny lay curled down within herself, amazed and watchful, staring at the point of light that was herself; her body was now only a deeper mass of shadow in an endless darkness and this darkness would curl around the light and swallow it up. God, give a sign!

For the second time there was no sign. Again no bridegroom and the priest in the house. She could not remember any other sorrow because this grief wiped them all away. Oh, no, there's nothing more cruel than this— I'll never forgive it. She stretched herself with a deep breath and blew out the light.

Smoke

MARY ROBISON

arty Elber followed his mother's green sports car through Beverly Hills, but she was too good a driver for Marty to stay close, even on his motorcycle. The recently remarried Mrs. Audrey Elber Sharon caught the next-to-last corner before her new home at about sixty at the apex of the curve, tires twisting, exhaust pipes firing like pistol shots.

She was laughing, leaning out of the open driver's door of her car and brushing grains of sand from her bare feet, when Marty drove his bike onto the blacktop turnaround. He dropped his kickstand, sat back sideways on the bike saddle, and lighted a cigarette. He was wearing Levis, with suspenders and no shirt, and linesman's boots. He was twenty-six.

"I won," his mother said. "You couldn't catch me, and you had all the way from Santa Monica."

"All the way from Malibu," Marty said. "I saw you leaving the Mayfair Market. You made every single light, though. I had to stop a lot."

Audrey Sharon picked up a paper sack of groceries and a cluster of iced-tea cans from the passenger seat of her car. She cradled the groceries in her arm, hooked the cans with her free fingers, used her knee to slam the car door, and came toward Marty. "Give us a puff," she said.

Marty put his cigarette between his mother's lips. "I need to borrow a great deal of money," he said while Audrey inhaled. "Before the weekend."

"Don't talk to me," she said, "talk to Hoyt."

Marty wiggled his jaw and yanked his chin strap loose. He lifted off his motorcycle helmet. "I can't talk to Hoyt," he said.

Hoyt Sharon came around the corner from the side lawn, carrying a 9-iron and a perforated plastic golf ball. His white hair was cut to a fine bristle, and he wore a long-billed fishing cap and what looked to Marty like a crimson spacesuit—one-piece, with its Velcro closing straps undone from his throat to his belly.

"Marty! Great! Come in, come in," Hoyt said.

"Hey," Marty said, "how's the honeymoon?"

Hoyt had planted himself over the golf ball. He rolled his shoulders and swung the club. The ball clicked and flew up onto the slate-shingled garage roof. "So much for that soldier," Hoyt said. He came up behind Audrey and tried to take the groceries away from her.

"Will you please calm down?" she said to him. "Look at how much you're sweating."

"O.K. Sorry," Hoyt said.

"If you want to help me carry, get the food cooler and beach umbrella from the trunk," Audrey said.

"Remember to talk to him for me," Marty whispered to his mother as they trailed Hoyt across the lawn.

Hoyt dumped the umbrella and golf club he was carrying and opened the front door for Audrey and Marty. They entered a paneled foyer cluttered with plants and bright oil paintings of sinewy cowboys. Audrey went up three carpeted steps and through a swinging saloon door that led to the kitchen.

Hoyt led Marty through another foyer, which was being repapered with flocked maroon sheets; through the shadowy game room, where an old-fashioned dark-green billiard table stood on an emerald carpet; and into the library, which was two stories tall. Two of the library walls were glass, with louvered double doors, and in front of a third wall was a row of plush-covered theater seats, bolted to the floor. Above these, a mural depicted a cattle stampede and a cowboy being flung from the saddle of a panicky-looking horse.

Marty sat down in a large wooden armchair decorated with old cattle brands. Hoyt threw himself into the sofa, which was as long and deep as a rowboat.

"Your mom tell you about Henry Kissinger?" Hoyt said, clasping his hands behind his head. "It's the damnedest thing. She tell you? You won't believe it."

"I don't think so," Marty said. "No."

"Ben Deverow and his wife—you don't know them—go into the Derby for lunch and there he is, Henry Kissinger."

"Really?" Marty said.

"Yeah, having shrimp or something," Hoyt said. "Only, you won't believe this, but he's in drag. He's dressed up like a woman."

"Oh, come on," Marty said, reaching across the coffee table for a copy of *Sports Illustrated*.

"No. He's really Kissinger, but he's got a . . . a whatchamacallit. . . ." Hoyt pointed to the swordfish stitched on his cap.

"A wig?"

"No, he didn't even have a wig. He had a little . . . like a hat thing, you know? With a little lace veil?"

Marty said, "He couldn't do that. Everyone would know if he dressed up like a woman and went out in public."

"That's what you'd think," Hoyt said. "It's what I'd think, isn't it? But it was him. I swear it."

"You weren't even there," Marty said.

"You're too quick for me," Hoyt said. "I was lying. It wasn't Kissinger at all. It was Ronald Reagan."

"He give you the Kissinger thing?" Audrey said as she padded into the room. "Isn't that incredible?" She had put on a pair of jeans and combed her hair in a ponytail.

Hoyt took a red tablet from his shirt pocket. He put the pill on his tongue, hopped up from the couch, crossed the room, and gulped water from a cut-glass pitcher on the bar. "Forgot my Stresstab," he said apologetically.

Marty cleared his throat three or four times, turning the pages of his magazine.

"Marty needs money for his business, Hoyt," Audrey said.

"Why the hell didn't he come to me before?" Hoyt said. He slapped his palms on the seat of his spacesuit.

"He didn't need money before," Audrey said.

"Look," Hoyt said, "I get a kick out of helping young people. You know who helped me when I was stalled? Forty years ago, when Anaheim was just a crop of orange trees?"

"Gene Autry," Audrey said.

"Gene Autry is who," Hoyt said. "That's right, honey." He turned to Marty and said, "No, I don't see any problem here. What are we playing with? Land?"

"Smoke detectors," Marty said. "I can get in on a pretty safe operation, Hoyt. Some friends in Sacramento tell me they're thinking about making detectors mandatory in the next couple of years."

"Besides which, I believe in the damn things," Hoyt said. "They're like little alarms? You bet I do. They save lives. Friends of mine lost a kid in a fire once. I say 'a kid,' but I mean *infant*. You should have seen it." He parted his hands. "They had a teeny-tiny casket only this big."

Audrey switched on the television, and a local charity telethon appeared on the screen. A high-school orchestra was playing "High Hopes." Audrey sat down on the carpet in front of the set, and Hoyt leaned over and kissed one of her ears as they both watched the screen.

"Can I neck with you for a second?" the show's master of ceremonies said to a five-year-old girl whose legs were strapped into metal braces. The child had on a party dress. "Why can't I?" he said. "Are you married?" He dropped on one knee before the girl and squinted at her suspiciously.

"No, I'm too little," the child said.

"You aren't too little," the M.C. told her and the audience. "You're one of the very biggest people on this planet, because your heart is full of courage and hope."

Marty went over and pulled open the double glass doors. They moved easily on their runners. There was the smell of cut grass, the knock of a carpenter's hammer, the hiss of lawn sprinklers.

Hoyt turned abruptly and came across the room. He sprang back and forth on the balls of his feet, shooting fists in combinations like a prizefighter. "O.K., buddy," he said to Marty. "Your turn. Waltz with me a few rounds."

"I really can't, Hoyt," Marty said.

"You want a grubstake," Hoyt said. "You got to do a little dancing." He moved easily, but his face was red. He jabbed wide of Marty's throat, delicately pointing the knuckles of his half-closed fingers.

Audrey turned off the television set and watched the two men with her arms folded.

Hoyt stopped moving. Marty stood before him, flat-footed, with his arms half raised.

"The old monkey," Hoyt said. He swung a clowning roundhouse right that smashed into Marty's left temple.

"Jesus, Hoyt," Marty said. The blow had knocked him onto the carpet, where he lay on one elbow and hip.

"He's all right," Hoyt said to Audrey.

"I'm all right," Marty said, getting to his feet.

Hoyt danced toward him. "Cover up," Hoyt said, and Marty crouched and crossed his arms over his face.

"Breadbasket," Hoyt said and whipped his left fist at Marty's bare stomach. Marty walked away with his hands on his hips, trying to take a breath. He bent over and went into a squat.

"Leave him alone," Audrey said. "Poor Marty."

"Christ, Hoyt," Marty said.

"Woozy?" Audrey asked him. She pushed Marty forward until he went onto all fours, and then found a metal wastepaper basket, which she put down under his face.

"I'm sorry, Marty," Hoyt said. "That was nuts of me. Just wanted to get the blood running back to the pump, you know? Those weren't supposed to land."

"You didn't have to put his eye out," Audrey said.

"I think he did," Marty said. "I can't see out of it."

"Look at me," Audrey said, taking Marty's chin in her hand. "No. All it is is a little sliver-cut at the edge of the brow. You'll have a mouse that may close your eye a bit. I'll get you a cup of coffee." She left the room.

Marty sat on the couch. Hoyt paced in front of him. "Forget it, Marty, really," he said. "I didn't mean for those to land. You're a great kid for not hauling off and plastering me right back."

Marty said, "I wouldn't mess with you."

"What'd you say you'd need to get in on those alarm systems? Did you say three or four thousand?"

"Really, three thousand is more than it would take," Marty said. "Three thousand is great, sir."

"Not 'sir.' Don't call me 'sir.'" Hoyt went over to the door and took some deep breaths. He pounded his chest a few times. He put a finger on the side of his nose, closing off the nostril, and breathed deeply five or six more times. "Listen, though," he said. "Don't those fire alarms sometimes go off when there's no fire?"

"They're working on that," Marty said.

"Your mother's so mad at me," Hoyt said.

"I'll tell her everything's O.K.," Marty said.

When Audrey came back into the room, she was carrying a full cup of coffee for Marty. "Everything's all right here," Hoyt said. She and Marty smiled at each other. When Marty glanced over at Hoyt, he saw that Hoyt was grinning, too.

"We're in business," Hoyt said. "My father told me the only things you got to worry about are sex, death, and money. And he told me if you've got the right family you'll never have to worry about two of them. That just leaves death. Bear that in mind, friends."

The Blind Spot

SAKI

Y ou've just come back from Adelaide's funeral, haven't you?" said Sir
Lulworth to his nephew; "I suppose it was very like most other funerals?"

"I'll tell you all about it at lunch," said Egbert.

"You'll do nothing of the sort. It wouldn't be respectful either to
your great-aunt's memory or to the lunch. We begin with Spanish olives,
then a borsch, then more olives and a bird of some kind, and a rather entic-
ing Rhenish wine, not at all expensive as wines go in this country, but still
quite laudable in its way. Now there's absolutely nothing in that menu that
harmonizes in the least with the subject of your great-aunt Adelaide or her
funeral. She was a charming woman, and quite as intelligent as she had any
need to be, but somehow she always reminded me of an English cook's idea
of a Madras curry."

"She used to say you were frivolous," said Egbert. Something in tone
suggested that he rather endorsed the verdict.

"I believe I once considerably scandalized her by declaring that clear
soup was a more important factor in life than a clear conscience. She had
very little sense of proportion. By the way, she made you her principal heir,
didn't she?"

"Yes," said Egbert, "and executor as well. It's in that connection that I
particularly want to speak to you."

"Business is not my strong point at any time," said Sir Lulworth, "and
certainly not when we're on the immediate threshold of lunch."

"It isn't exactly business," explained Egbert, as he followed his uncle
into the dining-room. "It's something rather serious. Very serious."

"Then we can't possibly speak about it now," said Sir Lulworth; "no one
could talk seriously, during a borsch. A beautifully constructed borsch, such

as you are going to experience presently, ought not only to banish conversation but almost to annihilate thought. Later on, when we arrive at the second stage of olives, I shall be quite ready to discuss that new book on Borrow, or, if you prefer it, the present situation in the Grand Duchy of Luxemburg. But I absolutely decline to talk anything approaching business till we have finished with the bird."

For the greater part of the meal Egbert sat in an abstracted silence, the silence of a man whose mind is focussed on one topic. When the coffee stage had been reached he launched himself suddenly athwart his uncle's reminiscences of the court of Luxemburg.

"I think I told you that great-aunt Adelaide had made me her executor. There wasn't very much to be done in the way of legal matters, but I had to go through her papers."

"That would be a fairly heavy task in itself. I should imagine there were reams of family letters."

"Stacks of them, and most of them highly uninteresting. There was one packet, however, which I thought might repay a careful perusal. It was a bundle of correspondence from her brother Peter."

"The Canon of tragic memory," said Lulworth.

"Exactly, of tragic memory, as you say; a tragedy that has never been fathomed."

"Probably the simplest explanation was the correct one," said Sir Lulworth; "he slipped on the stone staircase and fractured his skull in falling."

Egbert shook his head. "The medical evidence all went to prove that the blow on the head was struck by some one coming up behind him. A wound caused by violent contact with the steps could not possibly have been inflicted at that angle of the skull. They experimented with a dummy figure falling in every conceivable position."

"But the motive?" exclaimed Sir Lulworth; "no one had any interest in doing away with him, and the number of people who destroy Canons of the Established Church for the mere fun of killing must be extremely limited. Of course there are individuals of weak mental balance who do that sort of thing, but they seldom conceal their handiwork; they are more generally inclined to parade it."

"His cook was under suspicion," said Egbert shortly.

"I know he was," said Sir Lulworth, "simply because he was about the only person on the premises at the time of the tragedy. But could anything be sillier than trying to fasten a charge of murder on to Sebastien? He had nothing to gain, in fact, a good deal to lose, from the death of his employer. The Canon was paying him quite as good wages as I was able to offer him when I took him over into my service. I have since raised them to something a little more in accordance with his real worth, but at the time he was glad to find a new place without troubling about an increase of wages. People were fighting rather shy of him, and he had no friends in this country. No; if any one in the world was interested in the prolonged life and unimpaired digestion of the Canon it would certainly be Sebastien."

"People don't always weigh the consequences of their rash acts," said Egbert, "otherwise there would be very few murders committed. Sebastien is a man of hot temper."

"He is a southerner," admitted Sir Lulworth; "to be geographically exact I believe he hails from the French slopes of the Pyrenees. I took that into consideration when he nearly killed the gardener's boy the other day for bringing him a spurious substitute for sorrel. One must always make allowances for origin and locality and early environment; 'Tell me your longitude and I'll know what latitude to allow you,' is my motto."

"There, you see," said Egbert, "he nearly killed the gardener's boy."

"My dear Egbert, between nearly killing a gardener's boy and altogether killing a Canon there is a wide difference. No doubt you have often felt a temporary desire to kill a gardener's boy; you have never given way to it, and I respect you for your self-control. But I don't suppose you have ever wanted to kill an octogenarian Canon. Besides, as far as we know, there had never been any quarrel or disagreement between the two men. The evidence at the inquest brought that out very clearly."

"Ah!" said Egbert, with the air of a man coming at last into a deferred inheritance of conversational importance, "that is precisely what I want to speak to you about."

He pushed away his coffee cup and drew a pocket-book from his inner breast-pocket. From the depths of the pocket-book he produced an envelope, and from the envelope he extracted a letter, closely written in a small, neat handwriting.

"One of the Canon's numerous letters to Aunt Adelaide," he explained, "written a few days before his death. Her memory was already failing when she received it, and I dare say she forgot the contents as soon as she had read it; otherwise, in the light of what subsequently happened, we should have heard something of this letter before now. If it had been produced at the inquest I fancy it would have made some difference in the course of affairs. The evidence, as you remarked just now, choked off suspicion against Sebastien by disclosing an utter absence of anything that could be considered a motive or provocation for the crime, if crime there was.

"Oh, read the letter," said Sir Lulworth impatiently.

"It's a long rambling affair, like most of his letters in his later years," said Egbert. "I'll read the part that bears immediately on the mystery.

"'I very much fear I shall have to get rid of Sebastien. He cooks divinely, but he has the temper of a fiend or an anthropoid ape, and I am really in bodily fear of him. We had a dispute the other day as to the correct sort of lunch to be served on Ash Wednesday, and I got so irritated and annoyed at his conceit and obstinacy that at last I threw a cupful of coffee in his face and called him at the same time an impudent jackanapes. Very little of the coffee went actually in his face, but I have never seen a human being show such deplorable lack of self-control. I laughed at the threat of killing me that he spluttered out in his rage, and thought the whole thing would blow over, but I have several times since caught him scowling and muttering in a highly unpleasant fashion, and lately I have fancied that he was dogging my footsteps about the grounds, particularly when I walk of an evening in the Italian Garden.'

"It was on the steps in the Italian Garden that the body was found," commented Egbert, and resumed reading.

"'I dare say the danger is imaginary; but I shall feel more at ease when he has quitted my service.'"

Egbert paused for a moment at the conclusion of the extract; then, as his uncle made no remark, he added: "If lack of motive was the only factor that saved Sebastien from prosecution I fancy this letter will put a different complexion on matters."

"Have you shown it to any one else?" asked Sir Lulworth, reaching out his hand for the incriminating piece of paper.

"No," said Egbert, handing it across the table, "I thought I would tell you about it first. Heavens, what are you doing?"

Egbert's voice rose almost to a scream. Sir Lulworth had flung the paper well and truly into the glowing centre of the grate. The small, neat handwriting shrivelled into black flaky nothingness.

"What on earth did you do that for?" gasped Egbert. "That letter was our one piece of evidence to connect Sebastien with the crime."

"That is why I destroyed it," said Sir Lulworth.

"But why should you want to shield him?" cried Egbert; "the man is a common murderer."

"A common murderer, possibly, but a very uncommon cook."

Twenty Minutes

JAMES SALTER

This happened near Carbondale to a woman named Jane Vare. I met her once at a party. She was sitting on a couch with her arms stretched out on either side and a drink in one hand. We talked about dogs.

She had an old greyhound. She'd bought him to save his life, she said. At the tracks they put them down rather than feed them when they stopped winning, sometimes three or four together, threw them in the back of a truck and drove to the dump. This dog was named Phil. He was stiff and nearly blind, but she admired his dignity. He sometimes lifted his leg against the wall, almost as high as the door handle, but he had a fine face.

Tack on the kitchen table, mud on the wide-board floor. In she strode like a young groom in a worn jacket and boots. She had what they called a good seat and ribbons layered like feathers on the wall. Her father had lived in Ireland where they rode into the dining room on Sunday morning and the host died fallen on the bed in full attire. Her own life had become like that. Money and dents in the side of her nearly new Swedish car. Her husband had been gone for a year.

Around Carbondale the river drops down and widens. There's a spidery trestle bridge, many times repainted, and they used to mine coal.

It was late in the afternoon and a shower had passed. The light was silvery and strange. Cars emerging from the rain drove with their headlights on and the windshield wipers going. The yellow road machinery parked along the shoulder seemed unnaturally bright.

It was the hour after work when irrigation water glistens high in the air, the hills have begun to darken and the meadows are like ponds.

She was riding alone up along the ridge. She was on a horse named

Fiume, big, well formed, but not very smart. He didn't hear things and sometimes stumbled when he walked. They had gone as far as the reservoir and then come back, riding to the west where the sun was going down. He could run, this horse. His hooves were pounding. The back of her shirt was filled with wind, the saddle was creaking, his huge neck was dark with sweat. They came along the ditch and toward a gate—they jumped it all the time.

At the last moment something happened. It took just an instant. He may have crossed his legs or hit a hole but he suddenly gave way. She went over his head and as if in slow motion he came after. He was upside down—she lay there watching him float toward her. He landed on her open lap.

It was as if she'd been hit by a car. She was stunned but felt unhurt. For a minute she imagined she might stand up and brush herself off.

The horse had gotten up. His legs were dirty and there was dirt on his back. In the silence she could hear the clink of the bridle and even the water flowing in the ditch. All around her were meadows and stillness. She felt sick to her stomach. It was all broken down there—she knew it although she could feel nothing. She knew she had some time. Twenty minutes, they always said.

The horse was pulling at some grass. She rose to her elbows and was immediately dizzy. "God damn you " she called. She was nearly crying. "Git! Go home!" Someone might see the empty saddle. She closed her eyes and tried to think. Somehow she could not believe it—nothing that had happened was true.

It was that way the morning they came and told her Privet had been hurt. The foreman was waiting in the pasture. "Her leg's broken," he said.

"How did it happen?"

He didn't know. "It looks like she got kicked," he guessed. The horse was lying under a tree. She knelt and stroked its boardlike nose. The large eyes seemed to be looking elsewhere. The vet would be driving up from Catherine Store trailing a plume of dust, but it turned out to be a long time before he came. He parked a little way off and walked over. Afterward he said what she had known he would say, they were going to have to put her down.

She lay remembering that. The day had ended. Lights were appearing in parts of distant houses. The six o'clock news was on. Far below she could see the hayfield of Piñones and much closer, a hundred yards off, a truck. It belonged to someone trying to build a house down there. It was upon blocks, it didn't run. There were other houses within a mile or so. On the other side of the ridge the metal roof, hidden in trees, of old man Vaughn who had once owned all of this and now could hardly walk. Further west the beautiful tan adobe Bill Millinger built before he went broke or whatever it was. He had wonderful taste. The house had the peeled log ceilings of the Southwest, Navajo rugs, and fireplaces in every room. Wide views of the mountains through windows of tinted glass. Anyone who knew enough to build a house like that knew everything.

She had given the famous dinner for him, unforgettable night. The clouds had been blowing off the top of Sopris all day, then came the snow. They talked in front of the fire. There were wine bottles crowded on the mantle and everyone in good clothes. Outside the snow poured down. She was wearing silk pants and her hair was loose. In the end she stood with him near the doorway to her kitchen. She was filled with warmth and a little drunk, was he?

He was watching her finger on the edge of his jacket lapel. Her heart thudded. "You're not going to make me spend the night alone?" she asked.

He had blond hair and small ears close to his head. "Oh . . ." he began. "What?"

"Don't you know? I'm the other way."

Which way, she insisted. It was such a waste. The roads were almost closed, the house lost in snow. She began to plead—she couldn't help it—and then became angry. The silk pants, the furniture, she hated it all.

In the morning his car was outside. She found him in the kitchen making breakfast. He'd slept on the couch, combed his longish hair with his fingers. On his cheeks was a blond stubble. "Sleep well, darling?" he asked.

Sometimes it was the other way around—in Saratoga in the bar where the idol was the tall Englishman who had made so much money at the sales. Did she live there? he asked. When you were close his eyes looked watery but in that English voice which was so pure, "It's marvelous to come to a place and see someone like you," he said.

She hadn't really decided whether to stay or leave and she had a drink with him. He smoked a cigarette.

"You haven't heard about those?" she said.

"No, what about them?"

"They'll give thee cancer."

"Thee?"

"It's what the Quakers say."

"Are you really a Quaker?"

"Oh, back a ways."

He had her by the elbow. "Do you know what I'd like? I'd like to fuck thee," he said.

She bent her arm to remove it.

"I mean it," he said. "Tonight."

"Some other time," she told him.

"I don't have another time. My wife's coming tomorrow, I only have tonight."

"That's too bad. I have every night."

She hadn't forgotten him, though she'd forgotten his name. His shirt had elegant blue stripes. "Oh, damn you," she suddenly cried. It was the horse. He hadn't gone. He was over by the fence. She began to call him, "Here, boy. Come here," she begged. He wouldn't move.

She didn't know what to do. Five minutes had passed, perhaps longer. Oh, God, she said, oh, Lord, oh God our Father. She could see the long stretch of road that came up from the highway, the unpaved surface very pale. Someone would come up that road and not turn off. The disastrous road. She had been driving it that day with her husband. There was something he had been meaning to tell her, Henry said, his head tilted back at a funny angle. He was making a change in his life. Her heart took a skip. He was breaking off with Mara, he said.

There was a silence.

Finally she said, "With who?"

He realized his mistake. "The girl who . . . in the architect's office. She's the draftsman."

"What do you mean, breaking it off?" It was hard for her to speak. She was looking at him as one would look at a fugitive.

"You knew about that, didn't you? I was sure you knew. Anyway it's over. I wanted to tell you. I wanted to put it all behind us."

"Stop the car," she said. "Don't say any more, stop here." He drove alongside her trying to explain but she was picking up the biggest stones she could find and throwing them at the car. Then she cut unsteadily across the fields, the sage bushes scratching her legs.

When she heard him drive up after midnight she jumped from bed and shouted from the window, "No, no! Go away!"

"What I never understood is why no one told me," she used to say. "They were supposed to be my friends."

Some failed, some divorced, some got shot in trailers like Doug Portis who had the excavation business and was seeing the policeman's wife. Some like her husband moved to Santa Barbara and became the extra man at dinner parties.

It was growing dark. Help me, someone, help me, she kept repeating. Someone would come, they had to. She tried not to be afraid. She thought of her father who could explain life in one sentence, "They knock you down and you get up. That's what it's all about." He recognized only one virtue. He would hear what had happened, that she merely lay there. She had to try to get home, even if she went only a little way, even a few yards.

Pushing with her palms she managed to drag herself, calling the horse as she did. Perhaps she could grab a stirrup if he came. She tried to find him. In the last of the light she saw the fading cottonwoods but the rest had disappeared. The fence posts were gone. The meadows had drifted away.

She tried to play a game, she wasn't lying near the ditch, she was in another place, in all the places, on Eleventh Street in that first apartment above the big skylight of the restaurant, the morning in Sausalito with the maid knocking on the door and Henry trying to call in Spanish, not now, not now! And postcards on the marble of the dresser and things they'd bought. Outside the hotel in Haiti the cabdrivers were leaning on their cars and calling out in soft voices, Hey, *blanc*, you like to go to a nice beach? Ibo beach? They wanted thirty dollars for the day, they said, which meant the price was probably about five. Go ahead, give it to him, she said. She could be there so easily, or in her own bed reading on a stormy day with the rain gusting against the window and the dogs near her feet. On the desk were photographs: horses, and her jumping, and one of her father at lunch outside when he was thirty, at Burning Tree. She had called him one day—she was getting married, she said. Married, he said, to whom? A man named Henry Vare, she said, who is wearing a beautiful suit, she wanted to add, and has wonderful wide hands. Tomorrow, she said.

"Tomorrow?" He sounded farther away. "Are you sure you're doing the right thing?"

"Absolutely."

"God bless you," he said.

That summer was the one they came here—it was where Henry had been living—and bought the place past the Macraes'. All year they fixed up the house and Henry started his landscaping business. They had their own world. Up through the fields in nothing but shorts, the earth warm under their feet, skin flecked with dirt from swimming in the ditch where the water was chilly and deep, like two sun-bleached children but far better, the screen door slamming, things on the kitchen table, catalogues, knives, new everything. Autumn with its brilliant blue skies and the first storms coming up from the west.

It was dark now, everywhere except up by the ridge. There were all the things she had meant to do, to go East again, to visit certain friends, to live a year by the sea. She could not believe it was over, that she was going to be left here on the ground.

Suddenly she started to call for help, wildly, the cords standing out in her neck. In the darkness the horse raised his head. She kept shouting. She already knew it was a thing she would pay for, she was loosing the demonic. At last she stopped. She could hear the pounding of her heart and beyond that something else. Oh, God, she began to beg. Lying there she heard the first solemn drumbeats, terrible and slow.

Whatever it was, however bad, I'm going to do it as my father would, she thought. Hurriedly she tried to imagine him and as she was doing it a length of something went through her, something iron. In one unbelievable instant she realized the power of it, where it would take her, what it meant.

Her face was wet and she was shivering. Now it was here. Now you must do it, she realized. She knew there was a God, she hoped it. She shut her eyes. When she opened them it had begun, so utterly unforeseen and with such speed. She saw something dark moving along the fence line. It was her pony, the one her father had given her long ago, her black pony going home, across the broad fields, across the grassland. Wait, wait for me! She began to scream.

Lights were jerking up and down along the ditch. It was a pickup coming over the uneven ground, the man who was sometimes building the lone house and a high school girl named Fern who worked at the golf course. They had the windows up and, turning, their lights swept close to the horse but they didn't see him. They saw him later, coming back in silence, the big handsome face in the darkness looking at them dumbly.

"He's saddled," Fern said in surprise.

He was standing calmly. That was how they found her. They put her in the back—she was limp, there was dirt in her ears—and drove into Glenwood at eighty miles an hour, not even stopping to call ahead.

That wasn't the right thing, as someone said later. It would have been better if they had gone the other way, about three miles up the road to Bob Lamb's. He was the vet but he might have done something. Whatever you said, he was the best doctor around.

They would have pulled in with the headlights blooming on the white farmhouse as happened so many nights. Everyone knew Bob Lamb. There were a hundred dogs, his own among them, buried in back of the barn.

A & P

JOHN UPDIKE

n walks these three girls in nothing but bathing suits. I'm in the second checkout slot, with my back to the door, so I don't see them until they're over by the bread. The one that caught my eye first was the one in the plaid green two-piece. She was a chunky kid, with a good tan and a sweet broad soft-looking can with those two crescents of white just under it, where the sun never seems to hit, at the top of the backs of her legs. I stood there with my hand on a box of Hi Ho crackers trying to remember if I rang it up or not. I ring it up again and the customer starts giving me hell. She's one of these cash-register-watchers, a witch about fifty with rouge on her cheekbones and no eyebrows, and I know it made her day to trip me up. She'd been watching cash registers for fifty years and probably never seen a mistake before.

By the time I got her feathers smoothed and her goodies into a bag—she gives me a little snort in passing, if she'd been born at the right time they would have hung her over in Salem—by the time I get her on her way the girls had circled around the bread and were coming back, without a pushcart, back my way along the counters, in the aisle between the checkouts and the Special bins. They didn't even have shoes on. There was this chunky one, with the two-piece—it was bright green and the seams on the bra were still sharp and her belly was still pretty pale so I guessed she just got it (the suit)—there was this one, with one of those chubby berry-faces, the lips all bunched together under her nose, this one, and a tall one, with black hair that hadn't quite frizzed right, and one of these sunburns right across under the eyes, and a chin that was too long—you know, the kind of girl that other girls think is very "striking" and "attractive" but never quite makes it, as they very well know, which is why they like her so much—and then the third one, who wasn't quite so tall. She was the queen. She kind of led them, the other two peeking around and hunching over a little. She didn't look around, not this queen, she just walked straight on slowly, on these long white prima-donna legs. She came down a little hard on her heels, as if she didn't walk in her bare feet that much, putting down her heels and then letting the weight move along to her toes as if she was testing the floor with every step, putting a little deliberate extra action into it. You never know for sure how girls' minds work (do you really think it's a mind in there or just a little buzz like a bee in a glass jar?) but you got the idea she had talked the other two into coming in here with her, and now she was showing them how to do it, walk slow and hold yourself straight.

She had on a kind of dirty-pink—beige maybe, I don't know—bathing suit with a little nubble all over it and, what got me, the straps were down. They were off her shoulders looped loose around the cool tops of her arms, and I guess as a result the suit had slipped a little on her, so all around the top of the cloth there was this shining rim. If it hadn't been there you wouldn't have known there could have been anything whiter than those shoulders. With the straps pushed off, there was nothing between the top of the suit and the top of her head except just *her*, this clean bare plane of the top of her chest down from the shoulder bones like a dented sheet of metal tilted in the light. I mean, it was more than pretty.

She had sort of oaky hair that the sun and salt had bleached, done up in a bun that was unravelling, and a kind of prim face. Walking into the A & P with your straps down, I suppose it's the only kind of face you *can* have. She held her head so high her neck, coming up out of those white shoulders, looked kind of stretched, but I didn't mind. The longer her neck was, the more of her there was.

She must have felt in the corner of her eye me and over my shoulder Stokesie in the first slot watching, but she didn't tip. Not this queen. She kept her eyes moving across the racks, and stopped, and turned so slow it made my stomach rub the inside of my apron, and buzzed to the other two, who kind of huddled against her for relief, and then they all three of them went up the cat-and-dog-food-breakfast-cereal-macaroni-rice-raisins-seasonings-spreads-spaghetti-soft-drinks-crackers-and-cookies aisle. From my slot I can look straight up this aisle to the meat counter, and I watched them all the way. The fat one with the tan sort of fumbled with the cookies, but on second thought she put the package back. The sheep pushing their carts down the aisle—the girls were walking against the usual traffic (not that we have one-way signs or anything)—were pretty hilarious. You could see them, when Queenie's white shoulders dawned on them, kind of jerk, or hop, or hiccup, but their eyes snapped back to their own baskets and on they pushed. I bet you could set off dynamite in an A & P and the people would by and large keep reaching and checking oatmeal off their lists and muttering, "Let me see, there was a third thing, began with A, asparagus, no, ah, yes, applesauce!" or whatever it is they do mutter. But there was no doubt, this jiggled them. A few houseslaves in pin curlers even looked around after pushing their carts past to make sure what they had seen was correct.

You know, it's one thing to have a girl in a bathing suit down on the beach, where what with the glare nobody can look at each other much anyway, and another thing in the cool of the A & P, under the fluorescent lights, against all those stacked packages, with her feet paddling along naked over our checkerboard green-and-cream rubber-tile floor.

"Oh, Daddy," Stokesie said beside me. "I feel so faint."

"Darling," I said. "Hold me tight." Stokesie's married, with two babies chalked up on his fuselage already, but as far as I can tell that's the only difference. He's twenty-two, and I was nineteen this April.

"Is it done?" he asks, the responsible married man finding his voice. I forgot to say he thinks he's going to be manager some sunny day, maybe in 1990 when it's called the Great Alexandrov and Petrooshki Tea Company or something.

What he meant was, our town is five miles from a beach, with a big summer colony out on the Point, but we're right in the middle of town, and the women generally put on a shirt or shorts or something before they get out of the car into the street. And anyway these are usually women with six children and varicose veins mapping their legs and nobody, including them, could care less. As I say, we're right in the middle of town, and if you stand at our front doors you can see two banks and the Congregational church and the newspaper store and three real-estate offices and about twenty-seven old freeloaders tearing up Central Street because the sewer broke again. It's not as if we're on the Cape; we're north of Boston and there's people in this town haven't seen the ocean for twenty years.

The girls had reached the meat counter and were asking McMahon something. He pointed, they pointed, and they shuffled out of sight behind a pyramid of Diet Delight peaches. All that was left for us to see was old

McMahon patting his mouth and looking after them sizing up their joints. Poor kids, I began to feel sorry for them, they couldn't help it.

Now here comes the sad part of the story, at least my family says it's sad, but I don't think it's so sad myself. The store's pretty empty, it being Thursday afternoon, so there was nothing much to do except lean on the register and wait for the girls to show up again. The whole store was like a pinball machine and I didn't know which tunnel they'd come out of. After a while they come around out of the far aisle, around the lightbulbs, records at discount of the Caribbean Six or Tony Martin Sings or some such gunk you wonder they waste the wax on, six-packs of candy bars, and plastic toys done up in cellophane that fall apart when a kid looks at them anyway. Around they come, Queenie still leading the way, and holding a little gray jar in her hand. Slots Three through Seven are unmanned and I could see her wondering between Stokes and me, but Stokesie with his usual luck draws an old party in baggy gray pants who stumbles up with four giant cans of pineapple juice (what do these bums *do* with all that pineapple juice? I've often asked myself) so the girls come to me. Queenie puts down the jar and I take it into my fingers icy cold. Kingfish Fancy Herring Snacks in Pure Sour Cream: 49¢. Now her hands are empty, not a ring or a bracelet, bare as God made them, and I wonder where the money's coming from. Still with that prim look she lifts a folded dollar bill out of the hollow at the center of her nubbled pink top. The jar went heavy in my hand. Really, I thought that was so cute.

Then everybody's luck begins to run out. Lengel comes in from haggling with a truck full of cabbages on the lot and is about to scuttle into that door marked MANAGER behind which he hides all day when the girls touch his eye. Lengel's pretty dreary, teaches Sunday school and the rest, but he doesn't miss that much. He comes over and says, "Girls, this isn't the beach."

Queenie blushes, though maybe it's just a brush of sunburn I was noticing for the first time, now that she was so close. "My mother asked me to pick up a jar of herring snacks." Her voice kind of startled me, the way voices do when you see the people first, coming out so flat and dumb yet kind of tony, too, the way it ticked over "pick up" and "snacks." All of a sudden I slid right down her voice into her living room. Her father and the other men were standing around in ice-cream coats and bow ties and the women were in sandals picking up herring snacks on toothpicks off a big glass plate and they were all holding drinks the color of water with olives and sprigs of mint in them. When my parents have somebody over they get lemonade and if it's a real racy affair Schlitz in tall glasses with "They'll Do It Every Time" cartoons stencilled on.

"That's all right," Lengel said. "But this isn't the beach." His repeating this struck me as funny, as if it had just occurred to him, and he had been thinking all these years the A & P was a great big dune and he was the head lifeguard. He didn't like my smiling—as I say, he doesn't miss much—but he concentrates on giving the girls that sad Sunday-school-superintendent stare.

Queenie's blush is no sunburn now, and the plump one in plaid, that I liked better from the back—a really sweet can—pipes up. "We weren't doing any shopping. We just came in for the one thing."

"That makes no difference," Lengel tells her, and I could see from the way his eyes went that he hadn't noticed she was wearing a two-piece before. "We want you decently dressed when you come in here."

"We *are* decent," Queenie says suddenly, her lower lip pushing, getting sore now that she remembers her place, a place from which the crowd that runs the A & P must look pretty crummy. Fancy Herring Snacks flashed in her very blue eyes.

"Girls, I don't want to argue with you. After this come in here with your shoulders covered. It's our policy." He turns his back. That's policy for you. Policy is what the kingpins want. What the others want is juvenile delinquency.

All this while, the customers had been showing up with their carts but, you know, sheep, seeing a scene, they had all bunched up on Stokesie, who shook open a paper bag as gently as peeling a peach, not wanting to miss a word. I could feel in the silence everybody getting nervous, most of all Lengel, who asks me, "Sammy, have you rung up their purchase?"

I thought and said "No" but it wasn't about that I was thinking. I go through the punches, 4, 9, GROC, TOT—it's more complicated than you think, and after you do it often enough, it begins to make a little song, that you hear words to, in my case "Hello (*bing*) there, you (*gung*) hap-py *pee*-pul (*splat*) "—the *splat* being the drawer flying out. I uncrease the bill, tenderly as you may imagine, it just having come from between the two smoothest scoops of vanilla I had ever known were there, and pass a half and a penny into her narrow pink palm, and nestle the herrings in a bag and twist its neck and hand it over, all the time thinking.

The girls, and who'd blame them, are in a hurry to get out, so I say "I quit" to Lengel quick enough for them to hear, hoping they'll stop and watch me, their unsuspected hero. They keep right on going, into the electric eye; the door flies open and they flicker across the lot to their car, Queenie and Plaid and Big Tall Goony-Goony (not that as raw material she was so bad), leaving me with Lengel and a kink in his eyebrow.

"Did you say something, Sammy?"

"I said I quit."

"I thought you did."

"You didn't have to embarrass them."

"It was they who were embarrassing us."

I started to say something that came out "Fiddle-de-doo." It's a saying of my grandmother's, and I know she would have been pleased.

"I don't think you know what you're saying," Lengel said.

"I know you don't," I said. "But I do." I pull the bow at the back of my apron and start shrugging it off my shoulders. A couple customers that had been heading for my slot begin to knock against each other, like scared pigs in a chute.

Lengel sighs and begins to look very patient and old and gray. He's been a friend of my parents for years. "Sammy, you don't want to do this to your mom and dad," he tells me. It's true, I don't. But it seems to me that once you begin a gesture it's fatal not to go through with it. I fold the apron, "Sammy" stitched in red on the pocket, and put it on the counter, and drop the bow tie on top of it. The bow tie is theirs, if you've ever wondered. "You'll feel this for the rest of your life," Lengel says, and I know that's true, too, but remembering how he made that pretty girl blush makes me so scrunchy inside I punch the No Sale tab and the machine whirs "*pee*-pul" and the drawer splats out. One advantage to this scene taking place in summer, I can follow it up with a clean exit, there's no fumbling around getting your coat and galoshes, I just saunter into the electric eye in my white shirt that my mother ironed the night before, and the door heaves itself open, and outside the sunshine is skating around on the asphalt.

I look around for my girls, but they're gone, of course. There wasn't anybody but some young married screaming with her children about some candy they didn't get by the door of a powder-blue Falcon station wagon. Looking back in the big windows, over the bags of peat moss and aluminum lawn furniture stacked on the pavement, I could see Lengel in my place in the second slot, checking the sheep through. His face was dark gray and his back stiff, as if he'd just had an injection of iron, and my stomach kind of fell as I felt how hard the world was going to be to me from here on in.

The Use of Force

WILLIAM CARLOS WILLIAMS

They were new patients to me, all I had was the name, Olson. Please come down as soon as you can, my daughter is very sick.

When I arrived I was met by the mother, a big startled looking woman, very clean and apologetic who merely said, Is this the doctor? and let me in. In the back, she added. You must excuse us, doctor, we have her in the kitchen where it is warm. It is very damp here sometimes.

The child was fully dressed and sitting on her father's lap near the kitchen table. He tried to get up, but I motioned for him not to bother, took off my overcoat and started to look things over. I could see that they were all very nervous, eyeing me up and down distrustfully. As often, in such cases, they weren't telling me more than they had to, it was up to me to tell them; that's why they were spending three dollars on me.

The child was fairly eating me up with her cold, steady eyes, and no expression to her face whatever. She did not move and seemed, inwardly, quiet; an unusually attractive little thing, and as strong as a heifer in appearance. But her face was flushed, she was breathing rapidly, and I realized that she had a high fever. She had magnificent blonde hair, in profusion. One of those picture children often reproduced in advertising leaflets and the photogravure sections of the Sunday papers.

She's had a fever for three days, began the father, and we don't know what it comes from. My wife has given her things, you know, like people do, but it don't do no good. And there's been a lot of sickness around. So we tho't you'd better look her over and tell us what is the matter.

As doctors often do I took a trial shot at it as a point of departure. Has she had a sore throat?

Both parents answered me together, No . . . No, she says her throat don't hurt her.

Does your throat hurt you? added the mother to the child. But the little girl's expression didn't change, nor did she move her eyes from my face.

Have you looked?

I tried to, said the mother, but I couldn't see.

As it happens, we had been having a number of cases of diphtheria in the school to which this child went during that month and we were all, quite apparently, thinking of that, though no one had as yet spoken of the thing.

Well, I said, suppose we take a look at the throat first. I smiled in my best professional manner and asking for the child's first name I said, come on, Mathilda, open your mouth and let's take a look at your throat.

Nothing doing.

Aw, come on, I coaxed, just open your mouth wide and let me take a look. Look, I said opening both hands wide, I haven't anything in my hands. Just open up and let me see.

Such a nice man, put in the mother. Look how kind he is to you. Come on, do what he tells you to. He won't hurt you.

At that I ground my teeth in disgust. If only they wouldn't use the word "hurt" I might be able to get somewhere. But I did not allow myself to be hurried or disturbed, but speaking quietly and slowly I approached the child again.

As I moved my chair a little nearer, suddenly with one catlike movement both her hands clawed instinctively for my eyes and she almost reached them too. In fact she knocked my glasses flying and they fell, though unbroken, several feet away from me on the kitchen floor.

Both the mother and father almost turned themselves inside out in embarrassment and apology. You bad girl, said the mother, taking her and shaking her by one arm, Look what you've done. The nice man.

For heaven's sake, I broke in. Don't call me a nice man to her. I'm here to look at her throat on the chance that she might have diphtheria and possibly die of it. But that's nothing to her. Look here, I said to the child, we're going to look at your throat. You're old enough to understand what I'm saying. Will you open it now by yourself or shall we have to open it for you?

Not a move. Even her expression hadn't changed. Her breaths however were coming faster and faster. Then the battle began. I had to do it. I had to have a throat culture for her own protection. But first I told the parents that it was entirely up to them. I explained the danger but said that I would not insist on a throat examination so long as they would take the responsibility.

If you don't do what the doctor says you'll have to go to the hospital, the mother admonished her severely.

Oh yeah? I had to smile to myself. After all, I had already fallen in love with the savage brat, the parents were contemptible to me. In the ensuing struggle they grew more and more abject, crushed, exhausted while she surely rose to magnificent heights of insane fury of effort bred of her terror of me.

The father tried his best, and he was a big man but the fact that she was his daughter, his shame at her behavior and his dread of hurting her made him release her just at the critical moment several times when I had almost achieved success, till I wanted to kill him. But his dread also that she might have diphtheria made him tell me to go on, go on though he himself was almost fainting, while the mother moved back and forth behind us raising and lowering her hands in an agony of apprehension.

Put her in front of you on your lap, I ordered, and hold both her wrists.

But as soon as he did the child let out a scream. Don't, you're hurting me. Let go of my hands. Let them go I tell you. Then she shrieked terrifyingly, hysterically. Stop it! Stop it! You're killing me!

Do you think she can stand it, doctor! said the mother.

You get out, said the husband to his wife. Do you want her to die of diphtheria?

Come on now, hold her, I said.

Then I grasped the child's head with my left hand and tried to get the wooden tongue depressor between her teeth. She fought, with clenched teeth, desperately! But now I also had grown furious—at a child. I tried to hold myself down but I couldn't. I know how to expose a throat for inspection. And I did my best. When finally I got the wooden spatula behind the last teeth and just the point of it into the mouth cavity, she opened up for an instant but before I could see anything she came down again and gripping the wooden blade between her molars she reduced it to splinters before I could get it out again.

Aren't you ashamed, the mother yelled at her. Aren't you ashamed to act like that in front of the doctor?

Get me a smooth-handled spoon of some sort, I told the mother. We're going through with this. The child's mouth was already bleeding. Her tongue was cut and she was screaming in wild hysterical shrieks. Perhaps I should have desisted and come back in an hour or more. No doubt it would have been better. But I have seen at least two children lying dead in bed of neglect in such cases, and feeling that I must get a diagnosis now or never I went at it again. But the worst of it was that I too had got beyond reason. I could have torn the child apart in my own fury and enjoyed it. It was a pleasure to attack her. My face was burning with it.

The damned little brat must be protected against her own idiocy, one says to one's self at such times. Others must be protected against her. It is social necessity. And all these things are true. But a blind fury, a feeling of adult shame, bred of a longing for muscular release are the operatives. One goes on to the end.

In a final unreasoning assault I overpowered the child's neck and jaws. I forced the heavy silver spoon back of her teeth and down her throat till she gagged. And there it was—both tonsils covered with membrane. She had fought valiantly to keep me from knowing her secret. She had been hiding that sore throat for three days at least and lying to her parents in order to escape just such an outcome as this.

Now truly she was furious. She had been on the defensive before but now she attacked. Tried to get off her father's lap and fly at me while tears of defeat blinded her eyes.

Bullet in the Brain

TOBIAS WOLFF

Anders couldn't get to the bank until just before it closed, so of course the line was endless and he got stuck behind two women whose loud, stupid conversation put him in a murderous temper. He was never in the best of tempers anyway, Anders—a book critic known for the weary, elegant savagery with which he dispatched almost everything he reviewed.

With the line still doubled around the rope, one of the tellers stuck a "POSITION CLOSED" sign in her window and walked to the back of the bank, where she leaned against a desk and began to pass the time with a man shuffling papers. The women in front of Anders broke off their conversation and watched the teller with hatred. "Oh, that's nice," one of them said. She turned to Anders and added, confident of his accord, "One of those little human touches that keep us coming back for more."

Anders had conceived his own towering hatred of the teller, but he immediately turned it on the presumptuous crybaby in front of him. "Damned unfair," he said. "Tragic, really. If they're not chopping off the wrong leg, or bombing your ancestral village, they're closing their positions."

She stood her ground. "I didn't say it was tragic," she said. "I just think it's a pretty lousy way to treat your customers."

"Unforgivable," Anders said. "Heaven will take note."

She sucked in her cheeks but stared past him and said nothing. Anders saw that the other woman, her friend, was looking in the same direction. And then the tellers stopped what they were doing, and the customers slowly turned, and silence came over the bank. Two men wearing black ski masks and blue business suits were standing to the side of the door. One of them had a pistol pressed against the guard's neck. The guard's eyes were closed, and his lips were moving. The other man had a sawed-off shotgun. "Keep your big mouth shut!" the man with the pistol said, though no one had spoken a word. "One of you tellers hits the alarm, you're all dead meat. Got it?"

The tellers nodded.

"Oh, bravo," Anders said. *"Dead meat."* He turned to the woman in front of him. "Great script, eh? The stern, brass-knuckled poetry of the dangerous classes."

She looked at him with drowning eyes.

The man with the shotgun pushed the guard to his knees. He handed the shotgun to his partner and yanked the guard's wrists up behind his back and locked them together with a pair of handcuffs. He toppled him onto the floor with a kick between the shoulder blades. Then he took his shotgun back and went over to the security gate at the end of the counter. He was short and heavy and moved with peculiar slowness, even torpor. "Buzz him in," his partner said. The man with the shotgun opened the gate and sauntered along the line of tellers, handing each of them a Hefty bag. When he came to the empty position he looked over at the man with the pistol, who said, "Whose slot is that?"

Anders watched the teller. She put her hand to her throat and turned to the man she'd been talking to. He nodded. "Mine," she said.

"Then get your ugly ass in gear and fill that bag."

"There you go," Anders said to the woman in front of him. "Justice is done."

"Hey! Bright boy! Did I tell you to talk?"

"No," Anders said.

"Then shut your trap."

"Did you hear that?" Anders said. "'Bright boy.' Right Out of 'The Killers.'"

"Please be quiet," the woman said.

"Hey, you deaf or what?" The man with the pistol walked over to Anders. He poked the weapon into Anders' gut. "You think I'm playing games?"

"No," Anders said, but the barrel tickled like a stiff finger and he had to fight back the titters. He did this by making himself stare into the man's eyes, which were clearly visible behind the holes in the mask: pale blue and rawly red-rimmed. The man's left eyelid kept twitching. He breathed out a piercing, ammoniac smell that shocked Anders more than anything that had happened, and he was beginning to develop a sense of unease when the man prodded him again with the pistol.

"You like me, bright boy?" he said. "You want to suck my dick?"

"No," Anders said.

"Then stop looking at me."

Anders fixed his gaze on the man's shiny wing-tip shoes.

"Not down there. Up there." He stuck the pistol under Anders' chin and pushed it upward until Anders was looking at the ceiling.

Anders had never paid much attention to that part of the bank, a pompous old building with marble floors and counters and pillars, and gilt scrollwork over the tellers' cages. The domed ceiling had been decorated with mythological figures whose fleshy, toga-draped ugliness Anders had taken in at a glance many years earlier and afterward declined to notice. Now he had no choice but to scrutinize the painter's work. It was even worse than he remembered, and all of it executed with the utmost gravity. The artist had a few tricks up his sleeve and used them again and again—a certain rosy blush on the underside of the clouds, a coy backward glance on the faces of the cupids and fauns. The ceiling was crowded with various dramas, but the one that caught Anders' eye was Zeus and Europa—portrayed, in this rendition, as a bull ogling a cow from behind a haystack. To make the cow sexy, the painter had canted her hips suggestively and given her long, droopy eyelashes through which she gazed back at the bull with sultry welcome. The bull wore a smirk and his eyebrows were arched. If there'd been a bubble coming out of his mouth, it would have said, "Hubba hubba."

"What's so funny, bright boy?"

"Nothing."

"You think I'm comical? You think I'm some kind of clown?"

"No."

"You think you can fuck with me?"

"No."

"Fuck with me again, you're history. *Capiche?*"

Anders burst out laughing. He covered his mouth with both hands and said, "I'm sorry, I'm sorry," then snorted helplessly through his fingers and said, "*Capiche* oh, God, *capiche*," and at that the man with the pistol raised the pistol and shot Anders right in the head.

The bullet smashed Anders' skull and ploughed through his brain and exited behind his right ear, scattering shards of bone into the cerebral cortex, the corpus callosum, back toward the basal ganglia, and down into the thal-amus. But before all this occurred, the first appearance of the bullet in the cerebrum set off a crackling chain of iron transports and neuro-transmis-sions. Because of their peculiar origin these traced a peculiar pattern, flukishly calling to life a summer afternoon some forty years past, and long since lost to memory. After striking the cranium the bullet was moving at 900 feet per second, a pathetically sluggish, glacial pace compared to the synaptic lightning that flashed around it. Once in the brain, that is, the bul-let came under the mediation of brain time, which gave Anders plenty of leisure to contemplate the scene that, in a phrase he would have abhorred, "passed before his eyes."

It is worth noting what Anders did not remember, given what he did remember. He did not remember his first lover, Sherry, or what he had most madly loved about her, before it came to irritate him—her unembarrassed carnality, and especially the cordial way she had with his unit, which she called Mr. Mole, as in, "Uh-oh, looks like Mr. Mole wants to play," and, "let's hide Mr. Mole!" Anders did not remember his wife, whom he had also loved before she exhausted him with her predictability, or his daughter, now a sullen professor of economics at Dartmouth. He did not remember standing just outside his daughter's door as she lectured her bear about his naughti-ness and described the truly appalling punishments Paws would receive unless he changed his ways. He did not remember a single line of the hun-dreds of poems he had committed to memory in his youth so that he could give himself the shivers at will—not "Silent, upon a peak in Darien," or "My God, I heard this day," or "All my pretty ones? Did you say all? O hell-kite All?" None of these did he remember; not one. Anders did not remember his dying mother saying of his father, "I should have stabbed him in his sleep."

He did not remember Professor Josephs telling his class how Athenian prisoners in Sicily had been released if they could recite Aeschylus, and then reciting Aeschylus himself, right there, in the Greek. Anders did not remem-ber how his eyes had burned at those sounds. He did not remember the surprise of seeing a college classmate's name on the jacket of a novel not long after they graduated, or the respect he had felt after reading the book. He did not remember the pleasure of giving respect.

Nor did Anders remember seeing a woman leap to her death from the building opposite his own just days after his daughter was born. He did not remember shouting, "Lord have mercy!" He did not remember deliberately crashing his father's car into a tree, or having his ribs kicked in by three policemen at an anti-war rally, or waking himself up with laughter. He did not remember when he began to regard the heap of books on his desk with boredom and dread, or when he grew angry at writers for writing them. He did not remember when everything began to remind him of something else.

This is what he remembered. Heat. A baseball field. Yellow grass, the whirr of insects, himself leaning against a tree as the boys of the neighborhood gather for a pickup game. He looks on as the others argue the relative genius of Mantle and Mays. They have been worrying this subject all summer, and it has become tedious to Anders: an oppression, like the heat.

Then the last two boys arrive, Coyle and a cousin of his from Mississippi. Anders has never met Coyle's cousin before and will never see him again. He says hi with the rest but takes no further notice of him until they've chosen sides and someone asks the cousin what position he wants to play. "Shortstop," the boy says. "Short's the best position they is." Anders turns and looks at him. He wants to hear Coyle's cousin repeat what he's just said, but he knows better than to ask. The others will think he's being a jerk, ragging the kid for his grammar. But that isn't it, not at all—it's that Anders is strangely roused, elated, by those final two words, their pure unexpectedness and their music. He takes the field in a trance, repeating them to himself.

The bullet is already in the brain; it won't be outrun forever, or charmed to a halt. In the end it will do its work and leave the troubled skull behind, dragging its comet's tail of memory and hope and talent and love into the marble hall of commerce. That can't be helped. But for now Anders can still make time. Time for the shadows to lengthen on the grass, time for the tethered dog to bark at the flying ball, time for the boy in right field to smack his sweat-blackened mitt and softly chant, *They is, they is, they is.*

About the Authors

STEVE ALMOND Born in 1966, Almond spent seven years as a newspaper reporter before turning to fiction writing. He writes novels, short stories, and commentaries. He has published stories in *Playboy, Tin House,* and *Ploughshares,* among others. His stories have won the Pushcart Prize and been anthologized in *New Stories from the South.*

JOHN BARTH Born in 1930, Barth has published numerous novels and short stories. His work is postmodernist and experimental. Some of his best-known stories are metafiction. They explore the transaction between the writer and the reader, examining the effect of writing on the writer and the effect of reading on the reader and the interplay between the two.

RICHARD BAUSCH After early starts as a stand up comic and a singer–song writer, Richard Bausch began writing and publishing to great acclaim. He has published ten novels as well as several important collections of short stories, essays, and novellas. His stories have been included in prize-winning anthologies such as *The Best American Short Stories*, Pushcart, and O'Henry. In 2004, he was awarded the PEN/Malmud Award for Excellence in the Short Story.

JORGES LUIS BORGES (1899–1986) Born in Argentina, and raised in Italy, Borges returned to Argentina as an adult. He wrote poetry, criticism, essays, and is best known for his short stories. He lived for most of the twentieth century and gained a prominent place in literary modernism. He was completely blind for the latter part of his adult life, and while this may have influenced, it did not hamper his work.

FREDERICK BUSCH (1941–2006) has written more than twenty-five books, mostly novels and short stories. He has received the PEN/Malamud award for his short fiction, won the National Jewish Book award, and been honored by the American Academy of Arts and Letters. He has also taught writing, and written about writing.

ROBERT OLEN BUTLER has published ten novels and two volumes of short stories. He won the 1993 Pulitzer Prize for *A Good Scent from a Strange Mountain*. He is the director of the Creative Writing Program at Florida State University.

RON CARLSON is the author of eight works of fiction. He has published several novels but is best known for his short stories. His work has appeared in the Best American Short Stories, The O'Henry Prize Series, and the Pushcart Prize Anthology. He was awarded a fellowship in Fiction from the National Endowment for the Arts. His life motto is "make haste to be kind," and this theme is evidenced in a variety of ways in his stories.

RAYMOND CARVER (1939–88) is considered a foremost writer of the postmodern period. His short stories appeared in respected journals and have been collected in several volumes, *Cathedral* and *What We Talk About When We Talk About Love* among them. He is best known for his minimalist, deceptively simple, voice-driven stories, although his later work has been characterized as more expansive and even optimistic. He was unique and famous enough to have been parodied in a New Yorker essay, "What We Talk About When We Talk About Doughnuts" by Michael Gerber and Jonathan Schwartz. Carver was awarded a Guggenheim Fellowship and twice received grants from the National Endowment for the Arts.

MICHAEL CHABON Born in 1963, Chabon has published both novels and short stories. He won the Pulitzer Prize in 2001 for *The Amazing Adventures of Kavalier & Clay*. His work has been praised for its inventiveness, scope, and graceful language. He co-wrote the screenplay for *Spider Man 2*.

ANTON CHEKHOV (1860–1904) is best known for his later plays with their bracing naturalistic style, and his shorts stories, of which there are hundreds. His unapologetically direct style was highly influential to later writers, and he is considered one of the world's preeminent short story writers. He was trained as a doctor, and it has been noted that he brings a clinical discernment to the limning of his characters and the details of the story.

KATE CHOPIN (1851–1904) Chopin enjoyed success for her short stories and sketches published regularly in periodicals of the day. In 1899 she published her novel *The Awakening*. This was largely condemned for its scandalous depiction of infidelity and adultery. Although the book gained popularity and even acclaim after a time, it effectively ended her writing career.

COLETTE (1873–1954) wrote more than fifty books—novels, stories, essays, and sketches. In her work she returned often to the theme of darkness in personal relationships, expressed in an explicit and intimate style. She lived mostly in Paris and led what some would consider a racy existence. Due to her lifestyle, she was refused Catholic rites when she died. She was, however, given a state funeral.

STEPHEN CRANE (1871–1900) Crane began his professional life as a freelance journalist, but soon began writing novels. He first published *Maggie: A Girl of the Streets* and then *The Red Badge of Courage*. He was an early practitioner of the social and ironic realism that would become so popular decades later. In addition to his novels, he wrote short stories and modernistic poetry. He traveled extensively and lived irreverently, before he finally settled in England. Tuberculosis killed him when he was still very young.

CHARLOTTE PERKINS GILMAN (1860–1935) Gilman attended the Rhode Island School of Design. She married, had a child and descended into a prolonged depression. After she recovered she wrote her well known story "The Yellow Wallpaper" partially as an expose and indictment of the treatment she received during her illness. In addition to novels and short stories, she wrote and lectured on feminist causes. Her second marriage was much happier.

ERNEST HEMINGWAY (1899–1961) was one of America's foremost writers. With an insistent style and a larger than life reputation, he was part of the "lost generation" and the modernist movement in fiction. He won the Nobel prize for Literature in 1954.

AMY HEMPEL was educated in California and at Columbia. Her stories have been anthologized, appeared in magazines such as *Vanity Fair* and *Harpers,* and been published in several collections, most recently, *The Dog of the Marriage: Stories.*

JAMES JOYCE (1882–1941) is one of the preeminent writers of the modern age, a forerunner of literary modernism. He published *Dubliners* in 1914. While some of the stories had appeared previously, there was great resistance to the collection as it was considered both too graphic and too negative and critical of its subjects. He was plagued by similar controversy most of his life. In later life he was mostly blind, and suffered greatly from ill-advised and unsuccessful eye operations to correct this. Joyce's genius and his far-reaching legacy, even beyond literature, cannot be overstated. As an illustration, the phrase "Three Quarks for Muster Mark" appears in *Finnegans Wake.* From this, the physicist Murray Gell-Man proposed naming one of the elementary particles a "quark."

DORIS LESSING Born in 1919 in Persia, Lessing dropped out of convent school at age thirteen. After that she was entirely self-educated. She has published more than twenty books: fiction, nonfiction, poetry. She is the recipient of numerous international literary awards, such as the Prince of Asturias Prize in Literature and the David Cohen British Literature Prize.

JACK LONDON (1876–1916) The author of more than fifty works of fiction, both novels and short stories, London's contribution to literature is as varied as it is vast. Many of his novels were more popular than literary, but his short stories are wonderfully and carefully crafted. He is best know for stories about the demanding and brutal existence in the Klondike gold rush.

KATHERINE MANSFIELD (1888–1923) Born and raised in New Zealand, Mansfield spent her adult life in Europe, primarily in England. She was an accomplished musician as well as a writer. She published several collections of short stories in her lifetime. Her stories are known for their cruel and pessimistic portrayal of middle-class family relations, bitter perhaps, but always unblinking. She is often compared to Chekhov.

GUY DE MAUPASSANT (1850–93) A prolific writer, Maupassant published over three hundred short stories, as well as novels, travel books, and a volume of verse. He fought in the Franco-Prussian war and returned to civilian life where he worked as a civil servant, a profession he loathed. His stories are funny, pessimistic, cynical, and incisive. He also wrote a number of horror stories in the style of Poe. He died in an institution, suffering from syphilitic mental illness.

LORRIE MOORE Lorrie Moore's stories have appeared in *The New Yorker* and been anthologized in *The Best American Short Stories*. She has published three collections of short stories and two novels. She currently lives and teaches in Madison, Wisconsin.

JOYCE CAROL OATES One of the most prolific and versatile writers of our time, Oates has received both the National Book Award and the PEN/Malamud award for excellence in short fiction. Oates is known for her intimate explorations of the human capacity for ambivalence, violence, and cruelty in the service of love.

GRACE PALEY Paley is known as an activist as well as a writer. She has published collections of short stories and collections of poetry. In 1993 she received the Rea award for the short story.

DOROTHY PARKER (1893–1967) Parker published numerous short stories and essays, many for *The New Yorker*. She also wrote poetry and plays. Parker is famous for her incisive wit and unflinching examination of "society." Her popularity is enduring.

KATHERINE ANNE PORTER (1890–1980) was a journalist who went on to write and publish short stories, novels, and essays. She won the Pulitzer Prize and the National Book Award for *Collected Stories*. She has been nominated three times for the Nobel Prize for literature.

MARY ROBISON studied with John Barth, writes mostly short stories, and has published two novels. Her stories have appeared in *The New Yorker* as well as *The Paris Review* and *Esquire*. Her fiction is known for its edgy minimalism and emotional resonance.

SAKI (HECTOR HUGO MUNRO) (1870–1916) Born in Burma, educated both in England and during extensive travels across Europe, H. H. Munro worked briefly for the Burma Police but quickly resigned. He was a foreign correspondent in the Balkans, Paris and Russia. He was also a prolific writer of short stories. His stories primarily address the viciousness and hypocrisy barely concealed by the genteel surfaces of the upper class lifestyle. He published under the pseudonym, Saki. He was killed in WWI.

JAMES SALTER graduated from West Point in 1945. He flew combat missions in Korea. These experiences formed the basis for his first novel, *The Hunters*. He won the PEN/Faulkner award for his collection *Dusk and Other Stories*. His work has been described as impressionistic and deeply layered.

JOHN UPDIKE has published more than fifty books, including twenty novels, and various collections of stories, poetry, and essays. He has won the Pulitzer Prize, the National Book Award, the American Book Award, the National Book Critics Circle Award, and The PEN/Faulkner Award for fiction.

WILLIAM CARLOS WILLIAMS (1883–1963) Primarily a poet, Williams also wrote stories, novels, and plays. He was posthumously awarded the Pulitzer Prize.

TOBIAS WOLFF has written novels, memoirs, and short stories, most recently, *Old School*, a novel published in 2003. His stories are known for their vividness and incisive descriptions of tiny moments between family members, lovers, or friends.

Credits

Almond, Steve. "The Soul Molecule" from *The Evil B.B. Chow*. Copyright © 2005 by Steve Almond. Reprinted by permission of Algonquin Books of Chapel Hill.

Barth, John. "Ad Infinitum" from *On With the Story*. Copyright © 1996 by John Barth, reprinted with the permission of The Wylie Agency.

Bausch, Richard. "The Voices from the Other Room" from *The Stories of Richard Bausch*. Copyright © 2004. Reprinted by permission of the author.

Borges, Jorge Luis. "August 25, 1983" from *Collected Fictions* translated by Andrew Hurley, copyright © 1998 by Maria Kodama; translation copyright © by Penguin Putnam Inc. Used by permission of Viking Penguin, a division of Penguin Group (USA) Inc.

Busch, Frederick. "The Ninth, In E Minor" from *Don't Tell Anyone*. Copyright © 2000 by Frederick Busch. Reprinted by permission of the author.

Butler, Robert Olen. "Crickets" from *A Good Scent From A Strange Mountain*. Copyright © 1992 by Robert Olen Butler. Reprinted by permission of Henry Holt and Company, LLC.

Carlson, Ron. "Olympus Hills" from *The News Of The World*. Copyright © 1987 by Ron Carlson. Used by permission of W. W. Norton & Company, Inc.

Made in the USA
Middletown, DE
15 January 2020